THE AGE
OF THE ECONOMIST

THE AGE
OF THE ECONOMIST
Fourth Edition

DANIEL R. FUSFELD

University of Michigan

Scott, Foresman and Company   Glenview, Illinois

Dallas, Tex. Oakland, N.J. Palo Alto, Cal. Tucker, Ga. London, England

Library of Congress Cataloging in Publication Data

Fusfeld, Daniel Roland, 1922-
    The age of the economist.

    Bibliography: p.
    Includes indexes.
    1. Economics—History.   I. Title
HB75.F87   1981   330'.09   81—9073
ISBN 0-673-15500-5   AACR2

Preface

This small volume surveys the history of economics from the days of Adam Smith and some of his predecessors to the developments of modern times, including the crises of the 1970s. This book is written for all those who wish to familiarize themselves with the background of modern economics, but who have no initial knowledge of the more complex aspects of the subject. It should prove as useful to the interested layman as to the student studying principles of economics, history, or an introduction to social sciences.

This edition has the same basic goals as the first edition. Through historical development of economics one can understand how the minds of the great economists worked—how the grand themes they dealt with were developed out of efforts to understand the problems and issues of the times, competing social philosophies, economic and social conflicts, and a changing economic structure. The discipline that emerged helps us obtain a fuller understanding of an intricate and dynamic economy. The ideas and events that influenced the great economists over the last 200 years are still at work today. By examining the interplay of these forces and current events and ideas, we can begin to understand what today's economists are saying and why they are saying it. An inquiry into the past helps us understand the present.

The first edition of this book was published in 1966, at a time when the world economy was approaching the peak of the great surge of economic growth that followed World War II, and just prior to the slowdown in economic growth and time of troubles that began in the late 1960s. In the mid-1960s, economic policies seemed to be working well, on the whole, and there was a broad concensus among economists about what was important and useful. But when economic conditions turned sour in the late 1960s and the 1970s, the consensus dissolved. The accepted economic truths of the 1960s became the raw materials for controversy. In the process, the view of the past as reflected in this small volume has changed.

In one respect, the changes have not been great: those chapters that discuss the development of economics up to 1945 remain very much as they were in the first edition, although errors were corrected and some additions and changes were made that reflect the reevaluations of the 1970s. This revision, for instance, added to the discussion of Marxism and neo-classical economics (particularly on general equilibrium concepts and the method of logical empiricism), and made other changes to clarify and strengthen the discussion. The later chapters, on the other hand, were modified to a greater extent, with emphasis on the economic problems of the 1970s, the limitations of economic policy, current economic controversies, and the consequent disorder within economics as a discipline. Yet the last few pages that deal with the future of economics have hardly been changed: the predictions made in the third edition were borne out and reinforced by the developing emphases in economics over the past five years. The economics of the future is being created in our time out of the hurly-burly of events, policy problems, ideological debate, and scholarly inquiry.

By the end of the book the reader will be drawn into some complex ideas. Economics has developed into what one philosopher called "one of the most elaborate constructions of sustained philosophical reasoning in existence."* The important building blocks of the subject are introduced in the early chapters in relatively simple form, and the complexities are gradually developed, as they were in reality, by examining their development in historical context. The careful reader will develop a broad understanding of the more important ideas of modern economics by progressing through the book.

The emphasis throughout is on the larger conceptual framework of economic ideas, to show how one discipline is related to the great issues that have troubled people in every age—order versus freedom, riches and poverty, privilege and equality, power and its control, human welfare, material and moral values, and others. It is easy to get so involved in the intricacies of economics that we lose sight of these larger issues. Here they are pushed to the front of the stage, for economics has always been an instrument through which we may achieve a better understanding of the great problems that have troubled humankind.

Ann Arbor, Michigan   DANIEL R. FUSFIELD

*David Braybrook, *The Encyclopedia of Philosophy* (New York: Macmillan, 1967), Vol. II, p. 454.

Contents

Introduction

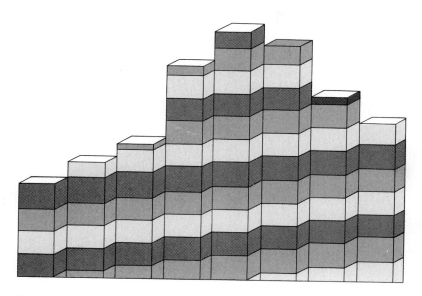

Edmund Burke called the eighteenth century "the age of the economist," and the label is equally appropriate for our own time. The writings of economists defined the major social philosophies of the past two hundred years. The chief ideological debates of the modern era involved the basic ideas of great economists like Adam Smith, Karl Marx, and John Maynard Keynes, who achieved their stature primarily because of the social philosophies involved in their economic theories rather than because of the scientific advances they made.

This fact was well understood by Keynes himself, who, doing battle with ideas he was convinced were wrong and pernicious, wrote:

> The ideas of economists and political philosophers, both when they are right and when they are wrong, are more powerful than is commonly understood. Indeed the world is ruled by little else. Practical men, who believe themselves to be quite exempt from any intellectual influences, are usually the slaves of some defunct economist. Madmen in authority, who hear voices in the air, are distilling their frenzy from some academic scribbler of a few years back.

Economists became the high priests of a world of money, wealth, and aspirations for material goods. Like the Schoolmen of the Middle Ages, they defined for a secular world the relationships between people, the individual

1

and nature, the individual and society. Their often esoteric and highly complex theories were translated into a folklore understood by millions and into policies adopted by nations. Although their base was usually in the relatively secluded atmosphere of the university, in recent years distinguished economists served as prime ministers of England, France, Germany, and Italy and as Secretary General of the United Nations. It would be hard to name another discipline that exerted as much influence on the modern world.

This was not always the case. Only two hundred years ago there were no economists known by that name, and economic theory was a branch of moral philosophy. Economics as we know it today hardly existed, and what did exist was called "political economy," indicating that it was part of national policy more than anything else and that it dealt with such matters as taxes, public debts, and foreign trade.

Until very recently economics was the only social science with a generally accepted body of theory whose validity almost every practitioner accepted. It is true that there were many differences of opinion among economists, who sometimes joked about obtaining five different opinions on any topic from any four economists, or about the old professor who asked the same examination questions year after year but changed the answers. There were many disputes among economists, too, but not about the fundamental principles of science. The disagreements arose over applications, over the proper policies to be adopted in given circumstances, over judgments about the importance of various factors in particular situations.

There was one major exception to this rule—the Marxists, who considered Western economics to be merely ideological justification of an exploitive system. They believed their own analysis of capitalism to be the correct one, laying bare the flaws that would lead ultimately to the downfall of the capitalist system. Their contempt for Western economics was reciprocated by the attitude toward Marxism of the orthodox economists, who considered that doctrine so wrong they didn't even bother to read Marx.

Today, however, the accepted principles of orthodox economics are in trouble. The issues and problems for which it provided answers—the way a market economy functions, how to maintain prosperity—have given way to new problems and issues for which answers are not readily available. Growth of big business, big government, and big unions brings economic power to the fore as a determinant of economic events. Economic growth and affluence bring problems of resources, pollution, and energy. An exploding world population seems to be a particularly intractable problem. The limits to growth inherent in a finite natural environment suggest that new economic institutions must be forged as we move from a growth-oriented way of thinking to a limits-oriented one. Great disparities in income and wealth within nations and between nations create political and ideological conflicts over how economic benefits are distributed. Capitalism itself faces the challenge of socialism. A changing world brings changing problems to a changing discipline. The economics of the future will be forged in today's cauldron of events. In addition, the responses of orthodox economists to the challenges of its ideological critics will be of prime importance in shaping our future economic institutions.

This procedure is not surprising, since economics is a social science, and ideological debates have always been important to its development. This presents a great paradox: some of the most important scientific advances in economics resulted from political debates over social policy. In this respect economics—like all other social sciences—differs radically from the physical and biological sciences, which grew step by step from facts and experimental evidence to theory, and from theory to further experiment and more general theories. Both the social and the physical sciences developed by means of grand integrating schemes, or "systems," intended to explain large interrelated portions of a discipline. In the physical sciences, the grand designs emerged primarily out of an ordering of facts and evidence; in economics, that source of scientific theory was supplemented by great political and philosophical debates. Ideological systems, each with its supporting facts, assumptions, and body of theory, spawned much that is valuable in economics.

The ideas developed by Adam Smith in the eighteenth century comprised one of those systems, and the theory of markets developed by Smith and his followers represented the first great body of generally accepted principles in modern economics. Challenged by Marx and others in the mid-nineteenth century, this "classical" system and its laissez-faire ideology were remade in the last quarter of the century into a new orthodoxy that prevailed until the 1930s, when John Maynard Keynes almost single-handedly built the modern theory of national income and justified a policy of government intervention in economic affairs. Between these last two developments, a variety of writers laid the foundations for today's welfare policies by criticizing the economic society and theories of their time. Throughout these debates ideas emerged that were useful either in supporting or attacking the existing order, its distribution of income and wealth, and its structure of power. Yet the arguments led to significant advances in our understanding of the complexities of economic life and to important new generalizations about how economic institutions function.

One of the great themes in the development of economics, then, is the interaction of ideology and science. Without ideology, the science could not have evolved. And because scientific economics was forged in the fire of ideological debate, it will always arouse emotions, no matter how "pure" its spokesmen may try to keep it.

A second great theme is the relationship between economic theories and practical problems. People everywhere have sought prosperity and justice, freedom and order, individual betterment and the social good. The quest for these sometimes contradictory goals always involved choices, and the theory of choice is a basic part of economic theory. One of the maxims of economic science is that the greater the economic surplus, the more numerous are the alternative courses of action and the easier it is to achieve a multiplicity of goals. As society brought a recalcitrant nature more effectively under its control, possible ways and means of organizing and utilizing economic resources became more numerous, and public policy toward economic affairs became more important. With control comes choice, and choice begets policy. The need for policy decisions brought forth the economist, to analyze and advise and to develop a scientific basis for the choices.

For example, at the close of World War II the American people debated whether or not to institute an extensive program of loans to aid the reconstruction of Europe. The issue would have been strictly academic had not the United States had a large surplus of production above its minimum needs that could be allocated to foreign aid. Since the surplus was available, however, economists were called in to advise on how best to mobilize it (whether under public or private auspices), the form it should take (loans or grants, or both), and the uses to which it should be put (consumer goods or machinery, or both). These are economic decisions, involving choices among alternatives.

A third theme in the development of economics is its close relationship to the climate of opinion. A problem is never analyzed in a vacuum. The function of theory is to provide a context in which facts can be systematically organized. But solutions to problems must be practical and acceptable to the general public as well as to political leaders. If economics is to have any usefulness, the economic theory of an era must be consistent with the beliefs and concerns of the public and it must provide useful and meaningful results. In this sense, economics has always been political economy.

Scholars often overlook the importance of the climate of opinion. They seek the origins of ideas in the solid advances made by earlier scholars, tracing an intellectual genealogy from one generation of thinkers to another, finding the origins of modern ideas in the Old Testament, Aesop, and the Upanishads. In some respects this is a worthwhile task, for older generations were just as intelligent as we are; it is true more often than not that if an idea is any good someone else thought of it first. But in the social sciences, at least, the more meaningful question is not "when did the idea first appear?" but "why is the idea important now?" The answer to the latter question involves the uses to which the idea can be put, the special interests of those who use it, and its consistency with other beliefs of the people affected by it. This climate of opinion is often more important than logical consistency for the development and survival of ideas—more important in the case of economic ideas, perhaps, than of those in any other social science, because of the close relationship between economics and public policy. Economists cannot escape the times in which they live—the times determine the very questions asked—and nearly every adult is, in some respects, an economist.

A fourth theme is the development of economics as a science. Over a period of 250 years—a quarter of a millennium—basic principles were developed concerning the ways in which markets function, the process of economic growth, the determinants of the level of economic activity, and many other topics. Like any science, economics evolved a vocabulary of concepts that defines its subject matter, and methods by which hypotheses are tested, modified, and verified. Generations of theorists developed systematic analyses, demonstrable conclusions, and broad propositions.

There is a tendency to write the history of any discipline as if the entire past were prologue, leading inevitably to the discovery of the truths of the present, with the implication that the process will continue into the future as scientists move ever closer to a fuller understanding of the subject. To some extent that is true of economics: we know today far more about how a market-oriented economy functions than we did a hundred or two hundred years ago. But this view is an oversimplification. People in past eras were just as smart as we are, and, although technology was perhaps simpler, the problems they had to wrestle with were just as intricate as those of today. Their world was different from ours, and their view of that world differed also. Inevitably, the social theories of the past were different from those of today. Whether our theories are "better" or more advanced is debatable.

For example, the "classical" economists of the early nineteenth century emphasized the economics of production and distribution in their analysis of the economy, and assumed that the level of economic activity was not a significant problem. That view is rejected today, when the emphasis is on exchange rather than production and on how to maintain "full employment" levels of output. We might describe classical economics as if it were merely a prelude to today's truths, but that would be a distortion of both classical economics and the process by which we came to our present understanding of market economics. It would also distort our understanding of the path into the future, for if the past really is prologue we know that many of the truths of the present will become the falsehoods of the future.

Economics is an ever-changing discipline. Partly a product of the great ideological debates over the way human society ought to be organized, it also influences the outcome of those debates. Partly based on a theoretical search for abstract truths, it is also rooted in the realities of public policy and the climate of opinion. Partly an explanation of how and why an economic system functions, it is affected by the ways in which economic systems change. Economics is a complex amalgam of scientific theory, political ideology, public policy, and accepted truths.

Yet development of the discipline to its present position could not have taken place without the work of many ordinary and extraordinary individuals. The story of economics is also the story of a Scottish philosopher, a London stockbroker, an Episcopalian minister, a German philosopher and revolutionist, a Cambridge professor, a Norwegian-American skeptic, and a host of others. The story reflects their personalities and their convictions, their strengths and their weaknesses, their successes and their failures. This book is an account of their work and of the discipline they helped to build, of the interaction among facts, problems, policy, philosophy, and institutions in the building process, and of how we have come to think as we do about one of the most important aspects of our lives.

All of these forces are at work today, for economics is in one of those periodic crises that in the past have led to fundamental changes in the discipline. A changing world and the emergence of new issues, ideological conflict, and theoretical advances on the frontiers of the subject have forced economists to reconsider some of their basic ideas and how they relate to each other. Many of the older ideas retain their relevance or are being revived. Today the entire discipline is in flux as economists all over the world have gone back to reconsider the fundamentals of their science as they respond to the needs of our time. The economics of the future is emerging from this process.

CHAPTER 1

Economics and the Market Economy

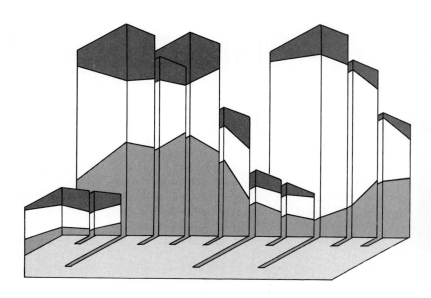

THE RISE OF THE MARKET ECONOMY

The modern market economy is such an intimate part of our way of life that most of us do not realize that it is a relatively recent development. The organization of economic life around an interrelated system of markets— markets which adjust prices, output, and incomes in an impersonal system— did not emerge on a large scale until after the Middle Ages, that is, from the fifteenth century onward. Prior to that time the bulk of Europe's population lived in an economy largely based upon a social system of rights and obligations rather than on an acquisitive, profit-oriented economy of buying and selling.

This transformation of society and its economy was observed by contemporaries. Thomas Becon, an English cleric of the mid-sixteenth century, for example, decried the growing materialism of his era and inveighed against "greedy gentlemen, which are sheepmongers and graziers" who "study for their own private commodity." Thomas Wilson, writing fifty years later, noted how even the aristocracy was affected by the change:

> *The gentlemen, which were wont to addict themselves to warres, are now for the most part growen to become good husbands and know well how to improve their lands to the uttermost as the farmer or countryman, so that*

they make their farmes into their handes as the leases expire, and eyther till themselves or else lett them out to those who will give most.

Becon and Wilson observed what many others of the time could also see. The traditional pattern, in which each person was born to a definite place and fulfilled a definite function through life, was passing away. Peasants, long accustomed to providing services and agricultural output for the lord of the manor, increasingly paid money rents and sold a portion of their product in order to get the money to do so. More than ever before, the lord used the rents to buy needed goods, and the more progressive landowners began to produce readily marketable products like wool. Others gradually raised the rents charged their tenants, who were forced similarly to orient their crops toward marketable products. Middlemen traders increased in number, wealth, and importance as a result of the growing market.

The Middle Ages—that era from the breakdown of the ancient Roman Empire to the mid-fifteenth century—were not without trade, commerce, and markets, but the trade was in large part a long-distance and interregional trade in luxury products consumed by the nobility and the wealthy. Peasant communities, rural and largely self-sufficient, produced a surplus paid to the lord in products, in labor, and sometimes in cash. This surplus was the basis for purchases of luxuries by the aristocracy—things like fine textiles, metal products, wine, and other items of the "good life." A dual economy grew up, comprising the peasant village on the one hand and the commercial town on the other. It was a regulated economy of organized groups such as manor, town, and guild rather than one which operated through free decisions freely negotiated. In its fundamental structure it was much like the economic system that prevailed throughout the rest of the civilized world eastward to the Near and Middle East, southeast Asia, and the Far East.

Then, in the fifteenth century, the great transformation of Europe to a market economy began. The geographical discoveries of the fifteenth and sixteenth centuries opened up tremendous opportunities for trade and commerce and set in motion a large flow of capital into Europe in the form of gold and silver treasures from both the New World and the East. The rise of national states largely destroyed the political power of two bulwarks of the old order, the nobility and the Church. New methods of warfare used by the emerging rulers, featuring paid infantries and large navies, required money and administration: national tax systems emerged, and a flow of purchasing power from taxpayer through government and back to the public further stimulated the growth of markets. Cities like London and Amsterdam became centers of commerce; they looked overseas for their profits and expansion, and they were supported by governments eager to increase the tax base by expanding the wealth of the nation.

The new economy generated new attitudes. Medieval people, accustomed to thinking and acting in traditional ways, gave way to market-oriented people who would sink or swim by virtue of their individual decisions. The successful ones were those who saved, who plowed profits back into the enterprise, who calculated prices and costs carefully, who took risks in order to make gains. In particular, there was little place for the attitudes of the old nobility, who set great store by blood lineage and the traditions of feudal warfare and jousting. The future lay with commercial profits and commercial wealth.

The new economy also generated the study of economics. The developing market orientation of production and distribution led to new relationships between the individual and society and among individuals, with all the ethical issues that those relationships imply. The morality of the new economic order had to be carefully analyzed and accepted rules for ethical behavior devised. Theologians became the first "economists."

RELIGION AND ECONOMIC LIFE

The theologians were concerned with reconstructing the ethical basis of economic life. The older medieval point of view had subordinated economic life to both individual salvation and the needs of society as a whole. Theologians had argued that earthly life was merely a prelude to eternity, and moral laws had to prevail in all aspects of human endeavor. This meant that in all human relationships, including the economic, the individual had to keep the law of God continually in mind. The Church knew that people must eat and clothe and house themselves, that the ordinary functions of production and distribution had to be carried on; but those functions had to be placed in proper perspective—salvation was the proper business of life, and one must never forget it. Seeking wealth for its own sake was sinful, since it took one's attention away from salvation and pursuit of the moral life.

The economic attitudes embodied in the orthodox moral philosophy of the Middle Ages were summed up in a famous parable. A monk on a pilgrimage to Rome purchased a silver chalice for his cathedral. Traveling back to Germany with a band of merchants, he showed them the vessel and told what he had paid for it. The merchants congratulated him on his purchase, telling him that he had bought it for far less than its true value, and laughed that an unworldly monk could drive a better bargain than any of them. Horrified, the monk left immediately, made his way back to Rome, and paid the seller of the chalice enough to make up the fair price. It was the only moral thing to do.

Such attitudes may have been consistent with an economy of customary prices and accepted economic relationships, but they were out of tune with the success-oriented, profit-motivated behavior of the market economy. They may have been appropriate to people concerned with eternal salvation, but they did not suit people who sought material wealth and success. They may have worked in a society organized in stable groups, but they were incompatible with an individualistic social order and a desire to rise in wealth and status.

The rise of a market economy created a moral dilemma for the people of the early modern era. On the one hand, the ethical teachings of religion told them that each individual was morally responsible for others. These ideas were found in the Old Testament story of Cain and Abel and in the New Testament parable of the Good Samaritan, to give only two widely known examples. On the other hand, survival and success in a market economy required that each person try to outreach, outsmart, and overcome others. Rivalry, not brotherhood, was the necessary mode of behavior, and the principle of *caveat emptor*—"let the buyer beware"—prevailed. Market relationships were impersonal and transient compared with the permanent and face-to-face relationships of an unchanging rural village. People were judged more by their success in acquiring wealth than by the morality of their behavior.

This moral dilemma—the conflict between salvation and success—was an important factor in setting the stage for the Reformation. It was hard for an urban merchant to believe that the business way of life was less proper than that of others. It was difficult to understand that the competition necessary for survival was antagonistic to the moral law, that the single-minded pursuit of profit which was fundamental to the very livelihood of business people was frowned upon by the divines. So doubts arose. Were the theologians right in their teachings about the modes of conduct required for salvation? After all, they were only human like everyone else and therefore subject to human error. What did the Bible itself say about these matters? Such questions led to the Protestant heresy—doubt of the infallibility of the Church and a desire to go directly to the Bible as the repository of God's law, without the priest as intermediary.

The theological arguments of the Reformation are of little interest to us here, but out of them came a new economic ethic that gave the profit-motivated market economy its moral letters of credit. Underlying the new morality was the idea that God in his infinite wisdom had intended a place on earth for each individual, through which the individual could work out his destiny. This place, or "calling," had to be sought and found by personal soul-searching, and once found it had to be diligently pursued. Salvation was earned by hard work in one's calling, and any calling—even that of the merchant—was equal in merit to any other in the eyes of God. But how was one to identify one's calling? The theologians answered: partly through inner feelings and partly through success. Worldly success indicated that one had found his or her calling and that God had approved. As for success, avoid idleness, temptation, and luxury . . . work hard and save. These were the prescriptions for ethical behavior hammered out during a half-century of religious controversy, sermonizing, and polemics. They fitted the needs of the growing urban middle class and promoted the hard work and capital accumulation that led to economic expansion.

By the eighteenth century the new economic ethic had lost much of its religious sanction and had become an almost universal way of life. That American sage, Benjamin Franklin, stated it in the form of aphorisms, which were repeated endlessly to generations of young people:

Early to bed, early to rise, makes a man healthy, wealthy, and wise.
The sound of your hammer at five in the morning, or at nine at night, heard by a creditor, makes him easy six months longer.
What maintains one vice would bring up two children.

The new ethic was the basis of a secular and materialistic value system that has dominated the climate of opinion in Western Europe and North America ever since.

But even though attitudes changed and the accepted goals of individual action became heavily materialistic, a moral problem remained. Was it true that economic failure meant unworthiness, that success and salvation were synonymous? Did not the individual have a responsibility to others that went beyond merely meeting one's contractual obligations in the marketplace?

Had the monk been correct in returning to Rome to pay the merchant more for the chalice than his bargain called for?

The problem arises because of the inherent conflict between an ethical principle—all humanity is one—and the competitive rivalry of the market economy expressed in the legal principle of *caveat emptor*—"let the buyer beware." The ethical principle requires the individual to take responsibility for others, while the legal principle calls for the individual to look out only for himself.

This moral dilemma has puzzled philosophers and ecclesiastics from the sixteenth century onward. Attempted solutions appeared in the religious controversies of the sixteenth century, in the eighteenth-century philosophy of *noblesse oblige,* in the writings of nineteenth-century socialists, and in the welfare legislation of the twentieth century. Present in all these approaches to the problem is a belief that the social system should not allow an individual to be crushed and destroyed by the operation of impersonal market forces. But the dilemma remains, and economists must be, in part, moral philosophers, while philosophers must also deal with economic issues.

CHAPTER 2

The Early Days

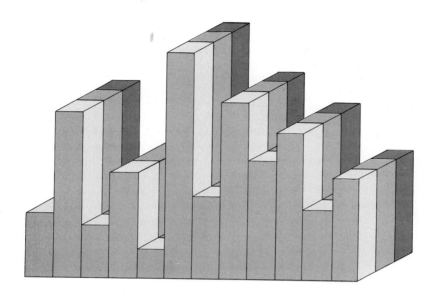

Practical people often argue over the most esoteric of subjects, for policy decisions sometimes rest upon the most intricate of theories. One of these debates took place during the eighteenth century, and from it emerged the foundations of modern economics. The question at issue was the ultimate source of national wealth, which some saw in trade, others in agriculture and the natural forces of life, and still others in human labor. Although the issue may seem at first glance to be devoid of practical significance, the whole range of government economic policy depended on the outcome.

THE MERCANTILISTS

The mercantilists were the first to take the field. These writers were concerned with the national states that developed during the sixteenth and seventeenth centuries. They faced two different but related problems, one internal and one external.

The domestic problem was one of unity. National power had to be built from the localism of the Middle Ages. For the economy this meant a unified coinage and monetary system, a national system of weights and measures, elimination of internal tolls on roads and rivers, and a national system of taxes and tariffs. These institutions, which today we take for granted, were slowly forged by national rulers against the opposition of feudal lords who tried to keep as much control as possible over the economy of their regions. The building of a national economy was predicated on the growing political power of the monarchs against the great nobles.

In this struggle the monarchs found natural allies in several places. First in importance were the rising commercial interests of the towns and cities. Merchants benefited from the widened trade made possible by a unified economy in which local barriers to commerce were reduced. In turn, the merchants augmented the monarchs' power by helping to finance the armies needed to subordinate the nobility. The interests of monarchs and merchants further coincided in that both benefited from expanded foreign trade. Merchants earned profits from trade with the newly opened lands in Asia and the New World. To the extent that the merchants of one country dominated trade with another area, profits would flow to the homeland and domestic manufacturers would be stimulated by the export market. The state gained from the tariff revenues derived from large trade, from the sale of trade monopolies, from the development of strategic military industries and personnel—shipbuilding and ship supplies, sailors and captains—and from the general economic growth that provided a firm economic base for national power. One of the basic goals of national policy, therefore, became the development of commerce and the growth of power in international affairs.

A second group allied with the monarchs consisted of the smaller landowners, who looked to the state as a counterweight to the powers of the barons. This group was more interested in commercial agriculture than in warfare, jousts, and family power and wanted the state to maintain order and promote the growing markets from which they profited. They knew that as the power of the state increased vis-à-vis the great lords, their own wealth and power in local affairs would also increase.

Two other groups emerged from the rising market economy and national states. One was the legal profession, whose members were needed to interpret and define the vastly complicated economic relationships that developed out of free association and private contract in the market environment. Old and familiar legal relationships were being replaced by new ones, and lawyers were needed to systematize them. The second group comprised public administrators and the court. Although small in numbers, these two groups were of great strategic importance. A "white-collar" superstructure, allied with and dependent upon business and government, supported the policies designed to strengthen unity and power.

Out of the political and economic alliances among crown, merchants, gentry, and professional people emerged economic policies designed to unify the nation under a single strong ruler, develop its military and naval strength, and increase its wealth through both domestic production and foreign trade. These and the theories underlying them have come to be called *mercantilism*. It was the first systematic body of modern economic thought.

One of the clearest statements of mercantilist policy was made by Phillip von Hornick (1638–1712), an Austrian civil servant writing for a backward country constantly threatened by the Turks. He wrote in 1684 a widely read tract called *Austria Over All, If She Only Will*, listing "nine principal rules of national economy":

To inspect the country's soil with the greatest care, and not to leave the agricultural possibilities of a single corner or clod of earth unconsidered … all commodities found in a country, which cannot be used in their natural state, should be worked up within the country … attention should be given to the population, that it may be as large as the country can support … gold and silver once in the country are under no circumstances to be taken out for any purpose … the inhabitants should make every effort to get along with their domestic products … [foreign commodities] should be obtained not for gold or silver, but in exchange for other domestic wares … and should be imported in unfinished form, and worked up within the country … opportunities should be sought night and day for selling the country's superfluous goods to these foreigners in manufactured form … no importation should be allowed under any circumstances of which there is a sufficient supply of suitable quality at home.

These basic policies of nationalism, self-sufficiency, and national power were adopted in varying degrees by all the states of Europe. Manufacturing was encouraged by subsidies, special privileges, patents, and monopolies. Foreign trade was stimulated by acquisition of colonies and efforts to keep wages down and regulated by tariffs, navigation laws, and trade restrictions. Agriculture was fostered by a variety of policies: in England imports of food were taxed in order to keep out foreign competition, while in France exports of agricultural products were taxed in order to keep domestic production at home. In particular, the munitions industries were promoted—guns, gunpowder, ships, and ship supplies.

In England, where trade quickly became the basis for increased wealth and national power, a great deal of emphasis was placed on expansion of the money supply as a stimulus to economic growth. In those days of limited markets and inadequate purchasing power, one of the barriers to economic growth was a lack of both hard cash in the hands of consumers and credit available for business. Rulers often borrowed, too, and they would similarly benefit from readily available cash and credit and from low interest rates. Modern banking was only in its infancy, and the availability of money and credit depended very heavily on the cash available—and that meant gold and silver coins. It was inevitable, then, that monetary policy was a major concern of the mercantilist economists. Basically, they favored what we would call an "easy money" policy—plenty of money to stimulate trade and keep interest rates down. On the other hand, they had to keep inflationary pressures in check, for two reasons: (1) rising prices created difficulties for the workers and the poor, because wage rates tended to lag behind price increases, and political unrest would therefore follow; (2) rising prices would reduce foreign demand for domestic manufactures and ultimately result in worsened economic conditions at home.

Domestic and international economic policies, therefore, became closely intertwined, and the English mercantilists were quick to realize that the world economy was a web of interconnections. Hard experience as well as sharp analysis taught them that if the domestic money supply and purchasing power expanded more rapidly than the supply of goods available for sale, domestic prices would rise, imports would increase, and exports would fall. The fall in exports and rise in imports would then result in an export of gold and silver to make up for the "unfavorable" balance of trade. This in turn would reduce the money supply at home and cause the domestic economy to languish. These relationships were soon well understood, and a cardinal tenet of the mercantilists was encouragement of a "favorable" balance of trade. If exports exceeded imports, they argued, gold and silver would enter the country, plenty of money would be available, economic growth would be stimulated, and national wealth would grow.

It should not be assumed that mercantilism was everywhere the same. There were great differences between countries. In France, for example, where luxury products like silks and linens, tapestries, furniture, and wine were of major importance, close regulation of the quality of goods was emphasized. Under the leadership of Jean Baptiste Colbert (1619–1683), minister of finance for more than twenty years during the reign of Louis XIV, national guilds were set up to regulate the major industries. Only craftsmen who were guild members could operate, and they were subject to the regulations of the national organization. The royal power, supported by steady revenues from the salt tax, was strong enough to enforce the regulations effectively, and the guilds remained powerful until the French Revolution at the end of the eighteenth century.

In England, by contrast, regulation of domestic industry was not success-ful because the government, always short of money, was never strong enough to administer regulations effectively. English mercantilism was devoted primarily to expansion of trade and encouragement of manu-factures. One result of this situation was that the medieval guilds disinte-grated, especially when cloth production developed in rural areas, and industrial processes were far freer of restrictions than were those of France. When the Industrial Revolution began in the late eighteenth century, this absence of guilds gave English industry a long head start over France and the other continental countries that had copied the French example.

Nor was there always agreement on policies within nations. Popular revulsion in England against government grants of monopoly to individuals and companies was so great that in 1601 Queen Elizabeth herself had to appear before Parliament to quell the objections and promise reforms. Two years later, in the famous "Case of Monopolies," the courts decided in a path-breaking decision that even monopoly grants by the Crown were subject to the common-law prohibitions on restraint of trade. Parliament finally prohibited government grants of monopoly in 1624, completing the legal foundations on which American antitrust laws are based.

The mercantilists recognized that wealth was produced by human effort, in general, but felt that it would not be realized unless trade and commerce were encouraged—unless exchange of goods enabled producers to make a profit. For this reason they emphasized the growth of trade and commerce as the key to increased national wealth, and expansion of the money supply as the key to increased trade. To the question, "What is the source of the wealth of nations?" the mercantilists gave the first answer: "Commerce."

In many respects they were right for their time. In the sixteenth and seventeenth centuries the most powerful nations of Europe were those that had developed their international and overseas trade to the greatest extent. Trade seemed to stimulate both manufacturing and agriculture and to bring prosperity, wealth, and power to the entire nation. Mercantilist doctrines had a common-sense validity derived from what people could see going on around them.

OPPOSITION TO MERCANTILISM

By the middle of the eighteenth century the mercantilists' preoccupation with trade and national power had begun to grate on some of the economic interests of the growing market economy. Mercantilist policies were fine for the great merchants and financiers who operated in the international economy; the basic goals of national power suited the rulers; and government administrators and courtiers were often able to benefit substantially, either directly or through bribes, from government grants of special economic privilege. But the economy became more varied as it grew, and both agricultural and industrial interests were increasingly coming to find that mercantilist policies were not in their best interest. The policies were subjected to substantial criticism, and the theories on which they were based were questioned.

Small businesses, in particular, felt hemmed in by the monopolistic privileges granted to a few big financiers, and both they and the smaller farmers resented the taxes imposed to maintain a national power alien to their individual interests. A classic example is the issue of "taxation without representation" in Britain's American colonies. When the French and Indian Wars ended in 1765, the western frontiers of the colonies were relatively safe for colonization and development, and the colonists were well aware of the fact that much of their economic future lay in the West. But the British government, long committed to development of the fur trade and favoring the interests of the Hudson's Bay Company, had prohibited settlement beyond the Allegheny Mountains. Troops were stationed in the colonies to protect the frontier and enforce the prohibition, which protected the colonists from the Indians before 1765 but which restricted colonial economic growth after the frontier was pacified. To make matters worse, taxes on legal documents and tea were imposed in the colonies to pay for the troops, who were sometimes quartered in the homes of colonials: the colonists had to support the very troops who were protecting English business interests against their own! One wonders what attitude the colonists would have taken had the tax revenues been used to open the frontier rather than to close it.

The case of the American colonies, where the issue became political and helped lead to the nationalistic and anticolonial American Revolution, was a striking example of opposition to mercantilist policies. In Europe, however, a debate about purely economic issues arose. Was it true that economic expansion and growth was best achieved through regulation and direction? Would not better results be achieved in a free economy unhampered by the directing force of a mercantilist government? The debate over these questions was particularly strong in France and England.

In France, government regulation of production was so detailed as to specify the required number of threads per inch in the manufacture of cloth. There was a multiplicity of taxes and tolls, and regulation of imports and exports was strict. Yet the nobility was exempt from taxation while substantial levies were imposed on peasants and independent farmers. Moreover, the government was corrupt and inefficient—indeed, this condition probably made the system workable: the regulations and taxes could often be evaded by judicious bribes or clever evasions. The situation was so bad that one government inspector of trademarks, Vincent de Gournay (1712-1759), disenchanted with mercantilist regulation, is reputed to have originated the famous phrase, *"laissez faire, laissez passer,"* or "free enterprise, free trade."

THE PHYSIOCRATS

The most important French antimercantilists called themselves *physiocrats.* Their leader was François Quesnay (1694-1774), court physician to Louis XV. Quesnay disagreed with the mercantilist assumption that wealth originated in industry and trade. He argued that only agriculture, by virtue of the life-giving aspects of nature, could produce a surplus over and above the effort invested in production. Quesnay then went on in his famous *Economic Table* of 1758 to show how the surplus from agriculture flowed through the entire economy in the form of rent, wages, and purchases, supporting all the social classes as it went. Two policy conclusions stemmed from his analysis: (1) regulation of trade and industry impeded economic development by hindering the flow of income and commodities on which the economy depended; (2) all taxes should be paid by landowners (as distinguished from farmers) partly because they were not productive and partly because their luxurious way of living distorted the flow of income.

Quesnay had been greatly impressed by the discovery of the circulation of blood in the human body and likened the circulation of money and products to that biological process. He believed profoundly that all wealth came ultimately from the life-giving process created by God. A strong believer in the supremacy of natural law, he felt that a regime of economic freedom would be both beneficial and self-regulating.

Another physiocrat, Jacques Turgot (1727-1781), rose to be minister of finance. In two short years he introduced a variety of antifeudal and antimercantilist reforms and was supported by the king, but opposition from the nobility forced him out of office. Even the "absolute" ruler of France was unable to push through reforms over the opposition of the nobility, and a few years later the old regime was swept away.*

All the physiocrats agreed on one basic proposition, that wealth came ultimately from the land. Only land contained the life-giving forces of nature derived from God. Manufacturing could change only the form of wealth derived from nature, and commerce could change only its location and ownership. Land alone could produce a surplus. This was the second major theory of the source of wealth.

THE ECONOMIC LIBERALS

The physiocratic interlude was short, although its influence hung on even in the United States, where a long line of statesmen from Jefferson to Lincoln were convinced that the nation's future depended on encouraging the small

*During the Revolution another prominent physiocrat, Pierre du Pont de Nemours, emigrated to the United States, where he stayed for several years. In 1802 his son founded a small gunpowder factory near Wilmington, Delaware, the beginning of the great Du Pont chemical enterprise.

farmer. Far more important was the rise of *economic liberalism.* From small beginnings in the late seventeenth and early eighteenth centuries, it became the mainstream of economic thought in the nineteenth century and lives on today as the classic capitalist ideology.

The early economic liberals—those who advocated the doctrine before it was systematized by Adam Smith in the latter part of the eighteenth century—first attacked restrictions on international trade and fought for an end to tariffs, monopolies, and regulations. They based their argument on the social theory that individual motives, however selfish they might be, resulted in benefits to society as a whole.

The first important economic liberal in England was Dudley North (1641–1691), whose *Discourses Upon Trade* was published anonymously in the year of his death. Because North was a wealthy merchant and landowner who became a treasury official, it is understandable that he was cautious in publishing an attack on the nationalistic policies of mercantilism. His book made a strong case for free trade and attacked the mercantilist assumption that a favorable balance of trade was necessarily desirable. People trade, he argued, because it is advantageous to both parties, promoting specialization, division of labor, and the increase of wealth. Regulation interfered with these benefits by reducing and restricting trade and inevitably reduced real wealth.

North's argument was supported by the philosopher and historian David Hume (1711–1776), who in 1752 pointed out that an automatic economic process would cause any favorable balance of trade to disappear: a surplus of exports would be paid for by imports of gold and silver, which would increase the money supply and cause prices to rise, which in turn would cause a decline in exports until exports and imports were in balance. It was therefore impossible for mercantilist policy to continuously maintain both a favorable balance of trade and imports of gold and silver.

The logic of North and Hume made mincemeat of the mercantilist arguments for regulation of foreign trade. According to Hume, the policies would not work, and North showed that the results would be undesirable if they *did* work.

In the meantime, a fascinating, popular, and controversial book had appeared in 1704, a doggerel poem called *The Fable of the Bees,* written by Bernard de Mandeville (1670–1733), a Dutch doctor who had emigrated to England. The poem's basic argument was that advances in civilization were the result of vices, not virtues. Progress came from the selfish interests of the individual—desire for ease and comfort, luxury and pleasure—not from any natural propensity to work hard and save or from benevolent concern for others. Prosperity and economic growth would be increased by giving free play to the selfish motives of the individual, limited only by the maintenance of justice. The vice of selfishness would spur people on to maximize their gains and thereby add to the wealth of the nation:

> *Thus Vice nurs'd Ingenuity,*
> *Which joined with Time and Industry,*
> *Had carry'd Life's Conveniencies,*
> *Its real Pleasures, Comforts, Ease,*
> *To such a Height, the very Poor*
> *Liv'd better than the Rich before,*
> *And nothing could be added more.*

The book was suppressed by an embarrassed government, with the full support of the guardians of morality. Yet, together with the theory of natural economic adjustments described by North and Hume, the selfish motives lauded by Mandeville became the basis of the next great economic theory— economic liberalism.

The economic liberals of the eighteenth century found the source of wealth in neither trade nor agriculture but in human labor. It was through individual effort, they argued, that production takes place and the where-withal to satisfy human needs is provided. Nature produces few materials that people can use in natural form: almost all natural products must be transformed by human effort before they can satisfy human wants. Without productive effort, natural products are worthless.

This theory became known as the *labor theory of value.* It emphasized that the production of wealth had as its ultimate purpose the satisfaction of human wants. Wealth could not be considered an end in itself, nor was the aggrandizement of national power its proper end. Wealth *was* wealth because it made people better off. The production of wealth, furthermore, depended not on the fertility of the soil or on favorable trade balances but on the individual incentives of ordinary people. The motive for work was the need to provide food, clothing, shelter, and comforts. The greater the incentive to work, the greater would be the production of wealth and the faster would humanity move toward a more abundant society.

John Locke (1632-1704), the English philosopher, tied together these ideas about labor and production of wealth with private property, and in doing so he made the institution of property one of the cornerstones of the liberal ideology. By adding labor to natural resources, people added part of themselves to the final product, making the product "theirs" to use or consume. Both wealth and private property were simultaneously produced by human labor. In Locke's words:

God hath given the world to men in common. . . . Yet every man has a property in his own person. The labour of his body and the work of his hands we may say are properly his. Whatsoever, then, he removes out of the state that nature hath provided and left it in, he hath mixed his labour with, and joined to it something that is his own, and thereby makes it his property.

Later economic liberals made much of these connections between labor, wealth, and property. They argued that the first requisite for national economic growth was the protection of private property, for unless the right to property was sustained the incentive to work was reduced, and the production of wealth would fall.

A favorite illustration of this principle was a comparison of the wealth of the English and the poverty of the Turks. In ancient times, liberals pointed out, the domain of the Turk was the wealthiest in the world, with flourishing cities, prosperous agriculture, large exports, and world-famous manufactures. But a despotic and arbitrary government seized wealth without justification, imposed confiscatory taxes, and operated both justice and government through a system of bribery. These actions brought an end to prosperity. The Turk languished in poverty thereafter, unwilling to work, to produce, or to accumulate capital because it would be seized or destroyed by a corrupt government. Happy and prosperous England, on the other hand, was growing in wealth because individual initiative was protected by a rule of law that preserved for the individual the wealth he or she produced and saved. Justice was evenhanded, not arbitrary. The sanctity of private contracts was preserved, and no property could be taken for public use without just compensation. Whatever one earned could be used as the individual alone saw fit—within the limits of legality and decency. According to the economic liberal, the functions of government were few: protection of property, maintenance of justice, and national defense. The economy would operate within this framework without additional aid or regulation. Individual incentives would produce national wealth.

There were many variations on this theme. Some economic liberals would grant broader powers to the national government, others put more stress on the strength of individual incentives and competition, still others on the operation of supply and demand in free markets. But all agreed on the need to free individual initiative from the limitations imposed by mercantilist restrictions, on the importance of work in producing wealth, and on the necessity of protecting and preserving property rights as the cornerstone of economic policy.

CHAPTER 3

Adam Smith

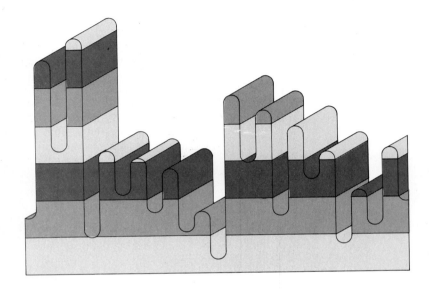

Adam Smith was the greatest of the economic liberals. A philosopher and college professor, he is considered today to be the founder of modern economics. Strangely enough, in his own lifetime he was known primarily for his writings in philosophy rather than economics, and had little influence on public policy. He cultivated his academic garden, and the flowers did not bloom until later.

THE PHILOSOPHICAL LIFE

Smith was born in Kirkaldy, Scotland, in 1723, a few months after his father's death. His childhood was quiet and uneventful, and at fourteen he entered the University of Glasgow. He did well enough to win a scholarship to Oxford, where he spent six years, dismayed by what he considered to be the low level of intellectual activity and the immorality of his fellow students. In 1751 he went to the University of Edinburgh to lecture, and the following year he became professor of logic at Glasgow when an opening suddenly appeared. Luck seemed to follow the young professor, for the next year the professorship of moral philosophy—Smith's favorite subject—became vacant, and he was appointed to that post. He lectured on ethics and his book *The Theory of Moral Sentiments* was published in 1759. To the modern reader it seems old-fashioned but interesting. Its basic idea is that ethical systems develop by a natural process out of individual personal relationships—a view that reflects the eighteenth-century interest in natural law. The individual decides that certain actions are proper or improper by observing the reactions of others to his behavior. A social consensus then develops, approving those patterns of behavior that benefit both society and the individual. The process amounts to an early "other-directed" theory of human action. The book was an immediate success and caught on well with the intelligentsia. Smith's reputation grew, and students even came from the Continent to study under him. He set to work writing a book on economics and began lecturing on "Police, Justice, Revenue and Arms" at the university.

Then came his greatest stroke of luck, but one that he had thoroughly earned. Charles Townshend, the politician who later as Chancellor of the Exchequer was responsible for the tea tax and other taxes that helped bring on the American Revolution, married a wealthy widow and acquired a teen-age stepson. An appropriate education for the young Duke of Buccleuch became important, and Townshend resolved to get the best. He had been very impressed by Adam Smith's book—and by the popular and critical esteem in which it was held—so he approached the forty-year-old philosopher to take a position as the young Duke's tutor. To the surprise of his friends, including the philosopher David Hume, Smith accepted the post: it involved a three-year sojourn in France and a lifetime pension of three hundred pounds a year (about fifteen hundred dollars, a large sum in those days).

Much of the time in France was spent in Toulouse, where Smith, bored, began writing his book on economics. Later, in Paris, Smith met the leading physiocrats Quesnay and Turgot and discussed their doctrines.

Returning to Scotland, Smith lived on his pension and continued writing his book. His friends wondered when it would be finished, for he seemed to work on it interminably. Finally, in 1776, *An Inquiry Into the Nature and Causes of the Wealth of Nations* was published.* The book was successful but not popular. Although it was read and appreciated by some, the general public ignored it. William Pitt seems to have based some of his tax proposals of the late 1780s on Smith's ideas, but it was not until twenty years after Smith's death that a new generation of writers, intent on building a new science of political economy, established Smith as the founder of their science and a major genius. In the meantime, the author returned to Scotland and in 1778 was appointed commissioner of the customs, a post his father had held. His death in 1790 passed almost unnoticed by his contemporaries.

Adam Smith did not lead a spectacular life. As a child of three he was kidnaped by gypsies for a few hours, and as a grown man he was once confronted briefly by a robber but otherwise he had few adventures. Typically, he was absent-minded. Strolling in his garden at Kirkaldy one Sunday morning, wearing a dressing gown and lost in concentration, he took a wrong turn down the turnpike and walked fifteen miles to Dunfermline before his thoughts were interrupted by the church bells. But despite the colorless personality of its author, the *Wealth of Nations* is a great book because it resolved the key problem of social philosophy in its time.

*Other important events occurred in 1776. Jeremy Bentham's *Fragment on Government* and Richard Price's *On Civil Liberty* were published, as was Edward Gibbon's *Decline and Fall of the Roman Empire*. Parliament rejected a bill that would have provided for universal male suffrage. Discontent continued in the American colonies, culminating in the *Declaration of Independence.* And the Boulton and Watt steam engine was applied to factory machinery for the first time.

THE PROBLEM IN SOCIAL PHILOSOPHY: ORDER OR CHAOS IN SOCIETY

The key problem of social philosophy in the eighteenth century was how social order emerges out of the potential chaos of an individualistic society. The problem arose because the spreading market economy, penetrating deeply into the daily lives of ordinary people, was gradually eliminating the medieval patterns of social status and defined obligations.

In medieval times each person had his place as part of one or more organized groups, each with its rights and duties. Lord and peasant, miller and priest, were each part of a village community that continued to function on the basis of traditional and often inherited obligations to others. Craftsman and merchant were members of guilds and citizens of towns, and each had his place and function, at least in theory if not in practice, based on the charter of guild or town. Religious doctrine held that there was a universal natural law, ordained by God, that underlay both the order of nature and the order of society. If many people worked to support a few who governed and fought, while others prayed, it was because God had established a social order designed to carry out all of those needed tasks.

Yet the medieval social system was rapidly passing and by the mid-eighteenth century had largely disappeared in the bustling cities like London, oriented toward international trade, banking and finance, and the making of money. What was to take the place of a social system of organized groups and established rights and duties? Could society function at all when composed only of individual units—and selfish ones at that—following their own bent and trying to outreach each other? How could social harmony be achieved in this environment of individualistic chaos?

INDIVIDUALISM IN ENGLISH LIFE

England in the eighteenth century was an open society in almost every area of life outside of politics. Individual initiative and innovation were becoming mass phenomena. In the practical and fine arts, it was the golden age of English pottery and of the great furniture makers such as Chippendale and Sheraton. English painting reached its greatest heights with Gainsborough, Reynolds, Romney, and others, and Handel composed his great oratorios. New forms of literature appeared: the novel (Defoe's *Robinson Crusoe,* Richardson's *Pamela,* and Fielding's *Tom Jones),* biography of a new type (Boswell's *Life of Samuel Johnson),* popular history (Hume's *History of England* and Gibbon's *Decline and Fall of the Roman Empire),* and the periodical essay (those of Addison and Steele in *The Tatler* and *The Spectator).* The first daily newspapers were established in London, and the first monthly magazine appeared.

The British Empire was extended by the acquisition of Canada, Gibraltar, Malta, and Ceylon. Robert Clive and Warren Hastings achieved supremacy in India for the British. Captain James Cook explored the Pacific from Australia and New Zealand to California and Hawaii for more than a decade. George Vancouver explored the northwest coast of America. James Bruce penetrated Africa in a daring expedition and found the source of the Blue Nile. Commercial and naval supremacy were won from the Dutch early in the century, and London replaced Amsterdam as the foremost center of shipping and finance in Europe.

Technological changes were building the foundations of industrialism. The cotton textile industry was transformed by a series of innovations that created the modern form of cloth manufacture, ushered in the Industrial Revolution, and made Lancashire and Liverpool great manufacturing and shipping centers. In 1738 John Kay invented a "flying shuttle" which greatly speeded up weaving and created a shortage of yarn. This led to the development of a spinning machine in the mid-1760s by James Hargreaves, an illiterate weaver and carpenter. An improved spinning machine developed by Richard Arkwright, a former barber, appeared a few years later. By 1779 Samuel Crompton, son of a small farmer, had perfected a spinning "mule" that could produce the finest yarn in much larger quantities than before; Crompton's invention was stolen and he died in poverty, but he gave the English cotton textile industry its greatest stimulus. The ability to produce yarn in greater amounts vastly increased the demand for cotton, and in America Eli Whitney developed the cotton gin, which mechanically cleaned the cotton boll. The growing of cotton throughout the world was greatly expanded, as was the plantation slavery system in America.

Industrial innovations had been preceded by the development of new machinery and methods in agriculture. Jethro Tull, a gentleman farmer, early in the eighteenth century developed a drill for planting seeds and introduced the practice of planting in rows. Charles Townshend, grandfather of Adam Smith's benefactor and a prominent statesman, retired from political life in 1730 to devote his time to the development of new crops, especially fodder crops such as turnips and clover. This was an important breakthrough: formerly land had to remain fallow to recoup its fertility, but now it could grow animal feed crops and still be "rested" for a year. Robert Bakewell, another successful farmer, developed techniques of stock breeding and introduced improved methods of livestock management. Arthur Young, the great writer on agriculture, spent most of his life publicizing the new methods and advocating enclosures as necessary to their adoption. The new agriculture techniques required larger farms, increased capital, and fenced-in fields, and from 1760 to 1830 the open lands of England were extensively fenced and hedged. Small farms and the village common disappeared in favor of larger acreage. Increased agricultural output and lower costs of production meant that greater numbers of the population could join the labor force in the growing industrial cities.

These were only a few of the leading events and the major personalities associated with them. Thousands of other people in commerce and industry, agriculture, exploration and empire building, the arts, and other aspects of English life took advantage of opportunities with initiative and imagination. Many were of humble origin. Even in politics, the last stronghold of privilege, a few newcomers like Edmund Burke were able to work up to positions of prominence and power.

This was the practical, everyday side of the social process that philosophers like Smith tried to analyze. They could see all around them an economy in ferment, with change the order of the day. Progress was being made because of the individual efforts of thousands of people acting for themselves alone. There seemed to be no order or reason behind the process, yet humanity was certainly moving onward—perhaps haltingly, but nevertheless onward—to what appeared to be a better world. In one respect there was a theoretical problem to solve—what were the principles that produced orderly social relationships in an individualistic, competitive, changing society? In another respect the problem was quite practical—would government regulation and control impede or advance the progress of such a society?

NATURAL LAW IN SCIENCE
AND POLITICAL THEORY

A new view of the world was emerging in Adam Smith's time, and within its framework writers in the social sciences were beginning to construct new explanations of human and social relationships. The Renaissance (fifteenth and sixteenth centuries) introduced a rational, scientific point of view, and the Reformation (sixteenth century) greatly weakened religious explanations of natural and social phenomena. In the seventeenth and eighteenth centuries the development of science and mathematics greatly strengthened naturalistic rather than theological explanations and led to theories in which natural forces alone were sufficient to explain events.

The greatest advance in the natural sciences was made by the English physicist Isaac Newton (1642-1727). His *Mathematical Principles of Natural Philosophy* (1687) pictured a mechanical universe operating under the influence of basic natural laws of motion, gravitation, and conservation of energy to achieve a balance of forces, or equilibrium, in which all objects had their proper place. A great theory, it was proved to the public by the return of Halley's Comet in 1759, just as Edmund Halley had predicted after calculating its orbit in 1682.

Other sciences were similarly developed on the basis of natural laws. Robert Boyle discovered in 1660 that the volume of a gas varies inversely with the pressure. Antoine Lavoisier proved the law of conservation of matter through quantitative chemical analysis: matter changes its form but not its quantity. In biology, William Harvey discovered and demonstrated the circulation of blood; and in the eighteenth century the regularity of nature was emphasized when plant and animal forms were systematically classified in interrelated groups by botanists and zoologists.

Political theory was the first area in the social sciences to develop an emphasis on natural law, regularity, and equilibrium. Hugo Grotius (1583-1645), the Dutch legal theorist and father of modern international law, stated the basic ideas. Grotius postulated that humans are inherently social beings and cannot survive without some form of social organization. Therefore, he argued, certain minimal conditions, or natural laws of society, must be realized if human society is to exist. Grotius listed the natural conditions of society as security of property, good faith and fair dealing, and correspondence between individual efforts and rewards.

It was in England, however, that natural law theories of the state evolved most fully. The English were engaged, throughout the seventeenth and eighteenth centuries, in changing a monarchy that claimed absolute authority because of divine right to a constitutional government based on the consent of the governed. The classical theory of democracy emerged from the events and the debate.

People are inherently selfish, it was argued, and they institute governments in order to protect their natural rights as individuals—life, liberty, and ownership of property. A supporter of absolute monarchy, Thomas Hobbes (1588-1679), argued for absolutism on the grounds that the stronger the power exercised by the sovereign, the more successful would be the social restraint on the selfish, combative element in human nature. John Locke (1632-1704), on the other hand, argued that order and freedom were compatible: people institute governments to avoid chaos and perserve their natural rights, but absolute power is granted to no one. The function of the state is to enforce the laws of nature and punish infractions of them, and the laws of nature are superior even to acts of the state. Within this structure, Locke said, individual action could be given free play. To these foundations of democratic theory Locke and his followers added the theory of majority rule: the interests of everyone in preservation of order were essentially similar, and the best method of determining the common good was decision making by a majority of all. Only the individual could know what was in his or her own best interest, and while a single person could be wrong in any one instance, it was highly unlikely that the consensus of a large group would be seriously in error. Finally, the Jewish philosopher Baruch Spinoza (1632-1677) added the last link to the liberal political philosophy: checks and balances within the government were necessary in order to temper power with justice, and English political theorists quickly integrated that idea into democratic theory.

By the early years of the eighteenth century the political philosophers had developed a theory of liberal democracy based on natural-law precepts. An analysis of the economy in similar terms was next on the agenda. Toward the middle of the century there were several unsuccessful attempts by a variety of writers to produce systematic treatises on the natural laws of economic life and their relationship to individual freedom and government action. It was to this problem in social philosophy that Adam Smith directed his efforts. The *Wealth of Nations* was the result.

SMITH'S SYSTEM OF NATURAL LIBERTY

Adam Smith advocated a "system of natural liberty," in which each individual would be left free to pursue and advance his own interests. This system, he argued, would result in the greatest wealth both for the individual and for society. Indeed, the very effort of the individual to serve himself would bring maximum benefits for society as a whole and for other individuals. This was the simple principle that would enable social order to develop in an individualistic society.

The advocates of mercantilism and government regulation had assumed that the selfish desires of individuals would lead to less wealth for all unless human actions were regulated and controlled. More for me means less for you, was the assumption, unless personal efforts were directed toward more for all.

This argument was wrong, said Smith. If I want something from you, I must produce something you want and exchange it for what you have. Both of us benefit, because we both give up something that has less value to us than does the product we receive in exchange; hence the welfare of both is increased over what it would otherwise be. As Smith phrased it:

> It is not from the benevolence of the butcher, the brewer, or the baker, that we expect our dinner, but from their regard to their own interest. We address ourselves, not to their humanity but to their self-love, and never talk to them of our own necessities but of their advantages.

According to Smith, self-interest in a free society would lead to the most rapid progress and growth a nation was capable of achieving. People would save in order to improve their own positions and in so doing would add more capital to the nation's resources. They would use that capital in the most profitable way and in so doing produce the things that others wanted most. Even where laws and regulations impeded freedom to invest, these motives would be so strong that they would still lead to growth and wealth:

> The uniform, constant, and uninterrupted effort of every man to better his condition, the principle from which public and national, as well as private opulence is originally derived, is frequently powerful enough to maintain the natural progress of things toward improvement, in spite both of the extravagance of government, and of the greatest errors of administration.

The greatest hindrance to economic progress was government, in Adam Smith's view. In the system of natural liberty there were only three legitimate functions of government: the establishment and maintenance of justice, national defense, and "erecting and maintaining certain public works and certain public institutions, which it can never be for the interest of any individual, or small number of individuals, to erect and maintain." Smith did not admit much into this last category, however. Roads and communications, yes—but their cost should be borne by the user through tolls rather than by the general taxpayer. Education and religious instruction, maybe—they were of general benefit but could be provided by private enterprise or voluntary contributions as well as by government. Any other government undertaking would be more harmful than beneficial, even though the best of motives were behind it:

> Every system which endeavors . . . to draw towards a particular species of industry a greater share of the capital of the society than what would naturally go to it . . . . retards, instead of accelerating, the progress of the society toward real wealth and greatness.

Although Smith definitely looked with disfavor upon government enterprise, it should not be supposed that he would give business a completely free hand. He was aware of the tendency of businessmen to conspire to their own advantage against the public:

> People of the same trade seldom meet together, even for merriment and diversion, but the conversation ends in a conspiracy against the public, or in some contrivance to raise prices.

Nevertheless, Smith was not afraid of monopoly. He lived in a simpler age than ours, before the growth of great enterprises and giant industrial plants. The only example of industrial production in his book is a pin factory in which some two dozen handicraft workers were employed. In those days the capital required for entry into almost any trade was small, technology was simple and available to all, and monopoly existed only where special privileges were granted and protected by government. Smith was confident that no private monopoly unprotected by government could long endure: monopoly profits would immediately invite competition, which would destroy the monopoly.

THE SELF-ADJUSTING MARKET

If self-interest was the driving force of the economy, the mechanism through which it worked was a system of self-adjusting markets. Competition among sellers in an effort to make profits would naturally result in a pattern of production fitted to the needs and desires of consumers, while profits would be held to a minimum amount just large enough to motivate producers.

Every commodity, according to Smith, has a "natural" price. In primitive societies it is determined by the amount of labor needed for production. In more advanced societies, those in which private property has developed, the natural price depends on costs of production—the amount that must be paid for wages, rent, and profit. Whenever the market price of a commodity differs from its natural price, market forces are set in motion to move it back. As Smith explains it:

> When the price of any commodity is neither more nor less than what is sufficient to pay the rent of the land, the wages of the labour, and the profits of the stock employed in raising, preparing, and bringing it to market, according to their natural rates, the commodity is then sold for what may be called its natural price . . . precisely for what it is worth, or for what it really costs the person who brings it to market. . . .
>
> When the quantity of any commodity which is brought to market falls short of the effectual demand, all those who are willing to pay . . . cannot be supplied with the quantity which they want. . . . Some of them will be willing to give more. A competition will immediately begin among them, and the market price will rise. . . .
>
> When the quantity brought to market exceeds the effectual demand, it cannot be all sold to those who are willing to pay the whole value of the rent, wages and profit, which must be paid in order to bring it thither. . . . The market price will sink. . . .

These changes in price set in motion corresponding changes in the amount produced. When the market price of a commodity is greater than its natural price, more of that commodity will be produced and brought to market. On the other hand, production will fall when the market price is below the natural price and when, therefore, the resources used in production cannot be paid at their natural rates. Again, Smith describes how production responds to price relationships:

> The quantity of every commodity brought to market naturally suits itself to the effectual demand. . . . If at any time it exceeds the effectual demand, some of the component parts of its price must be paid below their natural rate. If it is rent, the interest of the landlords will immediately prompt them to withdraw a part of their land; and if it is wages or profit, the interest of the

labourers in the one case, and of their employers in the other, will prompt them to withdraw a part of their labour or stock from this employment. The quantity brought to market will soon be no more than sufficient to supply the effectual demand. All the different parts of its price will rise to their natural rate, and the whole price to its natural price.

If on the contrary, the quantity brought to market should at any time fall short of the effectual demand, some of the component parts of its price must rise above their natural rate. If it is rent, the interest of all other landlords will naturally prompt them to prepare more land for the raising of this commodity; if it is wages or profit, the interest of all other labourers and dealers will soon prompt them to employ more labour and stock in preparing and bringing it to market. The quantity brought thither will soon be sufficient to supply the effectual demand. All the different parts of its price will soon sink to their natural rate, and its whole price to its natural price.

The natural price, therefore, is, as it were, the central price, to which the prices of all commodities are continually gravitating. Different accidents may sometimes keep them suspended a good deal above it, and sometimes force them down even somewhat below it. But whatever may be the obstacles which hinder them from settling in this center of repose and continuance, they are constantly tending towards it.

The whole quantity of industry annually employed in order to bring any commodity to market, naturally suits itself in this manner to the effectual demand. It naturally aims at bringing always the precise quantity thither which may be sufficient to supply, and no more than supply, that demand.

Little has been added in the last two centuries to this description of market equilibrium. Contemporary economists use the term *normal* rather than *natural* price, and they are more careful to spell out the exact conditions under which it prevails. A much more complex analysis of production costs has been developed, and the process by which the level of output responds to price has been analyzed in even greater detail. But the basic descriptions of how supply and demand determine an equilibrium price, of how competition pushes that price to a level that just covers production costs, and of how production responds to demand have remained fundamentally unchanged in the writings of successive generations of economists.

Smith's analysis of the self-adjusting market economy had tremendous significance. It showed that production will automatically adjust to the pattern of consumer demand, whatever that demand may be and however it may shift and change. It showed that competition among sellers will drive prices down to the lowest possible level consistent with continued production at levels satisfactory to consumers. It showed that resources will be used in the most efficient and economical manner—using as the criterion of efficiency and economy the satisfaction of consumer wants at the lowest possible prices consistent with continued production at the desired levels. And it showed that all this could be accomplished through the free operation of market forces, with no interference or direction from government or any other agency of economic management.

Smith emphasized, however, that these ideal results could be precluded by abridgements of full freedom in economic activity, such as "secrets in manufactures," "secrets in trade," "singularity of soil and situation," "monopoly," and "all those laws which restrain . . . competition." Smith was particularly opposed to monopoly in all of its forms, and some of his most pungent comments point to its evils:

> The monopolists, by keeping the market continually understocked, by never fully supplying the effectual demand, sell their commodities much above the natural price, and raise their emoluments, whether they consist in wages or profit, greatly above their natural rate.
> The price of monopoly . . . is upon every occasion the highest which can be squeezed out of the buyers. . . .

Whatever the source of the restrictions on economic freedom that led to monopoly—whether government, business, or labor—Adam Smith was opposed to it.

TWO QUALIFICATIONS

At this point it is important to note two limitations on Smith's analysis of the free market. These limitations were at the heart of criticisms developed by socialists of the nineteenth century, and theories of later economists have not satisfactorily overcome them.

The first limitation concerns the nature of "effectual demand" and its dependence on the pattern of income distribution. It is fine to argue that production will match itself to the pattern of consumer demand, but if the distribution of income is highly unequal, that pattern will provide much to the rich and little to the poor. Unless the distribution of income is right and proper, it does little good to argue that production is efficient and economical. If the distribution of income is wrong, the pattern of production will be wrong also, no matter how efficiently the free market works to match production with demand. This basic problem was almost immediately raised by the socialists spawned by the early Industrial Revolution, and it was shortly thereafter expanded by Karl Marx into a theory of the breakdown of capitalism. Later generations of economists have attempted to provide answers to the problem—most successfully in the 1890–1910 period—with results that have not been fully satisfactory.

The second limitation, closely related to that of economic justice, concerns private property in land and capital. Adam Smith, as a good economic liberal, supported the institution of private property as both natural and necessary to the preservation of economic incentives. However, he granted its necessity only in advanced societies. In primitive society, only labor needed a reward as a factor of production, and the cost of production consisted of wages alone. In advanced societies, rent on land and profit on capital became part of the costs of production. In the case of rent and profit, the costs of production were clearly the products of *social organization,* not natural phenomena in the same sense as human labor and the motive of self-interest. This qualification spoiled Smith's grand scheme of an equilibrium of *natural* forces in the market.

Socialists were quick to seize upon these gaps in Smith's logic. Only a return to labor was natural, they argued, and only when the full value of output was gained by labor through social ownership of land and capital would the natural state of society be recaptured. Then economic justice could also be achieved, since the entire product of society would go to those who worked and the pattern of effectual demand would not be distorted by unearned income. In later chapters the dialogue on economic justice between the critics and the supporters of the existing order will be explored in greater detail.

ECONOMIC GROWTH

Adam Smith was not primarily concerned with these matters of justice in income distribution, and they did not become topics of major concern to economists until after the rise of socialism. Smith was far more concerned with economic growth and the advancement of society to higher levels, which he also explained in terms of human motives inherent in the psychology of the individual and hence natural and inevitable in a free society.

The "progress of opulence," according to Smith, is the direct result of three factors: division of labor, widening markets, and accumulation of capital. As productivity rises because of these developments, "a general plenty diffuses itself through all the different ranks of the society."

Specialization in production and *division of labor* rest upon an inherent human "propensity to truck, barter and exchange one thing for another," according to Smith. Only humans show this propensity: "nobody ever saw a dog make a fair and deliberate exchange of one bone for another with another dog." Moreover, the same psychological inclination that leads people to trade, and thus gives rise to specialization, also makes them dependent upon one another and thereby engenders the complex social fabric of the market economy. This is an old-fashioned view, however: the modern economist argues that people specialize in producing one thing rather than attempt to produce everything they need because their productivity and earnings are thereby increased.

Just as exchange gives rise to specialization and division of labor, Smith said, "the extent of this division must always be limited . . . by the extent of the market." When the market is small, no one can devote himself to producing only one product. But when the market expands, he can specialize and thereby gain the advantages of increased efficiency. Wider markets lead to greater specialization, higher productivity, and greater wealth, and to the use of money in an effort to overcome the difficulties of barter in a system of complex exchange relationships.

None of this economic growth can occur without large amounts of capital, gathered out of savings and used to further increase productivity and promote still greater specialization and widening of markets. *Accumulation of capital* was seen as the key to economic expansion. But the whole process depended on security of property:

> In all countries where there is tolerable security, every man of common understanding will endeavor to employ whatever stock he can command, in procuring either present enjoyment or future profit. . . . A man must be perfectly crazy who, where there is tolerable security, does not employ all the stock which he commands, whether it be his own or borrowed of other people. . . .

In those unfortunate countries, indeed, where men are continually afraid of the violence of their superiors, they frequently bury and conceal a great part of their stock ... a common practice in Turkey; in Indostan, and I believe in most other governments of Asia.

Smith was well aware that economic growth brings change and diversity. As capital is accumulated the natural progress of opulence proceeds from agriculture to manufacturing to commerce, and the affluent society exhibits prosperity in all three areas. A developing agriculture gives rise to the growth of towns, which in turn offer a larger market for agricultural products, and a developed urban and rural society offers widened opportunities for trade and shipping. Enlarged trade further stimulates manufacturing and specialized agricultural production for export. Population increases as productivity rises, facilitating still broader market expansion and stimulating still more specialization and capital accumulation.

By this process the economy moves forward to higher and higher levels of development, raising the whole social order with it. Yet it simultaneously maintains the orderly market equilibrium that continuously tends toward a pattern of production fitted to effectual demand. The system of natural liberty produces an equilibrium of forces moving always toward opulence.

SMITH'S ACHIEVEMENT

Adam Smith's analysis of the market economy emphasized that individualism resulted in order, not chaos. Even though each person competed with all others for wealth and profit, their very competition unleashed market forces that led to an orderly increase in the wealth of the nation. The desire for prosperity, coupled with a natural tendency to trade and exchange, led to specialization, investment of capital, and stable economic growth. The free economy served the individual, whose needs and desires were met by the natural tendency of producers to make and sell what consumers desired. The welfare of the community was thereby maximized.

The moral dilemma of earlier writers was resolved by Smith's analysis, in that there was no conflict between individual and social benefits. The whole structure rested on the free, competitive play of individual selfishness. The motives lauded by Mandeville a half-century earlier were shown by Smith to be the source of economic growth, social order, and general welfare. The path to brotherhood—at least in economic affairs—lay through competitive selfishness. Adam Smith had thus provided social philosophers and moralists with answers to problems that had gone unresolved for a century.

In addition, Smith presented future economists with the analytical framework of the science of economics. His vision of a competitive market equilibrium following a path of growth to affluence and abundance defined the problems that the science of economics has wrestled with ever since. His formulation of the solutions—the self-adjusting market and the process of capital accumulation—was the starting point for a complex theoretical system that later economists have richly elaborated. Smith's purely scientific contribution has been vast, and in its basic structure his framework still remains the heart of scientific economics.

It is easy to see why the *Wealth of Nations* is one of the great books of

Western civilization. At one level, it is a polemic written for its own time and directed against the existing practices and policies of government. At another, it is a philosophical treatise that deals with fundamental problems of order and chaos in human society. Finally, it is a scientific treatise that analyzes the principles on which the economic system functions. All three themes are so closely intertwined that no one aspect of the argument stands alone, but each supports the others. It is a fascinating amalgam of ideology, philosophy, and scientific analysis.

CHAPTER 4

Classical Economics

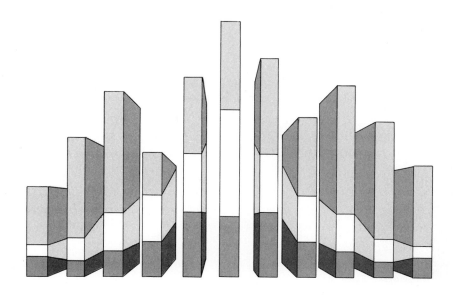

Adam Smith founded a "school" of economics. Particularly strong in England, Smith's followers dominated the field in both Europe and the United States for almost a century. They represented the orthodox approach to economic problems and policy up to the last quarter of the nineteenth century and were united by their acceptance of Smith's liberalism and his system of natural liberty. Their analytical system was founded on Smith's equilibrium of supply and demand in competitive markets, and they generally favored freedom of action for business enterprise and strong limitations on government. They were internationalists and stood for free trade and free movement of capital. "Classical economics" is the name usually given to this style of thinking.

Four other economists besides Smith made major contributions to the classical system. They were Thomas R. Malthus, David Ricardo, Jeremy Bentham, and Jean Baptiste Say. Working primarily in the turbulent first quarter of the nineteenth century, when the world economy was percolating with the changes wrought by war, revolution, economic change, population growth, new technologies, and political upheaval, they sought to analyze the economy in terms of a few basic underlying principles. In doing so, they turned economics into the first social "science."

ENGLAND'S REACTION TO THE FRENCH REVOLUTION

Adam Smith's *Wealth of Nations* had just been published when an age of revolution began—the great political and social revolutions in the American colonies and later in France that wiped away the last vestige of European feudalism and the old aristocratic order. There was a good deal of sympathy in England for the American revolutionists, since many Englishmen felt that their own society retained unwanted remnants of the old order. One of the reasons for the success of the American Revolution was undoubtedly the opposition of English liberals to continuing the war. Political reform was a particularly strong issue in England since many members of Parliament represented districts with very small populations, while some large cities, emerging as a result of economic change, had no representation whatsoever.

Many Englishmen looked with favor upon the French Revolution, too. They thought it would bring democracy to France, develop a society similar to that of England, and establish peace between two nations that had been at war intermittently for more than a hundred years. Charles James Fox, leader of the liberal Whig party, praised the fall of the Bastille, calling it the "greatest event . . . that ever happened in the world." Even William Pitt, the Tory prime minister, felt that the Revolution would enable France to become more like England, and he forecast fifteen years of peace and tranquility between the two nations.

There were, of course, conservatives who took a stand against the French Revolution from the very beginning. Edmund Burke, for example, in his *Reflections on the French Revolution* (1790), opposed the treatment of the French king and aristocrats by the French mob and feared that freedom, justice, and order would be destroyed by the growing radicalism of the "swinish multitudes."* When the Reign of Terror began, British opinion shifted to support the conservative position. The intellectual leaders who favored the Revolution—such as Thomas Paine, who wrote *The Rights of Man* in 1790 as an answer to Burke—were discredited. Some changed their minds to support the conservative position. Prime Minister William Pitt had come into office on a platform of social and economic reform but turned to a policy of uncompromising conservatism. At one point he stated, "Seeing that where the greatest changes have taken place, the most dreadful consequences have ensued . . . and . . . seeing that in this general shock the constitution of Great Britain has remained pure and unchanged in its vital principles . . . I think it right to declare my most decided opinion, that . . . even the slightest change in such a constitution must be considered an evil." The policy of the British government became one of maintaining the status quo, resisting reform, and—worse—suppressing liberal points of view.

When the wars with France began, legal action was taken in England to "prevent disloyalty." In 1795 the Habeas Corpus Act was suspended for five years; all secret associations were banned; all lecture rooms where admission was charged were legally classified as brothels, in order to prevent meetings; any meeting attended by more than fifty persons had to be

---

*The title of this book is taken from a passage in Burke's *Reflections:* "The age of chivalry is dead, that of sophisters, oeconomists and calculators has succeeded, and the glory of Europe is extinguished forever." Even in those days the economist was considered to be a liberal reformer.

superintended by a magistrate; all printing presses had to be registered with the government; export of English newspapers was prohibited; the Corresponding Society, a group of liberals who tried to spread news of liberal causes by writing letters, was suppressed in 1799. In that year and the next the Anti-Combination Laws were passed, which prohibited any kind of combination of either workers or employers for the purpose of regulating conditions of employment. There is no record that the laws were enforced against employers, but workmen were prosecuted and nascent labor unions destroyed. An atmosphere of suppression prevailed.

Although reform was prevented, the march of events could not be halted. The war years of the late eighteenth and early nineteenth centuries were years of broad and rapid change. Industrialization was greatly stimulated by wartime demands. The agricultural revolution was speeded up by wartime increases in the price of food. Population was growing rapidly and shifting from rural to urban. As cities grew, slums, inadequate sewage and water systems, and all the other urban ills developed on a large scale. The multitude of economic and social problems generated by these vast changes went unsolved, while "the Establishment" concerned itself with holding the line and rooting out the "radicals."

MALTHUS AND THE THEORY OF POPULATION

One of the most pressing problems that emerged during the years of the French wars concerned the poor. They had always been present in England, but in the former aristocratic, rural society, each parish had traditionally cared for its own. A tax on landowners was expected to provide relief funds for those who could not support themselves, while the parish was supposed to find work for the able-bodied poor. A philosophy of *noblesse oblige* prevailed.

This ancient system broke down, however. Wartime increases in food prices, the agricultural revolution and the enclosures of common land which displaced many farmers from their small plots, the Industrial Revolution, and growing cities and population brought on serious problems of poverty. Displaced farmers might have found work in handicraft manufacture of cloth, which had long been a rural occupation, but industrialization destroyed that opportunity; indeed, a whole generation of rural cottagers lost their livelihood with the rise of textile mills in the growing cities. Growth of the armed forces offered a way out for some of the able-bodied young men, but it was not a general solution.

The conservative reaction engendered by the French Revolution meant that new measures to alleviate poverty were politically impossible. Anything smacking in the least degree of reform was anathema to English policymakers. Yet the great increase in the number of poor people put a tremendous financial burden on the wealthier landowners. Something had to give.

The solution was provided by an obscure young minister named Thomas Robert Malthus (1766–1834). Like all good conservatives in a time when serious problems abound, he found the cause of the crisis not in any recent developments or changes that might be amended by policy actions but in large forces over which governments have little or no control. The problem of the poor was essentially moral, he argued, and had its origins in two fundamental propositions. First, "food is necessary to the existence of man." Second, "the passion between the sexes is necessary and will remain nearly in its present state." These two facts led to the principle that "the power of population is infinitely greater than the power in the earth to produce subsistence for man."

In other words, population would tend to increase unless it was held in check by "misery and vice." If the supply of food were to increase, there would be a corresponding increase in population until the amount of food per person had fallen back to the subsistence level, at which point the increase in population would stop. Wages would always tend toward the subsistence level. Any increase in wages above that level would only cause the working population to grow and wages to fall back once more to subsistence. Conversely, if the price of food rose, wage rates would likewise be forced upward to maintain a subsistence level. One way or another, there was a natural rate of wages which always tended toward the level of subsistence.

Consider the implications of this doctrine. Paying relief would not solve the problem of poverty but would merely increase the income of the poor and enable them to raise more children. Poverty would continue because there would be no increase in food supplies for the larger population. It was not necessary, therefore, to look to economic or social causes to explain the problems of the poor. They were caused by the old system of poor relief, which had continuously generated more poverty until the crisis had finally come. The solution was obviously to eliminate the relief system.

Assistance to the poor worsened the situation in another way. By increasing the numbers of the poor, the relief system shifted wealth from those who used it productively to an idle poverty-stricken population. Wealth that should have been invested to provide jobs was wasted on maintaining the poor in idleness, and the whole economic growth of the nation was slowed down.

The Malthusian view had other important implications. The causes of poverty were not rooted in the structure of society, in the distribution of income, in inequalities in the ownership of wealth, or in any of the many institutions of society. Neither the wealthy nor society as a whole was at fault. The poor were responsible for their own fate. All they had to do to eliminate their poverty was to have fewer children.

Even the formation of labor unions was useless, according to Malthus. Higher wages would result only in a larger population and a rise in the cost of food as more people used the wage increases to bid up food prices. The end result would be a shift of wealth from businessmen through the hands of workers into the pockets of unproductive landowners. The amount of capital available for economic expansion would be reduced just as population increased, leaving the nation worse off in the long run. Furthermore, unions meant strikes, and strikes meant reduced output, lower profits, and less capital accumulation. No, labor unions were not a solution.

Malthus' principle of population was indeed a dismal theorem—for the poor. But it was a great doctrine for conservatives, because it gave them the best of reasons for doing nothing about a serious problem. Malthus himself, an educated, religious gentleman, felt compassion and pity for the poor. He expressed it many times, and there is no reason to doubt his sincerity. But his analysis told him that social action would only hinder instead of help. The only permanent solution was moral reform of the individual.

The Malthusian principle of population was to become one of the major building blocks of classical economics and it remained the basis of wage theories for a century. Despite its essentially pessimistic point of view, however, it did provide one avenue of hope for economic growth. Economic expansion could provide increased food supplies which would cause increases in the labor force necessary to achieve further economic growth. Malthus showed that the size of the labor force was not a barrier to economic expansion. Manpower resources would emerge as the economy grew. All that was needed was capital to get the process started.

Malthus also helped later economists clarify one of the key relationships necessary for betterment of the human condition. Production had to increase faster than population if there was to be any major improvement in living standards. Europe and North America, in the ensuing era of industrialization, succeeded in achieving that relationship and are vastly better off today than they were in Malthus' time. Many other countries, in which population growth exceeds expansion of production, have millions of people who are doomed to the "misery and vice" of the Malthusian analysis.

RICARDO AND ECONOMIC GROWTH

David Ricardo (1772–1823) was the apostle of capital accumulation. In his view, the growth of capital was the great source of economic expansion, and all economic policy should be directed toward promoting it. To prove his point he developed a theoretical model of the economy that dominated the thinking of economists for fifty years. He believed that economic freedom led to maximum profits, that profits were the source of investment capital, and that a competitive economy would lead to profit-maximizing investments. In Ricardo's view, policies that benefited business would lead to maximum economic growth.

Born in London of Jewish parents, Ricardo married a Quaker girl when he reached the age of twenty-one, causing a break between himself and his stockbroker father. Financed by friends, he became a trader on the London Exchange. So adept was he at the intricate and risky business of speculation that by the age of twenty-six he had amassed a large fortune. He retired to a country estate in 1814, bought an Irish pocket-borough seat in Parliament in 1819, and devoted the rest of his life to public affairs and economics. A "millionaire radical," he advocated reforms in banking and currency, poor relief, and the tariff, and supported freedom of press and speech, as well as other reform causes. His only book on economics carries the formidable title *Principles of Political Economy and Taxation.* Its content is even more formidable, but it had tremendous influence in its day.

In the years around 1815, at the close of the Napoleonic wars, one of the great political and social issues in England was whether the nation should try to preserve its agriculturally-based economy or become more heavily industrialized. Involved in the debate was the whole question of the place of the landed aristocracy in the English social and political system. The issue was fought out in Parliament over the Corn Laws, which dealt with the import of wheat into England. (Englishmen call wheat "corn," and corn is "Indian corn.") English laws related to the import of wheat were intended to promote domestic agriculture without causing major increases in the price of food. When the price of wheat fell in England, tariffs were raised on imports of wheat in order to keep out the foreign grain that was depressing domestic prices and injuring the business of domestic farmers; when the price of wheat rose above a given level, import duties were reduced, thus encouraging more imports and keeping domestic prices from rising further. In short, the British government tried to keep grain prices between an upper and a lower limit by means of a sliding scale of tariffs.

Nevertheless, during the French wars the price of food rose substantially and farmers were well off. Their production costs also rose and remained high when peace came, wartime demand slackened, and the price of food fell. Farmers began clamoring for higher duties on imported wheat, fearing that they faced ruin unless protected by enforcement of the Corn Laws. The landowner's point of view was reinforced by arguments that a sound agriculture was necessary for England's national defense and for the preservation of the old traditions and national vigor. There was a revival of the physiocratic doctrine that economic growth depended on the natural productivity of the soil. Pamphlets appeared, such as one entitled "England Independent of Commerce," which argued for the protection and preservation of agricultural interests.

Business interests, on the other hand, opposed tariff increases, which, they declared, would raise food prices and force wages upward. The result would be reduced profits, decreased exports of manufactured products, and ruin for English industry. Business interests argued that England's future lay with industrial expansion, not with agriculture, and they demanded outright repeal of the Corn Laws.

This was the state of the issue when Ricardo and other economists entered the debate over Corn Law policy. Ricardo was on the business side of the argument. He believed that landowners, not farmers, would be the chief beneficiaries if the price of wheat in England was raised by a higher tariff. The high price of wheat would enable cultivation to be extended to areas that would otherwise be unprofitable. In older wheat-growing areas, rents would be raised to take advantage of the higher prices farmers were receiving. A larger proportion of the total national income would then flow into the hands of landowners, and this parasitic group would use its increased wealth for luxury expenditures such as servants and country houses, not for productive investment.

In addition, the enlarged cultivation of land would draw capital and labor away from industry and distort the whole production pattern of the country. Artificially high food prices would lead to a misallocation of productive resources into agriculture and out of manufacturing, thereby hindering the nation's natural development of industry.

Ricardo also pointed out that high prices for food would require high wage rates and high costs of production in manufacturing. Since England had to sell her manufactures throughout the world, competing with the products of other countries, higher costs in England industry would result in reduced business for English exports and a reduced level of output for English manufacturers. Profits would also be reduced, and there would be a slower pace of capital accumulation and economic expansion, due to the lack of both incentive and funds to invest.

This was Ricardo's indictment of the Corn Laws (although he did not advocate their complete repeal). It supported the business position on the issue with a theoretical model of the economy that gave substance and validity to his policy conclusions. Ricardo's theory was more than a treatment of a contemporary policy problem. If that were all it had been, it would have died as interest in the problem died. But Ricardo took it much further and generalized it into a comprehensive theory of economic growth.

In the early stages of a nation's growth, he argued, the population would be small and only a portion of the land would be cultivated. Under these conditions the rent paid to landowners would be a relatively small proportion, and profits a large proportion, of the total national income. The profits, plowed back into industrial development, would result in a greater demand for labor, which—following Malthus—would cause population to grow while wages remained at the subsistence level. The growth in population would require an extension of the cultivated area in order to provide larger amounts of food. This extension could be accomplished only by raising food prices to cover the higher costs of production incurred by bringing less fertile lands into cultivation. The higher price of food would enable landowners to raise the rents charged on the older cultivated lands, because the higher food prices charged could bear higher rents. At the same time, the higher cost of food would force employers to pay higher *money* wages in order to maintain wage rates at the subsistence level. This in turn would raise the cost of manufactured goods and thereby reduce the profits obtained by business-men. The reduced profits would then leave less wealth available for expansion and would also reduce incentives to invest. Ricardo envisaged that this process of economic growth would continue, with capital accumula-tion and growth gradually slowing down, until growth halted after many decades of expansion. At this stage of development the population would be large, cultivation extended, industry developed, production high—but sav-ings and capital accumulation would be adequate only for replacement of capital, not further expansion.

The picture Ricardo drew was one in which the economy, if left alone, would achieve the maximum growth possible. To that end, business would have to be freed of all restrictions that might reduce ability to maximize profits, so that the maximum amount of saving and capital accumulation could take place. Government intervention in the economy would lead to a lower rather than a higher level of economic activity. Right or wrong, the theory was on the side of the coming rulers of the social order—business interests—and this in itself ensured it long life.

THE INTERNATIONAL ECONOMY

One of the strengths of Ricardian economics was its applicability to the international economy. For the first time, an analysis of the domestic economy based on the fundamentals of land, labor, and capital could be applied rigorously to international economic relationships. This represented a major step forward in the development of economics as a science. One of the goals of all scientific endeavor is the building of broader and broader generalizations that encompass an ever-widening body of phenomena. Science advances by stripping away details and constructing general laws, and Ricardian economics did this by reducing all economic phenomena to fundamental relationships between the factors of production.

The integration of the international economy into the Ricardian model was done in two ways. First, Ricardo showed that international specialization and division of labor was advantageous to all nations and that restrictive trade policies designed to protect domestic producers would injure the nation that imposed them. Free trade was the road to economic well-being internationally as well as domestically. The argument for this position, embodied in the famous *law of comparative advantage,* is complex, but Ricardo was able to prove its validity. He showed that as long as it costs less to produce cloth in England than it does to produce wheat, *compared with costs in other countries,* it will pay the English to shift their resources to cloth manufactures, export cloth, and import wheat from other countries.

For example, suppose it takes an English worker one day's labor to produce a yard of cloth and two days' labor to grow a bushel of wheat; then wheat costs twice as much effort as cloth. Suppose also that it takes the French one day's labor to produce each product. In this case, England should produce cloth (one day's labor), export it to France, trade it one-for-one for wheat, and import the wheat back to England. In this way the English would get, for one day's labor, the wheat it would otherwise take them two days to produce. The French would also benefit. They could produce wheat, ship it to England and trade one bushel for *two* yards of cloth, and ship the cloth back to France. They would also receive products worth two days' effort for one day's actual work. Both sides would benefit from this specialization and free exchange.

But the process would not end there. The export of English cloth to France would drive its selling price down, and increased domestic production would push costs of production up. The same would happen for French wheat. As these price changes took place, the growing import-export trade between the two countries would establish an equilibrium of prices and trade. England would both produce and export much cloth, but its output of wheat would be small and most of its supplies would be imported. The opposite would be true of France. The two commodities would sell for equivalent prices in the two countries, for if they did not, further shifts in production, trade, prices, and costs would occur. In this way an international equilibrium would be established in which the world pattern of production would be optimized.

This analysis of international economic equilibrium was supplemented by a second approach, this time in the field of economic development. The preceding section of this chapter described the Ricardian theory of the stationary economy, in which the return to capital was so low that only replacement of worn-out capital equipment occurred. As the return to capital in one country fell, however, profit-maximizing investors would seek higher returns by investing in less well-developed countries abroad. Capital exports from the mature economies would flow quickly to the newly developing countries, and they in turn would be brought to higher levels of production and wealth. Of course, they would have to offer political stability and protection to private property, but aside from that qualification the classical economist could look forward to a whole world moving gradually toward opulence.

In this way Ricardo and his followers applied Adam Smith's concepts of orderly growth and market equilibrium to the international economic system. Only national rivalry, with its tariffs, trade restrictions, and wars, could interfere with the development process. It is perhaps ironic that the part of his theory which Ricardo thought most important—the theory of economic growth—has been largely discarded by modern economists, although they retain his stress on capital accumulation. But the theory of international economic equilibrium, which was only a minor part of the original analysis, remains an integral part of modern economics in almost its original form.

SAY'S LAW OF MARKETS

Only one major element had to be added to classical economics to complete its systematic analysis of the economy: an examination of production and employment levels. It had been shown that a free market would allocate resources so that production would adjust to consumer needs and wants, that output would grow through savings and capital accumulation, that income would be distributed among social classes according to natural laws, and that the same principles applied to both domestic and international economics relationships. Still to be determined was whether a free market would also maintain full employment of workers and capital.

The issue was not merely academic. The Industrial Revolution had brought economic instability, aggravated in the early years of the nineteenth century by the on-again, off-again wars against Napoleon. When peace came in 1815 the economic stimulus of government spending was withdrawn from the economies of both England and the Continent. Demand for industrial products fell from its wartime levels, and England was faced with competition from the Continent for the worldwide markets it had kept largely to itself. Soldiers and sailors returning to the civilian economy and handicraft workers displaced by factory production increased the numbers of workers seeking employment. These problems were compounded in England by the fact that industrialization had proceeded furthest there.

England's economic situation was further aggravated by government monetary policies that resulted in "tight" money and a shortage of credit just when the economy needed a stimulus. During the war years prices had risen substantially, credit had been much expanded, and the Bank of England had stopped redeeming its paper currency in gold. Increases in the national debt had been one of the major causes of the credit expansion and the price increases. Economists, led by Ricardo, blamed the inflation on excessive issuance of paper money and prescribed when the war ended that the Bank of England again redeem paper currency in gold at the levels that had prevailed before the war, even though there was not enough gold to sustain the existing amounts of currency and credit then outstanding. The economy was to be given a dose of deflation.

This early application of principles of sound finance was based on an incorrect diagnosis of the economic illness, and the remedy turned out to be worse than the disease. Inflation had been largely due to expansion of total spending during the war years, promoted in part by increases in the money supply, at a time when output could be increased only slowly. Prices had to rise, and the amount of currency and credit reflected this expansion of a relatively fully employed economy. By prescribing deflation as the cure for inflation, economists were able to bring prices down, but only at the expense of output and employment. Like any deflation after inflation, creditors and owners of financial assets benefited—to the detriment of unemployed workers and profitless businesses. The burden of England's economic difficulties was shifted from owners of monetary assets to producers.

Hardship was widespread and business activity was in a generally depressed state for thirty years after 1815. The economy had its ups and downs during this period, and economic growth continued, but there was hardly a year in which England had full employment by modern standards. In some years, unemployment apparently rose to 40 or 50 percent of the work force in the industrial cities of the midlands.

The instability of the economy had already aroused criticisms of industrialism and the new economic order. Even before 1815 Jean Simonde de Sismondi (1773-1842), a Frenchman traveling in England, had seen the industrial depressions and predicted that capital investment would periodically force the capacity to produce to outrun the ability to consume. His argument was echoed by an English physiocrat, William Spence (1783-1860), who pointed out in two pamphlets of 1807 and 1808 that capital investment in commerce and manufacturing created economic instability and insecurity, while the development of agriculture promoted economic stability and security. Spence called particular attention to the possibility that savings would reduce purchasing power and cause prosperity to disappear. Both Sismondi and Spence were disenchanted with industrialization, and each favored a different type of economic order—Spence the old aristocratic society and Sismondi a system that emphasized human and community values rather than individual gain. Their discussions of depressions were only part of more comprehensive attacks on the emerging business society.

Classical economists were quick to reply to these attacks. The basis of their rebuttal was a brief passage in a work by Jean Baptiste Say (1767-1832), a French popularizer of Adam Smith's work whose *A Treatise on Political Economy* had appeared in 1803. That work contained the first statement of the principle that came to be known as Say's Law of Markets, a concept that dominated the thinking of most economists on the level of economic activity until the Great Depression of the 1930s.

Say argued that there could never be a general deficiency of demand or a general glut of commodities throughout the whole economy. Certain industries or sectors of industry might be plagued by overproduction, due to miscalculation and excessive allocation of resources to those types of production, but elsewhere in the economy there would inevitably be shortages. The consequent fall of prices in one area and their rise in others would induce business firms to shift production, and the imbalances would be quickly corrected.

People produce, he pointed out, not for the sake of producing but only to exchange their products for other goods they need and want. Since, therefore, production *is* demand, it is impossible for production in general to outrun demand. "Production creates its own demand" became the answer of the classical economists to the problem of business depressions.

In England, Say's argument was put forth by James Mill (1773-1836), father of the renowned philosopher and economist John Stuart Mill, in an answer to Spence. The elder Mill wrote in 1807 that every increase in supply is an increase in demand—the more there is to sell, the more will be bought. The error in the theory of general glut, he maintained, is the confusion between a temporary dislocation in the process of exchange, which would be remedied by a new direction of industry, and the impossible case of an excess of wealth in general.

One economist remained unconvinced: Thomas R. Malthus. In his *Principles of Political Economy* (1820) Malthus devoted a long last chapter to developing a theory of economic stagnation based on inadequate "effectual demand." His argument, in brief, was that wages, being less than the total costs of production, cannot purchase the total output of industry, which causes prices to fall. The decline in prices reduces incentives to invest as well as profits that could be invested. The result is a general inadequacy of purchasing power that *could* continue indefinitely. A similar condition might result from excessive savings, which cause demand to fall, prices to decline, and stagnation to follow. The remedy, according to Malthus, was to reduce large incomes so that savings would not be excessive, to impose import tariffs and thereby promote a favorable balance of trade, and to spend for public works during bad times. A program of government intervention was needed because the free market economy could not regularly provide for full employment.

Malthus' argument was not developed with clarity and preciseness—he was not a rigorous theoretician—and his good friend David Ricardo made mincemeat of his theory of general glut in letters written to Malthus, in "Notes on Malthus' Principles of Political Economy" circulated among other economists, and in discussions at London's Political Economy Club. Since Ricardo's arguments *were* clear and precise, he carried the day.

Ricardo's answer to Malthus recapitulated Say's Law of Markets in slightly more elaborate form. Savings are made not as an end in themselves but in order to employ labor in production. Mistakes can lead to a glut of a single commodity, but demand for all other commodities is not thereby reduced. A reallocation of productive effort will occur. Furthermore, unemployment causes wages to fall, inducing businessmen to hire the idle laborers with the capital created by savings. In this way, all capital is put back into use and all willing workers are once again employed. The basic cure, therefore, is not income redistribution and public works but lower wages and higher profits.

Ricardo's answer was supplemented by an extraordinarily perceptive volume originally published in 1802, Henry Thornton's *The Paper Credit of Great Britain*. This book had been written during the controversy over paper money, gold, and inflation, but its argument was adapted to Say's Law and the discussion of gluts. Thornton observed that if savings tended to become excessive, the supply of funds in the money market would rise relative to demand and the interest rate would fall. The lowered interest rates would both encourage investment and discourage savings, the process continuing until the two were equal. Any funds not used for consumption would find their way into investment. Changes in the rate of interest would ensure that savings would be invested and the level of total spending maintained. There could be no surplus of savings and no general glut of commodities. Total spending on consumption and investment would then be adequate to purchase the total output of industry.

These complicated arguments were extraordinarily important. At the purely logical level they closed the theoretical system of classical economics by showing that a free market economy would utilize all its resources.

In terms of social philosophy or ideology they showed that unemployment and instability were not caused by a private enterprise economy but were the result of noneconomic factors, psychological factors, or some other cause not associated with the institutional structure and natural processes of economic life. Finally, they prescribed a policy treatment for whatever depressions might occur: (1) strengthen the financial sector of the economy so that the processes of savings and investment could work themselves out; (2) endure the crisis until declining wages and prices ultimately encouraged enough investment to bring the economy back to normal. Such is the strength of a logical and precise theory that these policies prevailed for more than a century—at tremendous social cost, for the waiting period often brought waves of bankruptcy and long-continued unemployment—until the theory was finally demolished by a countertheory propounded during the Great Depression of the 1930s.

BENTHAM AND INTERVENTIONIST LIBERALISM

No discussion of classical economics is complete without an account of the ideas of Jeremy Bentham (1748-1832), a lifelong reformer and nonpracticing lawyer. His *Fragment on Government,* published in 1776 anonymously when he was only twenty-eight, was a brilliant attack on the traditional legal interpretation of the English constitution as antithetical to progress. He sought to show how political reform toward greater democracy would promote "the greatest good for the greatest number." The book made a sensation, but as soon as it was revealed that the author was only a young upstart and not one of the leading constitutional lawyers of the day, it was quickly dismissed. Disillusioned, Bentham began his great philosophical work, *An Introduction to the Principles of Morals and Legislation,* which was privately printed in 1780 but not published for the general public until 1789, after another of his books, *A Defense of Usury,* had been a popular success.*

Principles of Morals and Legislation is the key work in utilitarian philosophy. In it Bentham argued that every act was morally valuable to the extent that it resulted in happiness. Both human actions and moral judgments were based upon the poles of pleasure and pain:

> Nature had placed mankind under the governance of two sovereign masters, pain and pleasure. It is for them alone to point out what we ought to do, as well as to determine what we shall do. On the one hand the standard of right and wrong, on the other the chain of causes and effects, are fastened to their throne.

This single principle was more complex than it appeared, however. Bentham meant that the social system should seek to maximize its total welfare and distribute it as widely as possible. A small increase in happiness for many

---

*Bentham's major work had been completed before he reached his fortieth birthday, but he lived to be eighty-four and to wield great influence over a small band of devoted followers. He was never again to write an influential book but spent much of his later life devising complicated plans for prison reform, poor relief, education, and legislative reform. He founded the University of London with an endowment, and his will provided that his body be embalmed and once a year seated at the meeting of the university's trustees as a reminder of the principles on which the university was established. This grisly ritual is still performed today!

was better than a large increase for a few, in his opinion. But, as critics were to point out, that conclusion is not self-evident.

An important problem it raised was that of measurement. Increasing human happiness involves choosing among alternatives, and the cost of one course of action is the elimination of others—that is, we can't have everything. This means that comparisons of the magnitudes of benefits and costs must be made in order to determine the best, or optimal, solutions. As long as the discussion involved only total benefits, the problem was insoluble. Not until the economists of the last quarter of the nineteenth century began analyzing *increments* in benefits and costs—the famous marginal analysis—were even partial solutions found.

A related question was whether happiness, or utility, could be quantified. Bentham thought it could, at least in principle, but others argued that only comparisons could be made—for example, "I greatly prefer Mary to Jane, but my preference for chocolate over vanilla ice cream is not very strong." The absolute amounts of happiness derived from being with Mary or eating chocolate ice cream are, according to this view, impossible to measure and, furthermore, are irrelevant to the choices made.

These fine points were less important to Bentham than was his argument that people, *in fact,* made decisions on the basis of the amounts of utility derived from the alternative course of action open to them. This "hedonistic calculus" was the principle underlying all human action, he declared, and the means by which the welfare of society was maximized. He believed that the selfishness of economic behavior was natural, rational, and desirable.

At this point in the argument, Bentham brought in morals and legislation. If people always act only for their own greatest pleasure when they *should* act for the greatest happiness of all, is there not a contradiction involved? Bentham said there was not, because moral and legislative sanctions caused individual action to coincide with the public interest. The sanctions rewarded individual action that benefited all and punished action that diminished public welfare. Both morality and government action (if it was majority action) had a utilitarian foundation and rested on the principle of greatest happiness. Bentham, then, was not opposed to government action if it was based on democratic processes and did not reflect the narrow interests of special groups. At the same time, he wished to give free play to individual decision making within the framework of moral and legislative sanctions. His goal was to reconcile individualism and social action.

Bentham's significance goes far beyond his rather narrow and outdated view of human nature. In the first place, his ideas were important throughout the nineteenth century and profoundly affected later developments in economics. His view of humans as pleasure machines, continually calculating the advantages and disadvantages of alternative courses of action, became the accepted view, and rational economic behavior was defined in those terms. The assumption that individual decisions would lead to maximum public welfare was inherent, of course, in the work of Adam Smith and the other classical economists, but Bentham made it explicit. All the later conclusions of orthodox economics were solidly based on, or at least closely related to, this concept of human nature.

Even more important than his influence on economic science was Bentham's impact on liberal social philosophy. He brought to it an interventionist emphasis quite at variance with the tradition of laissez faire, creating a problem that even today remains unsolved.

The classical liberalism of the eighteenth century emphasized individual freedom as the ultimate goal of all policy. Reacting against political centralization and economic regulation, its advocates argued that any restriction on freedom hindered the achievement of maximum welfare. At the hands of Adam Smith, its greatest explicator, this philosophy advocated minimizing the role of government, strictly limiting it to such essentials as police, justice, and arms.

Bentham, however, saw that this philosophy was based on the assumption that only individual action could create welfare. His practical mind told him that the actions of one person in his own interest might reduce the welfare of another. His legal training and his study of constitutional law told him that the institutional arrangements within which people act could significantly determine the outcome of their actions. The very fact that human society was organized by institutional arrangements created by people—that a social system existed—meant that conscious action could create social forms which would enable people to live better lives. Benthamite utilitarianism was potentially an interventionist doctrine.

Bentham and his followers in England—they called themselves philosophical radicals—included the economists James Mill, David Ricardo, and later John Stuart Mill. Advocates of democratic government and majority rule, their major target for reform was the political system, which in their day excluded large numbers of people from the right to vote and did not provide fully for freedom of speech and the press. They believed that the social system could bring the greatest good to the greatest number only if it were fully democratic and subject to true majority rule. They were also classical economists and expounded the advantages of a freely competitive market system and of laissez-faire policies. But their utilitarian political philosophy was to have the gravest consequences for their economic theories. Once political reform was achieved, the new power of the enfranchised voter was used as an instrument of economic reform, and the laissez-faire policy was discarded. The reforms were justified in terms of individual and social welfare, and the greatest-good argument was used again and again. The classical liberalism that had stressed individualism gave place to an interventionist liberalism that emphasized social welfare, and Bentham was its apostle.

The rise of Benthamite ideas gave to economics an extraordinarily wide applicability to questions of social policy. At one extreme, it could encompass the thoroughgoing laissez-faire individualist. At the other, it could include the most dedicated social reformer. The theories and methods of scientific analysis were similar, and all sides could agree on which concepts were correct. But the assumptions and preconceptions differed, as did the conclusions. This characteristic of the mainstream of economic thought continues today and enables the good economist to arrive at objective conclusions even though other economists may legitimately disagree.

CLASSICAL ECONOMICS TODAY

The great themes of classical economics are as important today as they were in Ricardo's time. The economy has changed, of course, from industrial revolution to mature industrial capitalism. But the interrelationships of resources, people, and capital remain central to problems of human welfare. As world population gallops toward ten billion and beyond, the Malthusian population trap takes on crucial importance. The advanced industrial nations were able to break the connecting link between production and population— rising output does not trigger population growth that prevents income per person from rising. But many less developed countries find that growing populations literally eat up the gains from economic expansion and billions of people remain embedded in poverty.

The Malthusian problem is complicated in less developed countries by a social structure that moves much of the gain from economic growth into the hands of large landowners, international corporations, and urban business firms. Population growth keeps wages down in the growing cities of the third world and creates vast unemployment in both rural and urban areas. Modernization brings population growth and extremes of poverty and wealth that cry out for amelioration.

Meanwhile, in the advanced countries the processes of capital accumulation and technological change continue to produce greater wealth and rising standards of living: the twenty-five years after World War II showed the largest and most sustained increases in material well-being in the history of Western civilization. This growth also put great pressure on the natural environment through both pollution and increased use of exhaustible resources. By the late 1960s it became clear that the rapid pace of growth could not continue indefinitely without great changes in the technology of production, and that the necessary technological changes could not come rapidly enough to sustain the pace of growth. A slowdown became inevitable, and indeed it came in the 1970s.

These developments in the economy itself brought back into prominence the fundamental relationships between population, accumulation of capital, technology, and economic growth that were the central concern of classical economics. Economic policy is increasingly concerned with those issues and, as we shall observe in Chapter 12, economists are returning both to them and to a renewed interest in the classical economists. Ricardo's prediction of an end to growth and an attainment of a "steady state" has a modern relevance.

CHAPTER 5

Socialism and Karl Marx

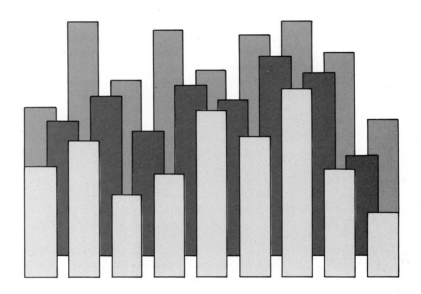

Modern socialism emerged as a response to the industrial era just as classical economics had, and just as the classical economists developed an ideology for the new order, the socialists developed a critique of it.

Some socialists were impractical, idealistic dreamers, some were hard-headed critics of the existing society and others were revolutionists, but all were united by their criticisms of the new industrial society and by their belief in common rather than private ownership of the means of production. Socialists had a different view of the nature of society than did the classical economists, arguing that the social fabric was an organic whole composed of classes, rather than independent individuals, as its essential elements. They stressed the cooperative element in human nature, rather than the materialistic profit motive of private capitalism, and they advocated equalitarianism in place of the unequal distribution of income that prevailed. The socialists could often point to actual economic conditions—real defects in industrial capitalism—to support their arguments.

SOCIALISM AND THE CLIMATE OF OPINION

The economic and political events of the half-century from 1775 to 1825 provide a background for an understanding of the rise of modern socialism. Of primary importance was the Industrial Revolution. It provided for substantial increases in living standards and opportunities for acquisition of great wealth for the new middle class. It was clear that the reasons for economic growth were industrialization, capital investment, and higher productivity and that every widening of market opportunities made still further advances possible.

To the socialist, however, industrialism had a different face. Workers in the new factories were paid low wages: although factory pay was high enough to draw labor from the countryside, unemployment in rural areas meant that workers were willing to accept very low wages. Hours of work were long, women and children were employed in substantial numbers and often in hard and dangerous jobs, factory discipline was often harsh and rigorous, and in some areas company-owned stores profited from exclusive selling rights among employees. Particularly in the textile and coal industries, competition kept selling prices low, and firms competed with each other by squeezing labor costs whenever possible. These shortcomings were particularly evident in the first half of the nineteenth century in England, where the Industrial Revolution began.

The realities of industrial life created sharp contrasts between the growing wealth of the new industrialists and bankers and the poverty of those without property who formed the work force in the factories of the slum-ridden cities. During the "hungry forties" in England, Benjamin Disraeli wrote of "the two nations"—the rich and the poor—while Charles Dickens examined *Hard Times* and the public read Thomas Hood's pathetic poem of the sewing woman, *Song of the Shirt.*

Poverty there had always been, and rich and poor had lived side by side for ages. Many always had to wrest a meager living from a recalcitrant nature. But industrialization promised abundance. For the first time it seemed as though it might be possible to produce everything people could want and that the great struggle for existence could be resolved. Yet the gray slums of Manchester and the black country of the coal mines told a different story. The promise and the reality were vastly different.

A similar difference between ideals and reality prevailed in politics. The French revolutionists of 1789 had proclaimed "liberty, equality, fraternity," and with that slogan the French had overthrown the privileges of the older order and marched through Europe to sweep away the last remnants of feudalism and aristocracy. New beliefs in freedom and democracy seemed to be creating a political order of full democracy, just as the Industrial Revolution seemed to portend an end to poverty.

But the defeat of Napoleon brought reaction and repression—and reestablishment of the old system of place and privilege. Even where parliamentary government existed, as in England and France, participation was limited to persons with property, and working people were excluded from the vote. Democracy, apparently, was fine for the middle class but dangerous if extended to the worker.

The Industrial Revolution and the French Revolution appeared to many as means of realizing some of the ageless and ancient ideals of Western civilization—abundance, an end to toil, and the triumph of brotherhood and equality. Yet in the darkness of the post-Napoleonic reaction all this was betrayed, and postwar depressions seemed to produce even greater poverty and want than before, since the unemployed worker did not have even a small plot of land on which to grow food. To the early socialists it was self-evident that private ownership of the means of production was the source of society's ills. Ownership of machines, factories, and other capital enabled the owner to reap rich rewards, to sit back and rake in profits while others worked. At the same time, his economic position gave him political power. In the eyes of the socialist, fifty years of social revolution had given wealth and power to a few owners of capital rather than to the great numbers of common people. Society as a whole had been betrayed for the benefit of a few, in the opinion of the critics.

ROBERT OWEN, UTOPIAN

The humanitarian and idealistic roots of early socialism are typified in the work and writings of the Englishman Robert Owen (1771–1858). Apprenticed to a linen-draper at ten years of age, he worked at various establishments in the textile industry through his youth, including one shop which "often worked their employees from 8 a.m. to 2 a.m." After failing in business for himself, he became manager of a textile mill when only nineteen years old. Seven years later he was able to buy control of textile mills at New Lanark, in Scotland, and in 1800 he took over their active management. The former management had used children from orphanages as part of its labor supply, along with adults, many of whom were "thieves, drunkards and criminals of every sort." The work day ran from 6 A M. to 7 P M. for children as well as adults, and the company town was composed of wooden one-room houses. Yet the working and living conditions were not considered bad for the time.

Owen was a religious man who believed that the workers of New Lanark were evil because of their surroundings, so he decided to turn New Lanark into a model community. He took no more children from workhouses or orphanages and allowed no child under ten to work. The working day was set at ten and one-half hours for both children and adults. He provided schools in the evening for the working children (imagine a child of ten going to school after working ten and one-half hours!) and set up nursery schools for younger ones. For his adult workers he established a "register of character" which recorded drunkenness and other delinquencies, such as illicit sexual behavior, so effectively that pubs quickly disappeared from the town and there were only twenty-eight illegitimate births in nine years. An elected committee, called "bug hunters" by the women, inspected domestic cleanliness once each week. A support fund for the injured, sick, and aged was established, into which workers were required to pay 1/60 of their wages. Thrift was encouraged by establishment of a savings bank and by provision of better houses for those who used the bank. Finally, Owen established a store that sold food and other products to workers, charging considerably lower prices and providing goods of higher quality than did private shopkeepers.

How could Owen do all this and still make money in the highly competitive textile industry? Apparently there were two reasons. First, his plants were located in an area of labor surplus and his wages were low: an investigating committee in 1819 reported that he paid 9 shillings, 11 pence—about $2.40—per week to men and 6 shillings—about $1.50—per week to women, figures that were below average for the time. Second, even though his methods were paternalistic, the attention he paid to workers seems to have brought relatively high labor productivity. In 1819 profits were 12.5 percent of the invested capital.

Owen himself recognized that the reforms at New Lanark had come from the patron rather than from the workers themselves, and that some form of industrial self-government would have to follow. He published his views in 1816 in one of the landmark books of the socialist movement, *The New View of Society,* at a time when England was debating the first factory act designed to limit the hours of work and establish a minimum age for child labor. Owen lobbied hard for the act, but failure of the bill adequately to cover child labor disappointed him, and the unwillingness of other employers to imitate the example of New Lanark drove him to more radical schemes.

He tried to establish cooperative communities, in which land was owned in common, and in 1824 came to the United States to open one at New Harmony, Indiana. But the community in America and others in England failed, with substantial financial loss to Owen. More successful were the cooperative retail stores established under Owen's leadership in England, beginning the far-flung consumers' cooperative movement that has been highly successful in England and Scandinavia and that has developed to some extent in the United States. Owen also tried to set up producers' cooperatives—groups of workers who owned the factory in which they worked—but these projects did not succeed.

Owen was a visionary who sought to reform society through worker-owned communities and enterprises in which profits were not permitted. He expected that in such communities the life of the individual would achieve a larger meaning through full integration into the cooperative life of the group. In an individualistic era, his efforts were doomed to fail. Perhaps he was right when he wrote to a business partner, "All the world is queer save thee and me, and methinks at times that thou art a little touched."

KARL MARX, REVOLUTIONARY

In sharp contrast to the idealistic and impractical Owen was the intense German, Karl Marx (1818-1883). Born and raised in the most economically advanced part of Germany, the Rhineland, and son of a petty legal official of the government, Marx displayed great intellectual ability at an early age. Sent to the universities at Bonn and Berlin, he first studied law with a view toward a governmental career, but his opposition to the autocratic governments in Germany precluded that. The young Marx then turned to philosophy, with the goal of a professorship, but his studies of philosophy and religion at Berlin—his doctoral dissertation was on the Stoic and Epicurean roots of Christian doctrine—led him to atheism, and this barred him from a university career. So Marx went into journalism and became editor of a liberal Cologne newspaper in 1842. It was there, while writing on economic problems, that he became convinced of the economic basis of politics—that underneath political theories and political power lay the economic interests of various groups in society. His newspaper was suppressed by the government for its liberal views, however, and Marx went to Paris where he married his childhood sweetheart, the daughter of a German baron, and became acquainted with a number of socialists.

One of them was Pierre Joseph Proudhon (1809-1865), a socialist leader who influenced him very strongly. Proudhon's chief work was a book called *What Is Property?* ("property is theft," he answered to his own question), a forceful statement of the idea that the whole product of industry should go to the worker and that private property in the means of production enabled the capitalist to appropriate wealth that rightfully belonged to the worker. This concept—not original with Proudhon—was a basic tenet of nineteenth-century socialism and fundamental to Marx's own view of capitalism. Another of Proudhon's books, subtitled *The Philosophy of Poverty,* attacked the orthodox economics of his time and especially the "iron law of wages"— the Malthusian argument that wage rates tended toward the subsistence level because of the population growth. Convinced that Proudhon's arguments were specious, Marx attacked his friend in a book sarcastically titled *The Poverty of Philosophy,* and legend has it that Proudhon never spoke to Marx again.

Another socialist whom Marx met in Paris was Friedrich Engels (1820-1895), son of a wealthy German textile manufacturer who owned mills in England as well as in Germany. Marx and Engels formed a friendship that lasted until Marx's death, and the two men collaborated in developing the ideas that Marx was later to publish. Engels supported Marx and his family for most of the next thirty-five years.

While in Paris Marx continued his journalistic career, writing articles especially critical of Prussia, and he was soon expelled from France at the request of the Prussian government. Moving to Brussels in 1848, just before the outbreak of the revolutions of that year, Marx and Engels wrote the *Communist Manifesto:* "A spectre is haunting Europe. . . . Workingmen of the world unite, you have nothing to lose but your chains!" Marx had entered on his career as active revolutionist.

When the revolution broke out Marx returned to Cologne, began his newspaper again, and publicized the revolution sweeping Europe. But the revolt was suppressed, and Marx, expelled from Germany and unwelcome in France, went to England, where he spent the rest of his life. He continued in journalism from time to time. For a while he was English correspondent for the *New York Tribune,* and he wrote on the French Commune of 1870 for the *London Times.* But most of his time was spent on scholarship, doing research on economics in the library of the British Museum and writing his great work, *Capital.* This book was both a denunciation of capitalism—Marx invented the word—and an explanation of why it must fail. The first volume appeared in 1867 and was the only part completed by Marx himself. The second volume appeared in 1885, two years after Marx's death, and was edited by Engels, while the last part was not issued until 1894.

Scholarship did not completely replace revolutionary agitation, however, for when the International—an international alliance of revolutionary parties —was formed in 1864, Marx took a leading part. It was not enough to be a theorist, he felt, for there had to be a revolutionary party to take control when capitalism collapsed. He wrote extensively in support of the proletarian revolutionary movement and in opposition to socialists whose views differed from his own. Marx set a precedent in the use of vitriolic denunciation that has continued to plague left-wing radicalism to the present day.

Marx died in 1883 after having given to revolutionary socialism its theoretical foundations. One wonders how different the world might be today had not the rigid authoritarianism of post-Napoleonic Prussia barred Marx from a career in government or university.

MARX'S VIEW OF CAPITALISM

It is difficult to condense the grand scheme of Marx's thought without doing injustice to the power and consistency of his reasoning. The very fact that Marx's argument is long and intricate, with all parts of it logically connected and integrated, makes almost any short summary a falsification. Nevertheless, it is important that it be understood, if only because it is the basis of one of the most powerful ideologies in the modern world.

Marx begins with the idea that economic relationships are the fundamental driving force in any society. Particularly under capitalism, however, people are motivated primarily by their economic interests—but let him say it in his own words, from the Preface to A Contribution to the Critique of Political Economy (1859):

> In the social production which men carry on they enter into definite relations that are indispensable and independent of their will; these relations of production correspond to a definite stage of development of their material powers of production. The sum total of these relations of production constitutes the economic structure of society—the real foundation, on which rise legal and political superstructures and to which correspond definite forms of social consciousness. The mode of production in material life determines the general character of the social, political and spiritual process of life.

In a capitalist society, according to Marx, the two great economic interests are those of capitalist and worker. These two classes stand in opposition to each other since the capitalist can prosper only if the worker is exploited. In this respect capitalism is only the latest in a series of social organizations in which one class exists at the expense of another. The Communist Manifesto (1848) puts it bluntly:

> The history of all hitherto existing society is the history of class struggles. Freeman and slave, patrician and plebian, lord and serf, guildmaster and journeyman, in a word, oppressor and oppressed, stood in constant opposition to one another. . . . The modern bourgeois society that has sprouted from the ruins of feudal society has not done away with class antagonisms. It has but established new classes, new conditions of oppression, new forms of struggle in place of the old ones.

Marx started his attack on capitalism with the *labor theory of value.* Recall that this theory, which was developed by the economic liberals and the classical economists, stated that the true value of any product or service was simply the amount of labor used in its production. So a table that takes ten hours of labor to make is worth twice as much as a chair that requires five hours of labor.

In Marx's view, labor under capitalism is exploited because it is not paid the full value of the products and services it produces. The capitalist employs the worker at the current wage rate and works him for as many hours each day as he can, making sure that the value of the worker's output is greater than the wage paid to him. It is this difference between wage and output value, which Marx called "surplus value," that becomes the capitalist's profit. Exploitation of the worker can be intensified, and the surplus value appropriated by the capitalist can be increased, by an employer's efforts to achieve lower wages, longer hours, and employment of a greater number of women and children. Thus Marx explained some of the more widely prevalent characteristics of the industrial economy of his time.

Exploitation exists in another sense as well. Marx saw capitalism as a gigantic mechanism through which the labor time of the worker is transformed first into profits and from profits into capital. Whereas labor time is owned by the worker, capital is the property of the capitalist. In this fashion the capitalist class grows increasingly wealthy out of the labor of the working class: "They coin our very life blood into gold," to quote a radical song from pre-World War I America.

This exploitation of workers is only the direct economic effect of capitalism upon the working class. It has psychological effects as well. Marx viewed work as a continuing interaction between people, nature, and the product of labor. Work was an essential element in the development of the human personality, so a full realization of the self required a full and rich development of the individual's relationship with the means of production and the product. Yet under capitalism the worker is separated from both the fruits of his labor and the tools of production, which are the property of the employer. Full development of the self and the personality is prevented. The result is a pervasive *alienation* that dehumanizes all personal and social relationships. Market exchange and money payments take the place of human feelings and human relationships, and life becomes dehumanized and pointless. The result is a range of social and psychological pathology that pervades all capitalist society and is inherent in its basic economic relationships.*

Exploitation and alienation are one side of capitalism. The other is accumulation of capital and growth of wealth. This side of the economic process also develops out of the relationships between capital and labor. However much the employer tries to squeeze his labor, the labor market itself will determine the level of wage rates, while hours of work are limited by human endurance, and employment of women and children is affected by a combination of technological factors and labor-market conditions. The employer has relatively little flexibility in these matters, and cannot readily gain a competitive advantage over other capitalists except by reinvesting the surplus value he earns in new machinery and equipment, which raises the productivity of his labor and increases his profits still further. Indeed, he is compelled to do so if he wishes to survive, because his competitors will do the same. The result is a continuing drive to expand investment. In this way Marx explained the process of capital accumulation and the growing productivity and increased output it generates.

*Marx did not give great emphasis to these extraordinary insights into modern society. He developed them in early essays that were not published until after World War II, and there are two chapters of *Capital* that deal with them in partial fashion. But even that was enough to influence profoundly a number of modern psychologists and give us the concept of alienation as a source of psychological disorders.

Capitalism, then, presents two faces: capital accumulation and growth on the one hand, with exploitation and alienation on the other.

THE BREAKDOWN OF CAPITALISM

Marx believed that capitalism was doomed, and he developed an intricate analysis of the "laws of motion" of capitalist society to prove it. At one level the argument has a moral basis: the inherent injustices of capitalism lead ultimately to economic and social conditions that cannot be maintained. At another level the argument is sociological: class conflict—between a decreasing number of increasingly wealthy capitalists and a growing and increasingly miserable working class—will lead ultimately to social revolution. And finally, the argument is economic: the accumulation of capital in private hands makes possible economic abundance, yet also leads to the economic breakdown of capitalism. At each level the idea of conflict is emphasized: conflict between ideal and reality, between capital and labor, between growth and stagnation. Out of conflict comes change, and for this basic reason, according to Marx, capitalism must give way to another form of society in which conflict is replaced by ethical, social, and economic harmony. Change through conflict is the "dialectical process" by which socialism was ultimately to replace capitalism. Marx felt that the process had an economic basis in the division of society into workers and capitalists. Their relationship was exploitive, with the owners of the means of production having the upper hand. Conflict was inherent in this situation, he argued, and it would build up until the whole fabric of society was torn apart.

Exploitation of labor is the starting point. It leads to inadequate purchasing power and, through surplus value and capitalist competition, to accumulation of capital. There is an inconsistency within capitalism here, however. When the economy is prosperous, business firms earn surplus value for their owners, who reinvest it for expanded output. But purchasing power eventually lags, partly because workers are not paid the full value of their labor and partly because capital investment pushes output capacity upward. Sooner or later a glut of unsold commodities appears on the market. Production is then cut back and prices fall: unemployment increases, profit declines and then disappears, and capital accumulation is halted. The capitalist "crisis" continues until the glut of commodities has been disposed of: prices recover, profits increase, and capital accumulation resumes, continuing until the next glut appears. This process, argued Marx, creates the recurring cycles of prosperity and depression that are an inherent failing of capitalism.

Marx also argued that the crises would become more severe—longer and deeper—as capitalism developed. The total capital and productive capacity of the economy increase from crisis to crisis, and the ratio of capital to labor rises. These changes cause the gluts to become larger and larger, to take longer and longer to be disposed of, and to necessitate greater and greater cutbacks in production.

But why, one might ask, would the glut appear in the first place? Will not rising prosperity cause increases in employment, wage rates, and purchasing power? Marx answered that even during prosperity the "reserve army" of the unemployed receives recruits—workers whose jobs are taken over by machines. Capital investment leads to substitution of capital for labor. Indeed, this is the only way in which the capitalist can increase the rate at which he accumulates surplus value. During prosperity, therefore, capital accumulation creates technological unemployment and pushes wages and purchasing power down, just as commodity gluts do during periods of depression. In either case, the result is the immizeration of the working class.

This is only half of the picture, however. Changes also take place within the capitalist class. First of all, the rate of profit declines as the businessman's investment in machinery and equipment gradually becomes an increasing proportion of his total investment. (Marx was thoroughly convinced of this when he wrote the first volume of *Capital,* but the notes he left for volume three showed that he was not quite so sure that profit rates must necessarily decline as capital accumulation proceeds.) Second, the business cycles engendered by capitalism enable the big capitalists to gobble up the little ones. The firms with the largest financial resources survive, and over the years the ownership of industry gradually becomes centralized in fewer and fewer hands until a few great financiers control all. This remaining capitalist class becomes increasingly wealthy, in contrast to the growing misery of the proletariat, which expands as small businessmen fail and join its ranks. The working class also becomes increasingly degraded as technological change breaks down complex jobs into simpler ones, skilled jobs become semiskilled, and semiskilled become unskilled. Ultimately the revolution occurs, a popular uprising of the vast majority against the wealthy few. Led by Communists, the working class seizes power and proceeds to build the new society.

Schematic Diagram of Marx's Theory of Capitalist Development

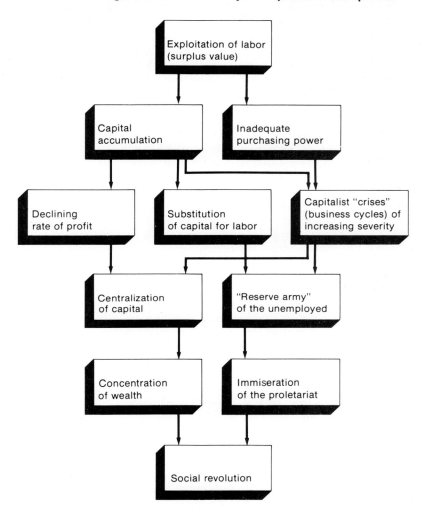

The Process of Capitalist Development

Exploitation of labor is the source of capital accumulation by capitalist enterprises, which seek to increase surplus value by substituting capital for labor. Loss of jobs, overproduction, and inadequate purchasing power bring on business cycles, which tend to become increasingly severe as the economy matures. The long-run trends (capital accumulation, substitution of capital for labor, declining profit rates), together with worsening economic crises, lead to (1) an increasingly wealthy capitalist class among whom ownership of wealth tends to become more highly concentrated, and (2) an increasingly immiserated working class that gradually becomes conscious of its own class interests and its systematic exploitation under a capitalist system.

Marx was quite aware of the possibility that these economic trends could be modified by political and social changes. Labor unions, originating in the conflict between capital and labor, could reduce exploitation of labor, but Marx feared that opportunistic union leaders might retreat from class conflict in favor of class accommodation. Governments, although dominated by capitalist political interests, could introduce social welfare legislation to strengthen the economic system as a whole. And parliamentary democracy could provide the appearance of popular participation even while the economic basis of political power was becoming more concentrated. Marx, however, was confident that the underlying economic trends and conflicts would predominate and ultimately create a revolutionary situation in which capitalism would be more or less rapidly transformed into socialism.

THE MARXIST VISION

Marx's analysis of capitalist development was based on the assumption that two great forces are continually at work in the development of human society. One is the struggle of people against nature to obtain subsistence and ease. The development of technology and improvements in methods of production are one result of that struggle, and in its early stages capitalism represented a major step toward abundance. Factory production and machine technology greatly increased human command over nature, and the competitive nature of capitalism forced business firms continually to reinvest their profits in new and better methods of production. Capitalism's failure lay in its inability to continue this process and in the periodic breakdowns, or crises, that occurred.

In Marx's view, the struggle for existence led to the second great force that causes economic and social change: the struggle of people against people. Human beings are one type of productive resource, and control over them is one way in which a few can increase their wealth and welfare. Therefore, argued Marx, the struggle for existence inevitably leads to exploitation of some by others. Early manifestations of this principle were the patriarchal family, the slave-based economy of ancient times, and feudalism. The latter, in turn, developed into the wage system of capitalism. Each of these social developments represented a victory in the battle against nature and marked an increase in human freedom—for some, if not all—and each was made possible by advances in technology and the social organization of production.

Ultimately, he argued, the economy could achieve widespread abundance and produce enough for all, and at this point in human history all people could be completely free, both politically and economically. Capitalism could not achieve this goal because it prevented the full development of modern technology, resulted in the periodic stoppage of capital accumulation, and created the conditions of social revolution. But socialism could achieve the goal because it eliminated exploitation and class distinctions and because it removed the roadblocks hindering the advance of production.

Marx concluded that an economy of abundance was possible only in a classless society. When the abundant economy arrived, there would no longer be any need for social or economic differences, and exploitation would long before have ended. Distribution of income would be based on the maxim "from each according to his abilities, to each according to his needs." At this point the two great struggles of humanity—people against nature and people against one another—would be ended. This was the positive side of Marxism—its vision of a great world of abundance, equality, and freedom.

WAS MARX RIGHT?

One of the least useful economic debates of the twentieth century has been over the correctness of Marx's analysis of capitalism. As proof of Marx's errors, his detractors point to the rising living standards of modern nations. The working class has not been subjected to growing misery, and labor unions have gained economic and political power in all the major industrialized countries. Moreover, the working class has shared the increased wealth, income, and economic benefits that have been spread widely throughout all social classes.

Marxists answer that the extremes of exploitation have been shifted from the domestic working class to that of colonial and less developed nations. Peoples dominated politically or economically by great capitalist nations now bear the greatest burden of exploitation, enabling the capitalists to ease their treatment of the working class at home and allow its living standards to rise. They also point to the continuing extremes of poverty and wealth within nations, to the rise of big business and the prevalence of monopoly, to the dominant influence wielded in politics by business interests, and to the failure of capitalist nations to find a cure for depressions and unemployment as indications that the Marxist analysis was essentially correct. In spite of all the "concessions" that have been made to the working class—social welfare legislation, union organization, higher living standards—the Marxists contend that the basic defects of capitalism remain, holding back economic growth and postponing indefinitely the emergence of the abundant society.

Yet even if the Marxist predictions of increased misery and a polarized society were wrong, Marx's arguments must give us pause. No society can long endure that excludes a substantial group of its citizens from enjoying its benefits, as was the case for many workers and their families in Marx's day and during the nineteenth-century decades of discontent and potential upheaval in Europe. In many respects Marx's analysis was a theoretical interpretation of actual conditions.

In the years after 1870, however, many great changes took place on the European scene. The right to vote—political democracy—was gradually extended to working people. National systems of welfare legislation provided protection against the worst effects of the industrial system. The growth of labor unions, and in Europe the appearance of labor's political parties, gave a new dignity to the worker and signified the place industrial labor was making for itself. The "safety valve" of emigration to North and South America and to Australia enabled many dissatisfied Europeans to start a new life in freer societies. And imperialism offered significant economic opportunities, whatever else might be said against it.

Social tensions would not have been sufficiently eased, however, in spite of these developments, without growth in the European economy. Industrialism opened many doors to the intelligent, ambitious man—Robert Owen is only one example. Although it has always been true that one gets ahead more easily if he begins near the top, it is also true that a growing and changing economy offers more opportunity than a stagnant one. Continued economic growth, both external and internal, gave Europe time to adapt to the stresses of industrialization by instituting reforms that gave political rights to workers and protected them from the harshest effects of the market economy. One moral to be derived from Marxism is that an economy must provide dignity and wide opportunities for all if society is to remain healthy.

The Marxist prediction of the triumph of socialism and the creation of a democratic, equalitarian, and nonexploitive society has not proved accurate. The prediction of increased concentration of economic power in the capitalist world has been borne out by events, although some economists would argue that the reasons for that trend differ from those advanced by Marx. And capitalism has been placed on the defensive by the rise of communist regimes in Russia and China, and by the spread of socialism through many of the less-developed countries. But in most instances, these noncapitalist regimes have developed authoritarian political regimes, new forms of economic and social inequality, and new aspects of exploitation. The humanistic goals that underlay Marx's rage at capitalism seem no closer to achievement in the noncapitalist regimes of the late twentieth century than in the capitalist. This situation has created something of a crisis among leftists in the remaining advanced capitalist countries, as they reevaluate Marxist theory to find out what went wrong.

Marxism, nevertheless, remains an important force in the modern world. It expresses a moral outrage at the condition of humanity. It holds up a grand vision of what the condition might be. It views modern capitalism as a dynamic system in which the very process of growth leads ultimately to a final crisis in which the system as a whole can no longer sustain itself. Its class-oriented view of the social order provides a framework within which much of what happens in the modern world can be analyzed. It provides a basis for political action and an ideology around which dissent can rally. These aspects of Marxism are far more important than whether its analysis of individual issues is right or wrong. Wherever people feel oppressed, Marxism can express their outrage and hope and offer a path to something better. It is this characteristic of Marxism that makes it a force to be reckoned with in the modern world.

CHAPTER **6**

The Philosophy of Individualism

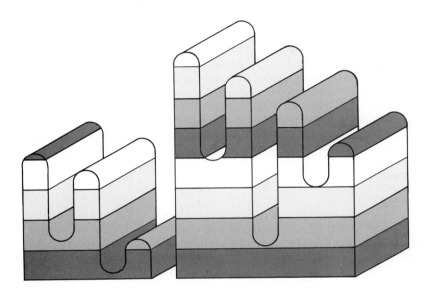

The rise of socialism and its demand for social justice forced the supporters of the existing order to raise their defenses. A theoretical refutation was also needed, because Marx's critique of capitalism was based on the assumptions of classical economics itself—on the labor theory of value and the theory of capital accumulation. He used the weapons of the dominant ideology to attack the very system those weapons defended.

One answer to Marx and socialism was the nineteenth-century philosophy of individualism, which developed as the ideology of a business civilization in the years between 1850 and the First World War. Just as Marxism had carried the disenchantment of the dispossessed and the alienated to a high level of theoretical analysis, so a revived and reinforced theory of laissez faire expressed the interests of the successful. Few of the protagonists of the new individualism could be called economists in the strict sense of the word—the most important were philosophers, jurists, and businessmen—but their economic thought left a far greater impact on their world than did the work of hundreds of academicians.

The second reaction to Marx was a reconstruction of economics itself, accomplished by stripping away its weak elements, strengthening its scientific validity, generalizing its basic concepts, and adapting it to the contemporary world. Economics as a science was greatly strengthened by the impact of socialist theory and criticism. But the tenor of the times and the climate of opinion within which the reconstructed economics emerged were set by other, more practical men of affairs.

THE PHILOSOPHY

An English philosopher, Herbert Spencer (1820–1903), and an American sociologist, William Graham Sumner (1840–1910), led the further development of the philosophy of individualism. These men worked out the ideology on which half a century of legislation, law, and and folklore was based.

Spencer was an evolutionist before Darwin. As early as 1850, in his *Social Statics*, he maintained that all social systems develop and change by a natural process that results in a maximization of individual welfare. This process of natural development stems from competition among individuals, he argued, and any interference on the part of the government prevents full achievement of the ideal goal. Spencer's early statement was followed by essays and a ten-volume *Synthetic Philosophy*, which sought to show that evolutionary progress occurred in all phenomena—in the biological world, in the human mind, in society, and in ethics. Where Darwin explained evolution in terms of "natural selection," Spencer invented the phrase "survival of the fittest" as the source of progress:

> *Any organism, including the social, changes through adaptation to outside influences, carried out in such a way as to benefit the organism involved. Those organisms which are best fitted to their environment, or which change to fit themselves to their environment, will survive.*
> *The least fit will die out, leaving the strongest and "best."*

In this way progress is made, and the weakest individuals and the least useful social institutions gradually are eliminated. Since the individual member of society is the decision-maker, the social organization that emerges from the process of change is more closely adapted to meeting the needs of the individual. Progress means that the welfare of the individual must be improved.

These ideas led to a description of the ideal society, conceived as static equilibrium between people and their surroundings brought about by full exercise of individual natural rights. Government, a necessary evil, was severely limited to protection of people and property and enforcement of private contracts—nothing else. As society moved from a primitive state of violence and military control to higher levels of industrialization and peace, even the protective role of government could be reduced and would ultimately wither away in the final utopia of philosophical anarchism. In the transition, however, there should be no government regulation of industry, no state church, no organized colonization, no relief for the poor, no social legislation, no public mint, no government-owned postal system, no public education. Unfettered individual action should be permitted, and nothing should be allowed to interfere with natural selection of the fittest—not even such measures as public sanitation, which protected and thereby perpetuated weaker types.

Spencer's philosophy had a greater impact in the United States than in his own country. His foremost American follower was William Graham Sumner, an Episcopalian minister and Yale University economist who became one of the foremost sociologists of his time. His major work is a sociological classic, *Folkways* (1907), which examined social "mores"—institutions and conventions that develop and continually change by a process of adaptation to individual and social needs. If such institutions do not contribute to welfare and survival, they are gradually replaced by more effective methods, and the social system evolves into a higher and better form. Social institutions that proved their usefulness in the past are given up only with reluctance, however, and only after new methods have been proven better. In Sumner's view, therefore, the social system is at one and the same time conservative and progressive, resistant to change and changing.

Within the social system, individuals are also rising and falling, according to Sumner. The person with ability, intelligence, and drive will rise to prominence by competing with all others. The lazy, ignorant, and weak will fall out of sight. The emergence of leading individuals brings progress, because these are the ones who innovate, who think, who develop new ideas. Competition among them results in both a more vigorous population and a better social structure.

In a long series of essays with such titles as "What Social Classes Owe to One Another," "The Forgotten Man," and "The Concentration of Wealth: Its Economic Justification," Sumner applied his theory of society to questions of contemporary policy. "The Forgotten Man" was the one who worked hard, produced, paid his taxes, saved, and invested, and thereby brought to society all the benefits of hard work and enterprise, in spite of bearing the burden of protective tariffs, government social services, and the high costs imposed by labor unions.* Concentrated wealth was justified because it was used to produce for others. Wealth that was squandered or allowed to lie idle never led to such concentration. The economic elite rose to the top only because, in competition with others, they expanded economic activity and produced the goods and services that society wanted and needed. Social classes owed nothing to one another; they had only to look out for themselves, and benefits to others would automatically follow.

This, then, was evolutionary philosophy applied to the social system. It justified unlimited individualism on the ground that only social good could come from competition. It justified great wealth on the ground that wealth existed only because it served others. It justified lack of responsibility for others on the ground that anyone destroyed by competition could be considered "unfit," not capable of making a large enough contribution to the social order to survive. It was a rigorous philosophy that associated success with right and failure with wrong, wealth with public service and poverty with uselessness.

INDIVIDUALISM AND THE LAW

The philosophy of individualism was applied to economic affairs most fully in the United States. The Civil War (1861–65) brought political dominance to the industrial interests of the northeast, and during the conflict several laws were passed that prepared the way for what one critic was to call "the great

*Ironically, Sumner's phrase "the forgotten man" was reversed by Franklin Roosevelt and used to describe the poor and downtrodden who would benefit by the welfare measures of the New Deal, an interventionist program that Sumner would have abhorred.

barbecue." The Morrill Tariff (1861) raised duties on imports and set the stage for high-tariff legislation after the war ended. The Homestead Act (1862) finally opened the west to large-scale settlement. The Pacific Railway Acts (1862 and 1864) provided federal subsidies for transcontinental railways. In 1864 contract labor was authorized to promote immigration by allowing employers to pay for the passage of immigrants in exchange for a work contract. The National Bank Act (1863) remade the monetary system to provide a limited and "sound" money supply. Finally, the ending of slavery created once and for all a free labor market for the entire country. The stage was set for the dominance of private enterprise in a business-oriented civilization, once the landed interests of the South went down to defeat in the war.

The philosophy of unrestricted individualism came to be embodied in the fundamental constitutional law. The person most responsible for this development was a now almost forgotten justice of the United States Supreme Court, Stephen J. Field (1816–1899). Field was the son of a prominent Congregational clergyman and the brother of two equally eminent men, Cyrus Field, the businessman who laid the first trans-Atlantic telegraph cable in 1866, and David Dudley Field, a prominent New York lawyer who led the movement for reform of legal codes in the 1860s and who later became the leader of an international movement to substitute arbitration for war, a forerunner of the League of Nations.

In his early thirties Stephen Field joined the gold rush in California. He was elected a judge and in 1850 to the state legislature. By 1857 he was on the state supreme court and became its chief justice in 1859. Field was a product of the developing West and its individualistic, open social structure in which a person could rise through his own efforts.

Abraham Lincoln appointed him to the United States Supreme Court in 1863, a position he held for thirty-four years, becoming one of the country's greatest authorities on constitutional law. In 1876 he was a member of the famous Electoral Commission that decided the presidency in favor of the Republican Rutherford B. Hayes against the Democrat Samuel J. Tilden, who had a larger total vote. During his career on the Supreme Court, Field's most important opinions related to protection of property and freedom of business enterprise, by application to corporations of the Fourteenth Amendment to the Constitution. At first in the minority, Field soon became the most important majority spokesman for the view that the Constitution guarantees individual and business enterprise against government intervention.

The famous Slaughterhouse Cases of 1873 enabled Field to state his position in unequivocal terms. Louisiana had passed laws intending to protect public health in New Orleans by limiting the operation of slaughterhouses and giving a monopoly of the business to a single company. The act was opposed by butchers and cattle dealers who asked for an injunction against enforcement on the grounds that the act was unconstitutional. They argued, among other things, that the monopoly deprived them of the right to follow their usual employment and, contrary to the Fourteenth Amendment, deprived them of property without due process of law and denied them equal protection under the law. Supporters of the legislation argued that it represented a valid expression of the police power of the state government. The case was ultimately appealed to the Supreme Court, where the majority held that the state was legitimately using its police powers and that no civil rights had been violated. Field, however, wrote a vigorous dissent. He felt that the right to operate a slaughterhouse or any other legitimate business enterprise was a right that could not be removed by government. "I cannot believe that what is termed in the Declaration of Independence a God-given and inalienable right can thus be ruthlessly taken from citizens, or that there can be any abridgement of that right except by regulations alike affecting all persons of the same age, sex and condition."

The argument for property as a natural right that no government can appropriate without due process of law was tested further in the ensuing years. Field dissented vigorously on several occasions when the majority of the Supreme Court supported state intervention in economic affairs. But opinion changed, and by 1886 the whole Court had come to accept Field's position. In a case concerning the validity of special taxes imposed on the Southern Pacific Railway by a California county, Field could say, "The Court does not want to hear the argument on the question whether the provision of the 14th amendment applies to these corporations. We are all of the opinion that it does." The constitutional amendment that originally had been intended to protect freed slaves was then applied to corporations and to business enterprise, and in this case the local taxes were declared invalid.

Once Field's position became part of the constitutional law of the United States, much state legislation was stricken down, including regulation of hours of work, child labor, factory conditions, and other aspects of economic life. At a time when industrial growth was creating many new problems, the philosophy of unrestricted laissez faire was the law of the land, and little interference with private enterprise and freedom of contract was permitted. In vain did Justice Oliver Wendell Holmes complain in one famous dissenting opinion that "the fourteenth amendment does not enact Mr. Herbert Spencer's *Social Statics.*"

THE FOLKLORE OF INDIVIDUALISM

The philosophy of individualism was translated into a folklore as well as legal principles. The lore told of the poor immigrant boy who started his career at the bottom of the business ladder, worked hard, saved his money, made shrewd investments, and ultimately rose to a position of business leadership. He married well, raised a happy family, and gained the respect of his fellows. Wise in his old age, he was an elder statesman consulted by Presidents and loved by his grandchildren.

Although relatively few business leaders followed this path to the top—most were sons of business or professional men, had more than an average education, and did not start at the bottom—a growing economy in which individual enterprise was unhindered and that had no income taxes did offer a fertile field to those bent on riches. A few actually were living examples of the folklore, although they did not rise within existing enterprises but built their own businesses with shrewdness, ability, and luck.

Andrew Carnegie, for example, was born in Scotland, son of a weaver who brought his family to America when power looms forced him out of business. The thirteen-year-old Andrew went to work in a textile plant near Pittsburgh as a bobbin boy at twenty cents a day His hard work earned him a promotion to the engine room, and his knowledge of arithmetic and his penmanship earned him another promotion to the clerical staff. Seeking newer fields with greater opportunity, Andrew became a telegraph messenger boy, learned telegraphy, became an operator, and in his spare time earned extra money as a newspaper telegraph reporter. Moving again to greener fields, he became a telegraph train dispatcher for the Pennsylvania Railroad and then secretary to the general superintendent. When his boss became president of the company, Andrew, then all of twenty-five years old, was appointed superintendent of the railroad's western division. Saving his money, he invested in a sleeping-car company and in oil lands, two new and dynamic industries at the time. During the Civil War Carnegie was in charge of all the eastern military railroads and telegraphs, and he ran them with the efficiency he had applied to all of his work.

Forecasting the superiority of iron and steel bridges over those made of wood, he organized the Keystone Bridge Works in 1862. Shortly after the Civil War ended, he built his own steel plant to supply raw material to his company and in 1868 introduced the Bessemer steel process into the United States. Building and expanding further, he acquired more plants, iron and coal mines, railroads, and all the other elements of the first fully integrated steel company in the country. Rather than run it himself, he took care to hire the best managerial talent available and gave his managers incentives to work with initiative and progressiveness. In 1901 he sold his company to the newly formed United States Steel Corporation for almost half a billion dollars. Carnegie himself received over $300 million.

Carnegie believed and lived the philosophy that wealth is held by the individual only as a stewardship and that it is to be used ultimately for the benefit of society as a whole. After selling his company, he devoted the remainder of his life to supporting education and research. He established and financed the Carnegie Institute of Technology in Pittsburgh, the Carnegie Institution of Washington for purposes of scientific research, the Carnegie Corporation of New York as a trust fund for support of education and research, the Carnegie Foundation for the Advancement of Teaching, the Carnegie Endowment for International Peace, and the Carnegie Hero Fund to provide rewards for heroic deeds, in addition to endowing libraries in hundreds of cities across the country. In all of these gifts he insisted on the principle of self-help: the recipient almost always had to provide some money himself.

Carnegie wrote several popular books expressing his philosophy of individualism and stewardship of wealth: *Triumphant Democracy* (1886), *The Gospel of Wealth* (1900), and *The Empire of Business* (1902). All of these works extolled the business system, individualism, free enterprise, and the idea that wealth was not to be used solely for individual benefit but devoted to community betterment. Typical of his opinions was an article on "Wealth" published in the *North American Review* in 1889:

> *The price which society pays for the law of competition... is also great; but the advantages of this law are also greater still, for it is to this law that we owe our wonderful material development, which brings improved conditions in its train.*
>
> *... While the law may be sometimes hard for the individual, it is best for the race, because it insures the survival of the fittest in every department.*

Accumulation of wealth by the few can lead to a "reign of harmony" and "reconciliation of the rich and the poor" as long as the wealthy use their riches "as a matter of duty" in the ways "best calculated to produce the most beneficial results for the community":

The laws of accumulation will be left free; the laws of distribution free. Individualism will continue, but the millionaire will be but a trustee for the poor; intrusted for a season with a great part of the increased wealth of the community, but administering it for the community far better than it could or would have done for itself.

Andrew Carnegie was a living embodiment of a folklore of individualism, which maintained that private property was a natural element of the social order, obtained by industry and thrift and demonstrating the moral superiority of its possessors. As Russell Conwell, a famous public speaker of the time, put it in his inspirational piece "Acres of Diamonds," "Godliness is in league with riches." Or as the Episcopalian bishop William Lawrence said, "In the long run it is only to the man of morality that wealth comes." By contrast, poverty was the result of laziness, or waste, or lack of ability—desirable only because it taught the need for hard work and saving. This philosophy was not merely a rationalization of wealth by the wealthy, although it was certainly that. It was also the faith of millions, including the great middle class and a large number of workers.

THE RESULTS OF INDIVIDUALISM

Individualism also had its seamy side. The apologists for wealth had much to apologize for. In 1900, when profits of the Carnegie Steel Company were more than $20 million for the year (most of it going to Andrew Carnegie himself), the average *annual* wage for steel workers was about $600. The justice of this division of society's income was not self-evident, and it threatened the polarization of social classes that Marx had predicted. Yet the more extreme adherents of the philosophy of laissez faire went merrily on their way, apparently unaware of the potentially explosive situation they were creating.

At one time, when the New York Central Railroad canceled a fast extra-fare train between New York and Chicago, a public outcry was raised. Interviewed by a newspaper reporter, William Vanderbilt, the company's president and majority stockholder, exploded, "The public be damned. I am working for my stockholders. If the public want the train why don't they pay for it?" The statement raised a storm of protest; Vanderbilt decided it was time to diversify his interests and sold $30 million of his Central stock.

It was a great age for the speculator, the promoter, and the freebooter. In 1869, Jay Gould and Jim Fisk, financial speculators who had learned their trade through almost certainly illegal watering of Erie Railroad stock, attempted to corner the free gold supply in the New York money market. Tying up the federal government's gold supply in the New York subtreasury by bringing President Grant's brother-in-law into the plot, they drove the price of gold to great heights. Their Washington connections brought advance warning of government action to break the corner, and they sold out in time to make large profits. When a financial panic ensued, they even allowed their own brokers to be bankrupted. This Black Friday of September 24, 1869, was only the most spectacular of the speculative games that unsettled the economy from time to time.

The builders of monopoly were also at work. The new industrial economy was particularly vulnerable to competitive price wars. In the railroad industry, for instance, capital costs were high, and rate cutting could bring returns down to well below total costs while still covering operating expenses. Rate wars could bankrupt the weaker lines, but, since railroad property could be used only for running trains, defeated companies would merely reorganize on a stronger financial basis and return to the industrial wars better able to survive than the lines that had won out the first time. It is little wonder that railroad companies merged, arranged agreements on rates and division of traffic, bought stock interests in one another, and formed "communities of interest."

Similar factors were at work in other industries as well: steel, agricultural equipment, sugar refining, oil refining and distribution, and public utilities. Giant trusts were formed to bring stability into industries made chaotic by the very competition that the theorists had claimed was the basis of economic order. In combining, financiers sometimes lost sight of economy benefits to company, stockholders, or public when large fees for legal and financial services beckoned. When J. P. Morgan began building large steel companies out of small ones in the 1890s, he discovered that issuing securities in amounts larger than the real value of the merged properties could bring high rewards. Capitalizing "good will" and potential monopoly profits could put money into the hands of bankers and lawyers. When Andrew Carnegie threatened to wreck the scheme by sharp competition, Morgan was forced to buy him out at Carnegie's price. The United States Steel Corporation was born, with stocks and bonds sold to the public and distributed to the promoters at prices equal to about twice the real value of the properties. The company's monopoly position enabled it ultimately to carry through, but the public paid through high prices for steel. Shortly after the Carnegie-Morgan deal was closed, the two men met on an ocean voyage. Carnegie is reported to have said, "I made one mistake, Pierpont, when I sold out to you. I should have asked you $100 million more than I did." To which Morgan replied, "I should have paid it."

This kind of free-wheeling individualism engendered an inevitable reaction. In 1877 the United States came close to revolution as a result of depression and industrial discontent. Layoffs and wage reductions on the railroads triggered local strikes that spread to other lines all over the country. Violence and fighting broke out and much railroad property was destroyed. Hardly a decade later, the Haymarket Square riot erupted in Chicago. A strike at the great McCormick Reaper Works, in which union membership was a major issue, was followed by a general strike throughout the city. Over fifty thousand workers left their jobs. Agitation by "practical" anarchists, who wanted to end capitalism and all government by destructive revolution, was especially strong, and after a riot before the McCormick Works in which a number of workers were injured, the tiny anarchist newspaper called for "revenge" for the "massacre." A meeting called the next evening at Haymarket Square attracted a large peaceful crowd, which had largely dispersed when police moved in to break it up. A bomb was thrown that killed seven policemen and wounded sixty-eight more. Eight anarchist leaders were arrested and tried for murder as accessories before the fact. Found guilty in a supercharged atmosphere of fear and hate, four were executed, one committed suicide in jail, and three were given long prison terms. No one ever found out who threw the bomb.

Again, in the 1890s, economic conflict bred violence. The hard times of that decade were called the "great depression"—until the 1930s. Unemployment was high, and basic industries such as steel, railroads, and agricultural equipment were hard hit. Fighting broke out in the summer of 1892 at Andrew Carnegie's Homestead steel plant near Pittsburgh. Wage cuts, refusal of the company to recognize a union or to bargain with the men, and importation of several hundred strikebreakers led to a pitched battle between workers and management forces. Twenty men were killed and perhaps fifty wounded, and Henry Frick, manager of the plant, later was shot and stabbed in his office by an agitator. The National Guard finally restored order, but the strike was broken.

Near Chicago, where George Pullman had paternalistically established a "model town" next to his railroad car factory, hard times resulted in layoffs and evictions, and the workers walked out. A sympathy boycott of Pullman cars by the American Railway Union, led by Eugene Debs, tied up the nation's transportation system, and serious fighting occurred in Chicago. An injunction against the strike was obtained by the attorney general of the United States, himself a former railroad lawyer, and President Cleveland called out national troops in spite of protests from Governor Altgeld that they were not needed. In the face of this power the strike failed and Debs was jailed, to emerge a fully convinced socialist.

The conservative leaders of business seemed to learn nothing and to forget nothing, however. When a strike in the anthracite coal mines in 1902 threatened to leave big-city consumers freezing through a long winter, George F. Baer, head of the employers' association that refused the union's offer to submit the dispute to arbitration, wrote to a complaining stockholder:

> Dear Mr. Clark: I have your letter of the 16th. I do not know who you are. I see that you are a religious man; but you are evidently biased in favor of the right of the workingman to control a business in which he has no other interest than to secure fair wages. I beg of you not to be discouraged. The rights and interests of the laboring man will be protected and cared for— not by agitators—but by the Christian gentlemen to whom God has given control of the property rights of the country. Pray earnestly that the right may triumph, always remembering that the Lord God omnipotent still reigns and that this reign is one of law and order, not violence and crime.

This bald statement of the divine right of capital so aroused public opinion that the federal government finally interposed itself between the two fighting parties of capital and labor. President Theodore Roosevelt threatened to seize the mines unless management agreed to arbitrate the dispute. For the first time, intervention by the federal government was on the side of labor rather than capital.

THE LIMITATIONS OF INDIVIDUALISM

The philosophy, law, and folklore of rugged individualism was on a collision course with labor. Its refusal to deal with problems of depression and unemployment, with monopoly and concentrated economic power, with problems of income distribution and economic justice, was bringing criticism and attack. Perhaps sound in theory, it did not deal with the great issues that Marxism had raised about capitalism or with the social problems that were encountered along the path of economic development. When lack of solutions to problems resulted in upheavals and violence, public opinion began to turn the other way. Reiteration of old theories and slogans was not enough. Economics, social theory, and public policy would have to come to terms with reality, and particularly the reality of economic conflict.

CHAPTER 7

Neoclassical Economics

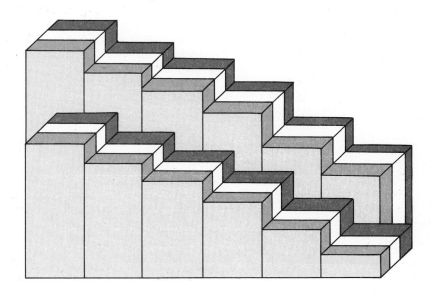

Economists, for the most part, did not accept the extreme position of the philosophy of individualism. They were concerned with social problems, and the influence of Benthamite utilitarianism made them willing to support government intervention in economic affairs if clear social benefits could be demonstrated. Nevertheless, most economists remained within the framework of the individualist philosophy, accepting government action only in limited amounts for limited goals. The emphasis on laissez faire remained, and economic theory reflected that point of view.

It reflected something else too: the Marxian critique of capitalism. In part consciously and in part unconsciously, the economists of 1870 to 1900 developed new theoretical formulations that served to refute the Marxist propositions about capitalism.

MARGINAL UTILITY AND INDIVIDUAL WELFARE

In the early 1870s three different economists, unaware of each other's ideas, developed a new theory of value to replace the old labor theory. An Englishman, a Frenchman, and an Austrian, they wrote in different languages, yet their theories were remarkably similar—another example of that often-observed phenomenon in the development of science, the independent and simultaneous discovery of a new principle. Within ten years the new ideas had swept triumphantly through the economics profession and had been hailed as a great breakthrough by all but a few diehards who clung obstinately to the old classical system. To compound the coincidence, the discovery came only a few years after Marx had published his attack on capitalism, using the labor theory of value as a base for his exploitation theory.

Later, it turned out that the new ideas were not so new after all. The basic principles of marginal utility had been stated by an Italian mathematician a century and a half before, and during the preceding fifty years had been published by a German engineer, a French public utilities expert, and several rather obscure English economists. Even Aristotle had used the idea in his treatise on ethics, and related concepts had been discussed by Catholic theologians in the sixteenth and seventeenth centuries. All of these writings had been ignored until Marx attacked the private-enterprise system. When that happened the labor theory of value had to go, and economists had to give serious attention to problems of income distribution and business cycles. A new approach to economics was born.

The new principle was a simple one: the value of a product or service is due not to the labor embodied in it but to the usefulness of the last unit purchased. That, in essence, was the famous *principle of marginal utility.*

Karl Menger (1840-1921), the Austrian codiscoverer, best stated the basic principle. He pointed out that the rational consumer, faced with a large number of alternatives on which to spend income, will seek to maximize satisfaction. This will be achieved when the consumer has allocated spending so that the last (or marginal) dollar spent on one commodity gives no more and no less satisfaction—or welfare, or utility—than the last dollar spent on anything else. If it is possible to shift a dollar of spending from one commodity to another and thereby raise the total satisfaction obtained, the rational consumer will do so, until utility "at the margin" is equalized. In this fashion the demand for any one commodity by any one consumer is determined. Menger pictured the consumer as a person who continually weighs the relative advantages of this or that course of action and always chooses the one that gives the greatest increment in welfare.

William Stanley Jevons (1835-1882), the English codiscoverer, emphasized another aspect of the principle by showing that utility at the margin diminishes: the more one has of a commodity, the less satisfaction one gets from consuming another unit and the less one is willing to pay for it. This means that plentiful commodities will be cheap because an additional unit is not worth much to the buyer, even though the commodity itself may be essential to sustain life—like water or bread. Scarce commodities, on the other hand, will be expensive because no one has much of them and one more unit will bring a great deal of satisfaction to the buyer—like diamonds or mink coats.

Léon Walras (1837-1910), the Frenchman who published the same principle in the early 1870s, had a still different emphasis. He explained how the entire economic system, including production of capital equipment and raw materials, was keyed to the spending decisions of the consumer. The economy was a seamless web of intricate relationships between prices and quantities purchased in which any change in the consumer's allocation of expenditures was felt throughout the entire system in tiny adjustments of production and prices. Especially in a competitive economy, the whole system automatically adjusted to match production to demand.

The theory of general equilibrium as developed by Walras was a complex mathematical model based on several important simplifying assumptions: people acted on the basis of their self interest; all markets were perfectly competitive; and implicitly, all economic relationships could be analyzed as a process of buying and selling within a system of markets. In spite of these limitations, which gave the theory an abstract and metaphysical air, Walrasian general equilibrium theory became the basis for most economic theorizing.

The new economics of marginal utility and general equilibrium found the roots of economic values on the demand side of the market, in the preferences of consumers. The old labor theory of value had focused on the supply side of the market and had explained value and price in terms of costs of production, which were reduced ultimately to costs of labor time. It was an English economist, Alfred Marshall (1842–1924) who reconciled these two approaches. He insisted that market price—that is, economic value—was determined by both supply and demand, which interact with one another in much the same way as Adam Smith described the operation of competitive markets. Marshall demonstrated that in the long run prices in competitive markets would tend toward the lowest possible costs of production at which the amounts desired by consumers would be provided. But although Marshall brought costs of production back into the picture, he and most other economists accepted the broader approach of Menger and Walras: the basic pattern of production was determined by the myriad independent decisions of millions of individual consumers.

One of the most important conclusions drawn from this line of thinking was that a system of free markets tended to maximize individual welfare. Since consumers were assumed to try to maximize their satisfactions, and since production was patterned after consumer wants, it followed that the result would be welfare maximizing. The analysis also showed that costs of production were pushed to the lowest possible level by the forces of competition. The whole economy, in a sense, was a pleasure-maximizing machine in which the difference between consumer benefits and production costs was increased to the highest level possible—if the economy were allowed to operate without constraints.

These ideas shifted the whole focus of economics away from the great issue of social classes and their economic interests, which had been emphasized by Ricardo and Marx, and centered economic theory upon the individual. The principles of income distribution on which Ricardo had based his analysis of the progress of industrialism and on which Marx had rested his theory of the breakdown of capitalism, were replaced by the individual consumer as the major determinant of economic activity and economic progress. The whole economic system was conceived as revolving around individual consumers and their needs.

Economics was transformed into a science consistent with the social philosophy developed by Herbert Spencer and William Graham Sumner, and that philosophy, of course, reflected the free-wheeling individualism that was remaking the face of the world. The economists and their highly abstract theories were part of the same social and intellectual development that brought forth the legal theories of Stephen Field and the folklore of the self-made individual.

ECONOMIC JUSTICE: INCOME DISTRIBUTION

This is not to say that the economists who used the marginal analysis ignored the problem of *income distribution.* Taking up the Marxist challenge, these new theologians of industrial society developed a theory proving that all factors of production—whether labor, land, or capital—earned a wage exactly equal to their contribution to the value of output. No one could exploit anyone else, there was no unearned surplus to be appropriated by the owners of capital, and full justice must prevail in the distribution of income. The worker received what he earned, no more and no less.

The new analysis of income distribution was called the *theory of marginal productivity.* Like the theory of marginal utility, it was based on the last, or marginal, unit, and its fundamental conclusion was very simple: workers would be paid a wage equal to the value of the last unit of output they produced. For example, consider a single manufacturing plant that turns out only one product. This plant will pay wages equal to those established in the competitive labor market. The manager will add to his work force as long as the added output per worker can be sold for more than the wage paid—that is, as long as profits rise because additional revenues exceed additional costs. The manager will stop hiring workers when increased output will not bring in enough additional revenue to cover the wage that must be paid. The plant's demand for labor is determined by the level at which wages equal the value of a worker's output at the margin. If an employer tried to pay a wage less than this value, the worker could, of course, get a job elsewhere with a competitive firm. It was a wonderful theory. The worker would get no more and no less than his contribution to society. If his productivity was high, he would earn high wages; if he was lazy or incompetent, his earnings would be low.

The same theory was applied to the boss, to profits earned on capital, and to the rent from land. Each of these elements in the production process was subject to the same economic law. No one could exploit anyone else because everyone got what he deserved. The economists even revived a theorem devised by a Swiss mathematician more than a hundred years before which proved that there could be no surplus value unaccounted for by payments to the various factors of production. Marx was dead.

The validity of the theory of marginal productivity depended upon the existence of that theoretical Nirvana, *perfect competition.* It also required that all factors of production be fully and freely substitutable for one another and that there be no change in costs of production per unit of output as the level of production rose or fell. But these highly restrictive assumptions did not bother many economists, who by this time were lost in the theoretical glories of a perfectly competitive economy.*

---

*It should be noted, however, that some economists never accepted the theory of marginal productivity. This dissident group included Alfred Marshall, the dominant figure in English economics from 1890 to after World War I.

PROSPERITY AND DEPRESSION: BUSINESS CYCLES

Wherever large-scale industrialization appeared, the economic system was subjected to alternating periods of prosperity and depression, often marked by a "crisis" in finance and business confidence. These breakdowns occurred with varying degrees of severity but with an apparent regularity that required explanation. During the nineteenth century financial crises followed by depressed economic conditions occurred in England in 1815, 1825, 1836, 1847, 1857, 1866, 1873, 1882, 1890, and 1900. In the United States crises were a little less frequent, perhaps because of the presence of an extensive land frontier, but they were still numerous: 1819, 1837, 1854, 1857, 1873, 1883, 1893. Furthermore, the world economy as a whole experienced three "great depressions" during the "hungry forties," the 1870s, and the 1890s.

At first the problem was ignored. Both the classical economists of the first half of the century and the neoclassical group that appeared after 1870 accepted the general propositions of Say's Law of Markets, according to which there should be no periodic economic breakdowns and the economy should continue to operate at uninterrupted high levels of output and employment. Those few who did investigate business cycles looked for causes outside the system of production and distribution, for Say's Law taught that demand was created by production and that, in the aggregate, the two could never get out of phase with one another.

Beginning in the 1860s British and French statisticians, rather than economists, first verified the periodic and cyclical nature of economic fluctuations. They identified several cycles of about ten years' duration and speculated on possible causes. Stanley Jevons in England was one of the few economists who gave much attention to the problem, and he attributed the causes of "great irregular fluctuations" to variations in agriculture, excessive investment or speculation, wars and political disturbances, or "other fortuitous occurrences which we cannot calculate upon, or allow for." Later Jevons developed a theory even more favorable to the adherents of Say's Law and the existing scheme of things. After finding a statistical correlation between cycles of sun spots and business fluctuations, he wrote in 1884:

> It seems probable that commercial crises are connected with a periodic variation of weather affecting all parts of the earth, and probably arising from increased waves of heat received from the sun at average intervals of ten years and a fraction.

But business cycles were creating problems for government, too, and hard-headed administrators responsible for policy need facts. Government men sat down to analyze the data. In 1886 Carroll Wright, in his first annual report as United States Commissioner of Labor, identified business investment as the most important fluctuating element in the economy. Natural causes, wars, and speculation were not the cause of crises: the culprit was overinvestment in capital equipment. Bad times came when opportunities for investment were inadequate. This emphasis on the process of investment was reiterated a few years later by Sir Hubert Llewellyn Smith, Wright's English counterpart as Commissioner of Labour in the Board of Trade, who reported to Parliament in 1895 that economic instability was concentrated in a few industries, such as machinery and other metals-producing industries, shipbuilding, construction, and mining, all of which were subject to "violent oscillation" in investment. Other sectors of the economy were relatively stable, and fluctuations there reflected the larger changes taking place in unstable industries.

These investigations by government servants did not have much effect on economists, however, who continued to pursue the clues given them by Say's Law. In its best and most complete formulation that law utilized the rate of interest as the automatic stabilizer of the economy, as the factor which ensured that savings would be directed into investment and prevent any break in the even flow of spending. But since breaks were obviously occurring and since the rate of interest was part of the monetary system, it was logical to look to that sector of the economy for the causes of difficulty: there could be problems in the monetary system even though production and distribution were sound.

By the last decade of the nineteenth century, economists began to agree that business cycles were caused by unwarranted expansion of the money supply. Easy credit would bring interest rates down and thereby stimulate excessive investment and speculation. Once the economy had over-expanded, a crisis was inevitable, since the normal operation of the system could not support the unnecessary production capacity and credit created during the wave of optimism. Once the crisis began, the economy would simply have to suffer until the high prices and unwise expansion were brought back to normal.

The preventive for this unfortunate sequence of events was to manage the monetary system properly. Limiting the expansion of credit to the legitimate needs of business through effective action by the central bank could prevent the process from starting or could stop it while the ensuing readjustment period might still be short and shallow. Stability in the monetary and credit system could bring stability to the economy as a whole.

This theory was spelled out by the Englishman Walter Bagehot as early as 1873 in *Lombard Street,* a classic work on the money markets. It was taught at Harvard around the turn of the century by Oliver M. W. Sprague, one of whose students was the young Franklin D. Roosevelt (who learned the lesson well but was critical enough to reject it as the basis of policy). It was the theoretical basis for the establishment of the Federal Reserve System in this country in 1914. President Herbert Hoover had this theory in mind when he said, shortly after the 1929 stock market crash, "The fundamental business of the country—that is, production and distribution—is sound." He didn't mention the monetary and credit system, which obviously was not sound and which he tried to strengthen by loans to banks and railroads (whose bonds were owned heavily by the large banks) and by trying to cut federal expenditures. But Hoover's policies pointed up the bias inherent in Say's Law of Markets and in the theory of business cycles it spawned. Production and distribution were *not* sound in 1929, even though the theory denied that causes and remedies could be found and applied in those areas.

SCIENTIFIC METHOD

One of the strong points of neoclassical economics was the use of scientific methods similar to those used in the natural sciences and mathematics. A rigorous methodology gave economics letters of credit in the intellectual community that could not be matched by any of the other social sciences. The method comprised several elements: analytical rigor, mathematical logic, and empirical studies. That combination enabled economists to develop "laws" of economic behavior and prescriptions for public policy that had the ring of scientific truth.

Analytical rigor was provided by the theory of competitive markets developed by Menger, Walras, and Marshall out of Adam Smith's original formulation. Start with the behavioral assumption that individuals seek to maximize their benefits. One line of deductive reasoning concludes that if all individuals maximize their benefits, the benefits to society as a whole will be maximized. A second line of reasoning analyzed demand, supply, and price in individual markets, showing how production responds to consumer demand. In the process, producers are shown to produce goods at the lowest possible cost consistent with a continuing supply at levels desired by consumers. A third line of reasoning showed how all portions of the market system were tied together in a seamless web, creating a benefit-maximizing and cost-minimizing general equilibrium.

This basic model was supplemented later by: analysis of the conditions necessary for optimal results, led by an Italian economist, Vilfredo Pareto (1848-1923); theories of imperfect competition and monopoly at the hands of Joan Robinson (English, born 1903), Edward H. Chamberlain (American, 1899-1967), Heinrich von Stackelberg (German, 1905-1946), and others; and concepts of entrepreneurship and innovation by Joseph A. Schumpeter (Austrian, 1883-1950), to list only a few of the chief developments—for those who would like to explore further. The fact that the central model could be extended meaningfully into many new directions by these economists and many others gave it a significant innovative appeal.

The analytical model derived much of its rigor from its simple theoretical structure. The boundaries of economic activity were clearly defined in the institutional structure of a system of self-adjusting markets. There were no complications derived from complex social institutions like family, religion, or state, which were hardly mentioned by the neoclassical economists. The driving force was also simple: the acquisitive nature of human beings, which was assumed to be a universal constant. This gave the results of theoretical analysis an aura of universal validity and applicability. Like Newtonian physics, it was a science of finite space in which inexorable natural forces worked out a stable equilibrium.

Economics also adopted the methodology of laboratory experiments from the natural sciences, but applied it to theoretical inquiries. The essential idea was to start from a static situation, or equilibrium, change a single variable while holding all others constant, and then observe and analyze the results. For example, in chemistry, an acid would be added to a stable compound, or a chemical would be heated. In economic analysis this method involved starting from a stable market equilibrium, postulating a change, and then analyzing the chain of events that would follow until a new market equilibrium were established. The postulated change might be an increase in demand for a product, imposition of a tax, or discovery of a cheaper method of production. Whatever the presumed change, the economist would work through his analytical model to arrive at the likely results. This methodology became known as *partial equilibrium analysis* (because only one variable was allowed to change) or *comparative statics* (because one static equilibrium situation could be compared with another).

Theoretical analysis was greatly facilitated by the use of symbolic logic and mathematical notation. When two English philosophers, Bertrand Russell and Alfred North Whitehead, showed in *Principia Mathematica* (1910–1913) that mathematical logic could be used to derive rigorously correct conclusions from prior assumptions, without confusions or ambiguities, it seemed as if the ancient Aristotelian ideal of perfect deduction from initial premises was at last possible. All subsequent work based on logical analysis was revolutionized, and mathematical theoretical models became an essential element in economic analysis. Earlier studies like Irving Fisher's *Mathematical Investigations Into the Theory of Value and Price* (1892) and Francis Y. Edgeworth's *Mathematical Psychics* (1881) became the models for a reformulation of economic principles on the new foundation of analytical logic.

However, as with any new methodology, a number of critics were quick to point out faults. The new methodology was criticized as being essentially static, like Newtonian physics, and not well adapted to analysis of an economy in constant flux and disequilibrium. It assumed the existence of a universal human nature—acquisitive economic humans—that was attacked as a distortion. There was no room for changes in the institutional structure of the economy in a method that assumed *ceteris paribus,* that is, "everything else remains the same." And there was no way to determine how much of a change would occur from one position of equilibrium to another. In brief, critics argued that the analytical concepts were limited, unrealistic, and not quantified.

This criticism led to the final element in the methodology of neoclassical economics: empirical studies to verify or disprove the results of theoretical analysis. Theory would provide an hypothesis, which would then be tested by empirical studies. For example, the conclusion that a higher price for automobiles would result in reduced purchases of gasoline could be verified or disproven by statistical studies relating automobile prices with demand for gasoline. This required that theoretical concepts would have to be at least potentially testable.

The method was complete. Theoretical analysis, refined by mathematical logic, would provide testable propositions. Statistical studies would then verify or correct the hypotheses, leading to more highly refined propositions that were a closer approximation to reality. In this way economic science could move towards greater understanding of the world, just like the physical sciences.

THE IDEOLOGY OF CAPITALISM

In spite of its scientific method, neoclassical economics had strong ideological implications. The theoretical model assumed the existence of a structure of economic institutions based on individuals functioning in an environment of self-adjusting markets. It pictured a private enterprise economy that produced what consumers wanted and therefore maximized welfare, distributed products justly, and normally operated at full employment levels. Economic growth through saving and capital accumulation was the source of progress. The model was essentially the same as Adam Smith's, modernized to eliminate the labor theory of value and to bring it into conformity with the philosophy of individualism and newer ideas about scientific method.

Unlike the social Darwinism of Spencer, Sumner, Field, and Carnegie, however, neoclassical economics was not a rigorous laissez-faire theory. One major exception was in the area of monetary policy, where responsibility for maintaining economic stability through proper management of the money supply was assigned to government acting through the central bank. But even in this area, policy discretion was to be limited: the criterion for monetary policy was that it limit expansion of credit to the legitimate needs of business—that is, to the needs of production and distribution. Both of those aspects of the economy were to be governed by the free play of market forces unhampered by government intervention. In the last analysis, what little monetary intervention was allowed was to be largely indicated by the free market.

Other types of intervention were also approved by most neoclassical economists. One was the effort to preserve competition by what in this country came to be called "antitrust" laws. Since their theories were based on the assumption of perfect competition in all markets, the economists were at least consistent when they argued for regulation of "natural" monopolies and for laws to prevent restraint of trade. Their commitment to competition and their support of antimonopoly legislation were not complete, however. Some economists argued that private monopolies, unsustained by government restrictions on competition, would inevitably fall from their positions of power because of efforts of other business firms to get a share of the excessive profits. Others wanted to move slowly for fear that antitrust action might reduce the advantages to be obtained from mass production. In spite of these relatively mild dissents, however, a fairly consistent emphasis on the advantages of competition was developed and has been sustained to this day.

Still other concessions to government intervention were made. For example, Henry Sidgwick, a prominent English economist, in a paper given in 1886 before the Economic Section of the British Association for the Advancement of Science, listed a number of "economic exceptions to laissez faire." They included actions based on moral considerations, such as sanitary regulations, control of narcotics and intoxicants, and restrictions on gambling; efforts to improve the productivity of individuals by education; measures that require total public participation for effectiveness, such as public health measures and flood control; and provision of services whose benefits are general and for which the individual cannot be charged, such as lighthouses on rocky shores or certain types of scientific research. No one of these exceptions seems especially significant to the modern mind, accustomed to almost a hundred years of growing government activity, but they do point up the fact that much of neoclassical economics represented accommodations to existing needs and that it was not the simple paean to individualism and laissez faire its critics sometimes made it out to be. Many neoclassical economists could look upon their discipline as a scientific and rational path to reform.

The new economics, however, had strong ideological implications. It was a complete answer to Marx. Where the classical economists had used the labor theory of value to justify private property, Marx had used it as the basis for his theory of exploitation. Once Marx had written his devastating attack on capitalism, it was inevitable that the ideology of the existing order jettison the labor theory of value, and it is the necessity of doing so that largely explains both the "discovery" of a "new" theory of value and its rapid sweep to acceptance.

Viewed in this light, the development of the new economics of the 1870s must give us pause. It suggests that ideas are not accepted because they are "right" and rejected because they are "wrong" but that they are accepted when they are useful and rejected when their usefulness ends. In this case, the labor theory of value was part of the accepted canon of economic ideas as long as it could be used as part of the ideology of capitalism. When Marx destroyed its usefulness, the theory was discarded and replaced by the theory of marginal utility, which could support the theory of free markets and be used to belabor the Marxists.

Indeed, the new theory made refutation of Marx unnecessary, for it enabled the theory of private-enterprise capitalism to be rebuilt on a new basis. As the Austrian economist Eugen Bohm-Bawerk (1851–1914) pointed out in 1884, the entire Marxian analysis became irrelevant. This disciple of Karl Menger spent much of his career attacking Marxism in great detail, but he always felt that the best single argument was that the labor theory of value was just plain wrong. In England, Philip Wicksteed (1844–1927) came to the same conclusion at about the same time; he wrote that the entire Marxian analysis was invalid because it was based on labor instead of utility. The consensus of orthodox economists of the late nineteenth and early twentieth centuries was perhaps most succinctly stated by another Austrian, Friedrich von Weiser (1851–1926), who rejected the Marxian theory of surplus value as follows:

This argument is not conclusive, if for no other reason than simply because it takes the ground of the labor-theory, which cannot be maintained for the developed conditions of national economy.

The ideology of capitalism had survived its first great crisis and had been reconstructed on new grounds.

CHAPTER 8

The Human Family

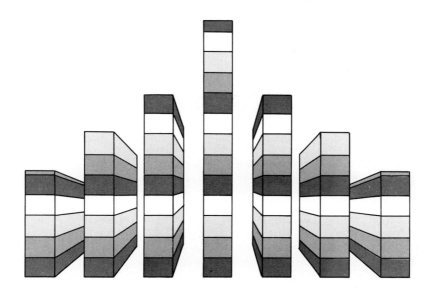

With the emergence of Marxism, the great debate over the economic system centered around the issue of socialism versus capitalism. The orthodox response based on the extremes of Darwinian individualism and the moderation of neoclassical economics served to further divide the antagonists. But the pattern of social thought is never simple. There are more than two or three possible responses in any ideological debate, and the issue of the proper organization of economic life brought forth a wide variety of ideas that opened up other dimensions of the problem. It was not just a question of socialized property and planning at one end of the scale versus private property and competitive enterprise at the other, with a variety of compromises forming a continuum between the two extremes. Other approaches, other formulations of the issue, and other solutions were offered.

One great middle ground involved the human race and its needs as a social unit. Marx had looked on the social system as being divided into antagonistic social classes, with social conflict as the source of change. Orthodox economists, on the other hand, saw society as a mass of individual units brought into an uneasy equilibrium by the forces of the market. Yet a third group of economic thinkers considered people and society as a single interrelated unit, with the individual motivated by self-interest, by feelings of brotherhood, by curiosity, by ethical values, by social and economic status. This complex view of the nature of people and society was developed in a wide variety of ways by different writers who, as a group, advocated a society in which human welfare was consciously sought as the chief objective of social policy. These thinkers were the architects of the philosophy of the welfare state. Pragmatic yet visionary, critical yet hopeful, they built many of the ideas on which the mixed economics of Western Europe and North America are based. Their influence on contemporary public policy far exceeded that of the socialists or the orthodox neoclassical economists.

PAPAL ECONOMICS

Pope Leo XIII (1810–1903) tried to find, in the abstract principles of social justice, a middle ground between the warring factions of capital and labor. In a famous encyclical of 1891 he defined the social problems of the age as essentially moral rather than economic and called for their solution on the basis of justice animated by charity. It was not a solution that could be measured by benefits and costs in the marketplace, and it was by no means "practical," but that was the whole point: morality and justice are not market phenomena but stand above the worldly considerations of profit and loss, wages and costs. Leo XIII called for consideration of economic issues in an entirely new dimension.

The Pope, who was born Gioacchino Vincenzo Pecci, had devoted his entire life to the service of the Roman Catholic Church. He was educated as a Jesuit, became a priest in 1837, and held a variety of administrative posts in the papal government, rising rapidly to become an archbishop in 1846 and a cardinal in 1853. He was elected Pope in 1878, at a time when the nationalism of the nineteenth century was causing severe problems for the relationship between Church and state in every European country and when industrialization was creating new social classes whose relationship to the Church was not yet clearly defined. Leo XIII held the papacy for a quarter of a century, and it was in large part through his efforts that the Catholic Church adapted itself to the new political and economic order.

In a series of encyclicals issued between 1878 and 1901, Leo XIII sought to analyze the problems of modern society and their remedies, the nature of the state and its relationship to the individual and the Church, and the fundamental economic problems of the age. One of his first encyclicals condemned socialism and upheld the right of private property, continuing a traditional position of the Church. But by 1891 he was prepared to take a position much more critical of the existing order. Problems of Church and state had largely been settled by compromise in France, Germany, Belgium, Switzerland, and Austria-Hungary, so that attention could be given to the struggle between capital and labor, between capitalist and socialist, that was threatening to tear apart the fabric of the European social order. In *Rerum Novarum*, sometimes called *On the Condition of Labor*, he argued that "a remedy must be found . . . for the misery and wretchedness which press so heavily at this moment on the large majority of the very poor." He continued with an indictment of laissez-faire policies:

Working men have been given over, isolated and defenseless, to the callousness of employers and the greed of unrestrained competition. The evil has been increased by rapacious usury ... still practiced by avaricious and grasping men. And to this must be added the custom of working by contract, and the concentration of so many branches of trade in the hands of a few individuals, so that a small number of very rich men have been able to lay upon the masses of the poor a yoke little better than slavery itself.

This passage, hardly distinguishable from the writings of avowed socialists, was followed, however, by a condemnation of socialism and a plea for private property as a natural right of the individual.

Leo XIII viewed the proper form of society as one in which the interests of the community as a whole transcended those of the individual and in which economic relationships were motivated by good will and concern for the interests of others rather than by pure profit-seeking acquisitiveness. Building on Catholic social thought that went back to Thomas Aquinas in the thirteenth century and beyond, Leo XIII saw larger community interests at stake than merely those of the market. He criticized the rugged individualism of the market economy and called for a return to human and community values.

In placing the interests of the community above those of the marketplace, Leo XIII assigned an important function to the state: it *ought to intervene* in economic affairs whenever the welfare and preservation of society as a whole might be endangered, but always with justice and fairness. It was quite proper for the state to limit hours of work, establish minimum wages, prohibit child labor, and provide other welfare legislation wherever required for the protection of society and its members. Labor unions were also proper, so long as they did not restrict membership and pursue selfish goals. Indeed, Leo XIII argued for the organization of a Catholic labor union to ensure that the labor movement gave proper consideration to ethical values. Viewed from the last quarter of the twentieth century, these papal pronouncements seem mild indeed, but at the turn of the century they were not, especially as they came from the leader of a religion that has generally supported conservatism in political and economic affairs.

The tradition of Leo XIII was continued by later popes, by the Catholic trade union movement, and by liberal theologians in the Church. Pope Pius XI commemorated the fortieth anniversary of *Rerum Novarum* in 1931 with another encyclical, *Quadragessimo Anno (Reconstructing the Social Order),* which applied the same principles to problems of the depression and the rise of fascism and communism in Europe. It tried to find a middle ground between those warring factions in a humanitarian concern for human welfare that rejected the philosophy of laissez faire as well. In 1961 Pope John XXIII issued *Mater et Magistra (Christianity and Social Progress)* to restate the idea that individuals and community were one and to emphasize that both individual freedoms and individual welfare had to be reconciled in a society that stressed community values and social justice. Although these ideas have not been translated into specific economic policies or reforms anywhere in the world, they have helped to create a climate of opinion that gives high priority to equity in economic life.

PHILOSOPHERS OF THE WELFARE STATE

In England John A. Hobson, the Fabian socialists, and Richard H. Tawney led the fight for a positive liberalism designed to cure the social ills of an industrial society. They defined government's role as one that fosters those social relationships and institutions that emphasize humanistic goals. The state should remove hindrances to the good life and promote conditions that enable the individual to do and enjoy the things worth doing and enjoying.

Under the influence of these ideas England witnessed a quarter century of reform, including legislation for factory safety (1891, 1895), limited working hours for women and children (1895), the beginnings of slum clearance (1890), widened powers for labor unions (1890-1900), compensation to workers for injuries suffered on the job and child-welfare legislation (1906), old-age pensions (1908), the beginnings of town planning and redevelopment (1909), and disability and sickness insurance (1911). The major components of the modern welfare state were being brought together.

John A. Hobson (1858-1940) was one of the chief exponents of the ideas behind this social legislation. He was denied a university post because of his unorthodox views, but from his pen flowed an unending stream of books and articles that shamed his orthodox contemporaries by their insight and criticisms. An early work, *The Physiology of Industry,* analyzed the causes of depressions and found them in inadequate consumer spending. *The Evolution of Modern Capitalism* criticized the industrial order for its monopoly, unequal income distribution, and depressions. *Imperialism* attacked the selfish expansion of the European states; its argument was later incorporated by Lenin into the communist ideology. *Incentives in the New Industrial Order* proclaimed that socialism could work because it would utilize a broad spectrum of motivations, not just those of big business capitalism. *Work and Wealth,* however, was Hobson's most important work. In it he argued for a concept of the good life in which government would be responsible for a more equitable distribution of income and for social controls to ensure full employment and high wages and to promote health, education, and recreation. Hobson believed that government action could end poverty, unemployment, and insecurity and establish a society in which human happiness would prevail. Utopian, yes—but this was the vision that lay behind English social legislation. Hobson did not originate it, but he was its best spokesman.

Hobson's ideals were similar to those of the Fabian Society, organized in 1883 by a group of English intellectuals whose ambitious goal was "reorganizing society in accordance with the highest moral possibilities" through a democratic socialist regime designed to promote "the greatest happiness of the greatest number." It was a small but very influential group; among the early members were the dramatist George Bernard Shaw, Sidney Webb, Graham Wallas, and Annie Besant, and they were joined later by the novelist H. G. Wells and by Beatrice Webb. The *Fabian Essays,* published in 1889 under Shaw's editorial leadership, advocated a gradual extension of state intervention in economic affairs to improve working conditions, replace monopoly with government ownership, and promote a more equalitarian distribution of income.

The society was named after the Roman general Fabius Maximus, "the delayer," who fought Hannibal, the Carthaginian commander, with what would now be called guerrilla tactics as opposed to full-scale battles. The name signified the society's political philosophy and plan of action. In opposition to the Marxists, the Fabians viewed the state not as an instrument of class warfare that had to be destroyed but as a means of social control that should be captured and used to promote social welfare. To this end they advocated formation of a labor party with a socialist program and were among the group that did successfully form such a party in 1906. They also sought to use local governments, which had been greatly strengthened by legislation of the late 1880s and early 1890s, to achieve their goals. The tactics of the Fabians involved political action within the framework of democratic, parliamentary government. They worked to institute their reforms by convincing the general public of the correctness of their views and by publicizing their stand in a series of research reports and popular pamphlets.

The Fabian band enjoyed considerable success. Their work helped push the welfare legislation of pre-1914 England through Parliament, and they helped organize the Labour party. Although they failed in their attempts to use local governments for social reform and to establish government ownership of large-scale industries (coal, steel, electric power, finance, and railroads), their ideas and tactics lived on in the Labour party and came to fruition after World War II, when the Fabian Society had a resurgence of activity and influence. Much of contemporary English welfare legislation and the socialization of transport, coal mining, and other basic industries can be traced back to the influence of the Fabians.

A different sort of influence was wielded by Richard H. Tawney (1880–1963), a scholar whose field of research was English economic history of the sixteenth century—a period considerably removed from the hurly-burly of political and economic issues of the twentieth century. But Tawney was a man of both ages. His masterly treatise on *The Agrarian Problem in the 16th Century* (1912) broke new ground in historical theory by analyzing the breakdown of the old agricultural, feudal order and the emergence of the modern market economy and society. Then, looking at modern society with the eyes of both an outraged reformer and an objective scholar, Tawney wrote three of the most important books of his time.

First came *The Acquisitive Society* (1920). Tawney compared the functional society of the Middle Ages, in which each individual had his place, his duties, and his rewards, with the modern industrial world, in which productive effort gains little reward while the promoter, speculator, and *rentier* collect large sums of unearned income. Modern society should be reorganized, argued Tawney, so that rewards are received by those who expend work and effort, by those who perform the tasks that society needs if it is to function for the welfare of all. "It is foolish to maintain property rights for which no service is performed," said Tawney, "for payment without service is waste." Society, he argued, should be reformed along the functional lines of a socialist society.

Then came the most influential of all of Tawney's works, *Religion and the Rise of Capitalism* (1926). Going back to his academic field of the sixteenth century, Tawney took up the scholarly debate begun by the Germans Werner Sombart and Max Weber over whether the Protestant Reformation created the intellectual climate that made possible the rise of modern capitalism. Tawney agreed that the two were related, and that each influenced the other, but the major thrust of his argument was that the business activities of modern society were completely amoral. Ever since the Protestant ethic of hard work and worldly success had become ends in themselves, without reference to broader or higher values, business had been carried on without moral principles. It was almost as if modern men and women were continually re-enacting the Faust legend, selling their souls for material prosperity while relegating ethical values to a quickly forgotten two hours on Sunday. Tawney described the modern world as "the smiling illusion of progress won from the mastery of the material environment by a race too selfish and superficial to determine the purpose to which its triumphs shall be applied."

This plea for values going beyond material wealth was followed by *Equality* (1931), which argued persuasively for a society that would provide an equalitarian distribution of wealth through "the pooling of surplus resources by means of taxation, and the use of the funds thus obtained to make accessible to all, irrespective of their income, occupation or social position, the conditions of civilization which, in the absence of such measures, can be enjoyed only by the rich." Such equalitarianism would, in turn, support and sustain the democratic political framework that made it possible.

Tawney was an interesting man. The foremost historical scholar in an obscure field, he used his detailed knowledge of the subject to cast new light on his own times. He developed a broad-ranging philosophy that raised basic criticisms of the economic life of his era. Tawney's solutions to the problems he described were socialistic because he believed that only through socialism could human values receive proper development.

VEBLEN AND COMMONS

The idea of the democratic welfare state developed in the United States on much more pragmatic grounds than in England. There were no economic philosophers like Hobson and Tawney and no group of intellectual activists like the Fabians. The American approach developed through the work of a small group of economists who investigated the economic problems of business cycles, labor relations, monopoly and big business, and social welfare, and through political leaders from the progressive era to the New Deal. The basic theme of both groups was that modern industrial society faced serious problems that would not solve themselves, and that the power of government should be used to protect both the social fabric and individuals within it from the often destructive forces of the market. The Americans sought workable solutions to specific problems within the traditional framework of American society, in contrast to the socialist philosophy that prevailed in England.

If any one writer were to be singled out as the most influential exponent of the philosophy underlying the American development, it would be Thorstein Veblen (1857–1929). Coming out of the rural Midwestern society that produced the Populist movement and William Jennings Bryan, this son of a Norwegian immigrant studied philosophy at Johns Hopkins and Yale and economics at Cornell. He made a career out of failure, never rising above the rank of assistant professor in a teaching career at Chicago, Stanford, and Missouri. Even when he lectured at the New School for Social Research in New York City during the early twenties, his salary was paid in part by contributions from his former students. But Veblen's books made him famous, and his ideas earned him the respect of his fellow economists. He was elected to the presidency of the American Economic Association in 1924, but declined the honor with the comment that the position was not offered when it might have done him some good professionally.

There are innumerable stories about Veblen. He left the University of Chicago in 1906 under a cloud created partly by his unorthodox ideas and partly by having taken a trans-Atlantic trip with a prominent Chicago woman. Although he was married, his extramarital escapades continued during his three years at Stanford, and the administration and several faculty members are said to have heaved great sighs of relief when he left.

Veblen did not enjoy teaching. When he went to the University of Missouri in 1911, his reputation as an economist preceded him. Students flocked to register for his classes, but they were met by a man who mumbled into his beard and who, on the first day of classes, filled the blackboards with a long list of readings on which they were to be examined in a week. This brought the class down to manageable size—about a dozen students. Moreover, Veblen did not give grades above "C," in order to discourage those hoping to be selected for Phi Beta Kappa.

Veblen shone in his books. In *The Theory of the Leisure Class* (1899), one of the most influential books of the last hundred years, Veblen criticized the materialistic criteria of success in a pecuniary culture. Since the survival of individuals and families depended on income, money and wealth became the standard by which all actions were judged. The wealthy spent their money conspicuously to prove their claims to success, and those with lesser incomes emulated the wealthy and their way of life: if the boss took a month-long vacation in Bermuda on his yacht, the secretary scrimped for years to take a one-week cruise to the Caribbean. Since leisure time was the greatest indication of success—showing that one did not have to work at all—the wealthy had many servants, did not allow wives or children to work, and spent their time seeking pleasure. "Conspicuous leisure," "conspicuous consumption," and "pecuniary emulation" were inherent in the market economy, and all led to a vast waste of resources, productive effort, and time. Veblen did not state his views as to what alternative value systems might be desirable, but he clearly rejected those of the pecuniary culture.

Veblen's next book, *The Theory of Business Enterprise* (1904), carried the argument further, with an analysis of the production side of the market. He distinguished between production for use and production for profit, pointing out that businessmen often prevented achievement of the former by pursuing the latter. The drive for profit led to restriction of output through monopoly. It held back technological advances, as business firms sought to protect their existing capital investment. It led to depressions and cutbacks in production, because of excessive extensions of credit and financial manipulations. It promoted separation of ownership and control in business, as efforts were made to control greater amounts of wealth with existing capital. It led to military expenditures and war through business control of political power. The single-minded pursuit of profit, in other words, prevented full realization of the gains that could be achieved by machine technology. Just as consumer attitudes led to waste in a pecuniary society, so also did the basic patterns of business behavior.

These two books, and Veblen's other writings, focused as much on economic and social change as they did on descriptions of the pecuniary society. The business and leisure classes might dominate a society, said Veblen, but change was inevitable. Technology had a life of its own, and scientists, engineers, and others were continually seeking better methods of production and more efficient systems of organization, irrespective of profits. On the other hand, businessmen and owners of wealth were "vested interests" who resisted change because it might upset their comfortable positions. A great conflict was therefore inherent between the march of technology and the conservatism of the existing order, between the interests of the community at large and those of the wealthy powers-that-be. A cultural lag inevitably must develop between the needs of society created by changing conditions and the established institutions supported by the leisure-class elite. Veblen saw this conflict polarizing around the two extremes of a technologically dominated socialism based on central planning and devoted to community welfare and useful production, on the one hand, and a military authoritarianism designed to protect the existing structure of power and wealth, on the other. He felt that the latter would triumph, as business managers sought to protect their own interest through state support of monopolistic controls combined with militarism and colonialism to create and preserve prosperity. Perhaps Veblen was influenced by the parallels between militarist Germany and the colonialism, big navy ideology, and strong presidency of Theodore Roosevelt. But whatever the source, as early as 1904, he had predicted the rise of fascism and the emergence of the corporate state: institutions that did indeed appear in the 1920s and 1930s in Germany, Japan, and Italy.

Veblen's viewpoint could not be ignored: fundamental forces of change were at work, he argued, requiring adaptations in social, economic, and political institutions that would inevitably be opposed by those who had achieved wealth and success. Veblen may not have originated this point of view, but he gave it a solid theoretical foundation in his concepts of the relation between change and the vested interests. Allied with his critique of the pecuniary society and the business system, these concepts gave direction as well as viewpoint to the movement for economic and social reform.

Veblen's books were widely read by the general public. In addition to these popular works, however, Veblen also presented to professional economists a devastating critique of neoclassical economics in a series of articles and book reviews in professional journals. Economics was old-fashioned, he argued, in its preoccupation with static equilibrium. Its assumption of the hedonistic psychology of the economic individual was a narrow interpretation of human nature. It ignored society as a whole in concentrating on the isolated individual. The importance of economic institutions and the processes of institutional change were excluded from analysis by use of the methodology of comparative statics. Its conclusions were almost wholly theoretical, and were interlaced with ideological justification of the existing order. This critique was, in fact, largely responsible for the development of empirical studies to supplement and refine theoretical analysis, which became a major feature of economics after Veblen.

Veblen's influence was widespread not only among the public, but also within the discipline of economics. His pupils and followers investigated in detail the issues he emphasized. Wesley Mitchell studied business cycles and founded the National Bureau for Economic Research. Adolf Berle and Gardner Means wrote on the separation of ownership and control in the large corporation. Means and Walton Hamilton analyzed the pricing policies of big business. Clarence Ayres looked at the impact of changing technology on economic institutions. Robert and Helen Lynd studied the structure of community power in books like *Middletown* and *Middletown in Transition,* and C. Wright Mills did the same on a national scale in *The Power Elite.* Even literary criticism was affected; for example, Vernon Parrington applied Veblenian ideas in his monumental *Main Currents in American Thought.*

Paralleling Veblen's work and influence was that of John R. Commons (1862-1945). Where Veblen had articulated the basic approach and viewpoint of the twentieth-century reform movement, Commons and his followers pioneered specific measures and legislation. Commons was also a Midwesterner and he also studied at Johns Hopkins University in the 1880s, when it was the foremost American graduate school. His teaching career took him first to Wesleyan, then to Oberlin, Indiana, and Syracuse. While at Syracuse he published a study which argued that the growth of the state paralleled the development of the institution of private property, as society sought to control the economic power that accompanied accumulation of property. Such ideas, plus Common's desire to add to the curriculum a course in labor problems, impelled the university administration to abolish his position. For the next four years, he worked with the United States Industrial Commission studying labor unions and labor-management relations and with the National Civic Federation promoting conciliation between labor and management.

In 1904 Commons returned to academia with a position at the University of Wisconsin, at the invitation of his old professor at Johns Hopkins, Richard T. Ely. He spent almost as much time on leave from the university to serve on government commissions as he did on the campus. His major interests were public utility regulation and labor problems. He helped draft Wisconsin's public utility law of 1907 and wrote extensively in favor of compensation to workers for injuries suffered on the job, unemployment insurance, and peaceful collective bargaining. In 1911 he helped set up the Wisconsin Industrial Commission, which sought to develop mediation and conciliation in labor disputes. In 1914 he served on a similar national commission in Washington and in 1915 wrote a report calling for a national labor board to promote settlement of labor disputes through collective bargaining. He then turned to unemployment insurance and began the movement that led to enactment of such a law in Wisconsin in 1932 and nationally a few years later. Realizing that unemployment insurance could not work effectively without economic stabilization, Commons entered that area and in the 1920s became president of the National Monetary Association, which sought programs to achieve stability of credit and prices.

All these programs and policies later became major parts of the public economy of the United States: public utility regulation as part of a regulatory system for businesses "affected with the public interest"; collective bargaining and mediation to settle disputes between labor and management on a voluntary basis; promotion of economic stability at high levels of output and employment; and social legislation (unemployment insurance, workers' compensation, and old-age insurance) to mitigate the chief harmful effects of the industrial system. Much of the New Deal legislation of the 1930s lay within the framework pioneered by Commons.

Underlying Commons' ideas was the concept of the economy as a "going concern." That is, the economy was a web of relationships among people who had diverging or conflicting interests, but who also had an interest in resolving those conflicts in order to keep the system functioning effectively. The development of modern industrial society may have created important social problems of monopoly, business cycles, labor-management conflict, and others, but everyone, Commons argued, could agree that all would be better off if those problems could be resolved. This approach led to a view of government as mediator between conflicting economic interests and between economic forces and the individual. Commons and other liberal reformers saw conflicts of interest, which had to be resolved with fairness to both sides, between business and the public, between labor and management, and in broader terms, between the free operation of market forces and individual welfare. This view of conflict differed sharply from those maintained by the other two chief ideological positions—from that of the neoclassical economists, who saw harmony emerging in all areas out of the equilibrating forces of the market, and from that of the Marxists, who argued that class conflict would inevitably tear the social order apart. Commons accepted both of these concepts but went beyond them; he argued that market forces could reconcile some but not all of the conflicting interests of the modern world and that a complex industrial society continually created new conflicts whose equitable resolution required government action.

THE NEW DEAL

The reforming, social welfare philosophy expressed by Veblen and the policies pioneered by Commons and his associates came to fruition during the 1930s under the New Deal administrations of Franklin D. Roosevelt, when the concept of the welfare state became dominant. It is true that old ideas began to change before the thirties: witness the welfare legislation of New York and Wisconsin, the conservation movement prior to World War I, and the gradual acceptance by government of the use of monetary policy to promote economic stability. Crusaders and critics from the Populists onward had been forging the social philosophy of the New Deal. But the years from 1929 to 1933 were a great watershed in American social thought, and the legislation of the five years after 1933 created the framework within which the American economy continues to function a half century later.

The most important aspect of the New Deal philosophy was the belief that society as a whole, functioning through government, must protect itself and its members against the disruptive forces inherent in an industrial, market-oriented economy. This represented a great shift away from the philosophy that the self-adjusting market should be given free sway and that people, resources, and wealth should be treated essentially as commodities.

The New Deal emphasized four main types of direct intervention in economic affairs to achieve its goals. First was its assumption of responsibility for maintaining full employment prosperity as nearly as possible, although the Great Depression's unemployment was not conquered until World War II. The most effective method developed by the New Deal was to use the federal budget to ensure an adequate level of total spending, and the budget deficits of the thirties sought to supplement inadequate private spending with public investment. This concept was embodied in the Employment Act of 1946 and institutionalized in the President's Council of Economic Advisers.

The second type of intervention was legislation establishing collective bargaining as a means of settling labor-management disputes. Ever since the 1890s the American Federation of Labor had sought gains for labor primarily through collective bargaining rather than radical political action or socialism. The Socialist Party and a radical union, the Industrial Workers of the World, were strong prior to World War I, but they were largely destroyed by repressive measures taken by the federal and state governments and courts during the war and immediately after—a dismal chapter in the history of civil rights in the United States—leaving collective bargaining as the only practical alternative for workers. Although the bulk of business opinion was opposed to unions and collective bargaining, typified by the National Association of Manufacturers, an important segment of the business community led by some leaders of major corporations saw in collective bargaining the answer to continued class conflict. Out of this meeting of minds of labor leaders and leaders of the corporate community, together with the stresses created by the Great Depression and the election of Franklin Roosevelt, came the National Labor Relations Act (1935), which made collective bargaining the national policy. Although modified by additional legislation after World War II, the policy remained as one of the cornerstones of the nation's economic constitution.

Thirdly, a less successful form of intervention was embodied in the National Recovery Administration (NRA), the great effort to promote economic stability through cooperation among business firms and between business and labor in individual industries. The experiment failed and has been one of the most heavily criticized of the New Deal programs. The New Deal itself abandoned it and in the later thirties turned full circle to the policy of promoting competition as recommended by the Temporary National Economic Committee. Whatever the merits of the case, the spirit of the NRA lived on in two natural resource industries—petroleum and coal—and in the military-industrial complex, although its philosophy is no longer part of the liberal creed. In the petroleum industry, a combination of state legislation, federal regulation, court decisions, and community of interest among major companies served to stabilize markets, prices, and profits until the early 1970s, when the Arab dominated Organization of Petroleum Exporting Countries (OPEC) took over, using control over production and prices to extort exorbitant profits from consumers all across the world. The coal industry for many years was characterized by a high degree of labor-management cooperation and coordination that had the effect of stabilizing output and market shares of major producers—an arrangement that crystallized in the 1940s on the foundation of government efforts to stabilize the industry in the 1930s. And, of course, the symbiosis of government, big business, and big labor in the armaments industries, a development of World War II and after, is a notorious example of the NRA philosophy in practice.

The fourth main type of government intervention in economic affairs was regional land-use planning based on water resources. Typified by the Tennessee Valley Authority, the principle of such planning was the outgrowth of a number of pre-New Deal policies—reclamation, waterway development, forest conservation, city planning, and the controversy over electric power development. Today we take for granted the desirability of unified development of water resources and related land uses, and the debates now center on far more complex issues of resource use.

The growth of government responsibility for economic affairs during the 1930s was supported by a new view of the individual's place in society. The older proposition—that the welfare-maximizing individual would contribute most to society as a whole, and the corollary that the unsuccessful ought to bear the cost burden themselves—was not tenable in a modern industrial society, particularly one plagued by a depression that crushed not only the unemployed, but even intelligent, hard-working business people. In its place arose the belief that society had a responsibility for the welfare of each person, partly because the individual contributed to society by working, by raising a family, and by participating generally in the activities of the social order, and partly because the problems of a complex society were often too great to be solved by the individual. It was felt that the individual functions more effectively, both in his own interest and as a contributor to society, in a secure environment. Another goal of New Deal policy was therefore to create sufficient economic security to release greater individual energies that would, in the long run, more than compensate for the costs involved. In practice this meant the passage of a range of "welfare measures"— unemployment insurance, social security, workers' compensation, and federal grants-in-aid in health and education—which also have achieved general acceptance today. Of course, such welfare measures are not simply humanitarian commitments maintained over time because they promote security. They also help stabilize consumer demand.

Another major tenet of New Deal social philosophy was that businessmen had social responsibilities beyond mere profit-making. In the pre-New Deal era, profit and success were their own justification; wealth reflected not only hard work and ability but also the fact that the search for wealth resulted in meeting the needs of others, "as if by an invisible hand." By contrast, the New Deal stressed that the market economy often ran roughshod over human and social values and that individual gain was not always synonymous with social good. Success and profit were not enough; business had to justify itself on other grounds. Nowhere was this requirement spelled out in detail, but New Deal legislation implied that it included a reasonably stable economy, broadly effective labor-management relations, reasonable prices, and straightforward financial activities.

Two further aspects of the changes of the 1930s had great significance for America and the world. First, reform and welfare programs greatly strengthened the nation's economic and social order. Through labor unions and collective bargaining, workers were able to achieve both higher standards of living and a new feeling of dignity and importance. Farmers were protected from some of the insecurity found in their highly unstable sector of the economy. Middle-income families were assisted in becoming homeowners, and their savings were protected. Some of the more objectionable practices of big business were prohibited, and government regulation of other business activities was expanded. The risks of old age and unemployment were ameliorated, and a beginning was made on a system of welfare payments to aid the poor. Although some groups were hardly affected, including most blacks, migrant workers, and the rural poor, and low-wage workers did not benefit significantly, the economic interests of many Americans were advanced—and their commitment to the existing order of things was strengthened. The New Deal, as America's answer to the challenge of change, was reform rather than revolution.

In a second respect, the legacy of the New Deal was less favorable. It set in motion a shift toward an American version of the corporate state that most Americans have been loath to recognize. As the federal government became the instrument of reform, and federal expenditures were increased to meet social needs, power tended to shift from the states to Washington. Within Washington, the executive branch of the government gained power at the expense of Congress, partly because the President took the initiative in promoting legislation, and partly because the enlarged federal expenditures were managed by the executive branch. This subtle shift did not go unnoticed at the time. Indeed, it was a favorite theme of New Deal critics. But its implications did not become clear until World War II and after, when the military and national security activities of the executive branch came to dominate national policy. This came about, in part, because of the very large amount of military-related spending, as well as because of national preoccupation with the "Cold War" and related international commitments. The New Deal reforms brought with them a growth in the power of the national government and its executive branch that later resulted in even greater power for the military.

This shift in the locus of power was validated by fundamental changes in constitutional law. A series of Supreme Court decisions in 1937-1939, upholding the chief New Deal legislation, greatly expanded the powers of the central government. Prior to 1930 the federal government could engage in those activities specifically designated by the constitution. By 1940 it was empowered to take action to "promote the general welfare." A constitution of limits was replaced by a constitution of largely open powers for the national government.

Nevertheless, the New Deal greatly strengthened the essential elements of the private enterprise economy. It preserved the individual's right to spend or save as he pleased, to choose his occupation, and to make his own business decisions. Although the New Deal restructured much of the country's social and economic framework, its methods never included detailed planning or controls. Nor did it encroach upon personal decision making—one of the basic tenets of American individualism. Furthermore, it left untouched the fundamental structure of economic power in an economy dominated increasingly by large corporations and it did little to shift the distribution of income and wealth.

The 1930s saw some basic changes in the economic institutions of the United States and a fundamental shift in economic philosophy. The outdated ideal of laissez-faire gave way to an interventionist, welfare-oriented economic philosophy. Yet the basic structure of a private enterprise economy and private accumulation of wealth was retained. In this respect developments in the United States were similar to those occurring in all of the advanced industrial nations. During the 1930s there was strong political and ideological conflict between the advocates of an expanded role of government and the protagonists of the older ideas and policies. Yet the decades following World War II were to see a growing symbiosis between corporate economic power in the private sector and the expanded economic, political, and military power of the national government. This was the type of development that Veblen predicted at the turn of the century, as a prelude to an eventual authoritarian and militarist industrial society. He may yet be proven right.

CHAPTER 9

The Keynesian Revolution

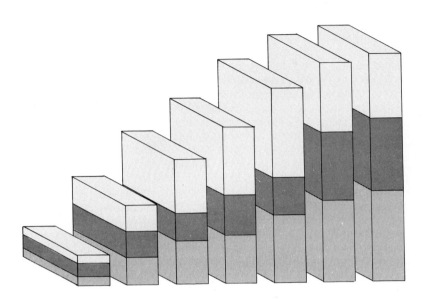

In 1936 the whole direction and emphasis of modern economics was transformed by the appearance of a single book. Its forbidding title was *The General Theory of Employment, Interest, and Money,* and it was written by the most controversial English economist of the time, John Maynard Keynes. It dealt with crucial problems of employment and unemployment at a time when the world economy was in the grip of the most disastrous and widespread depression it had ever experienced. Although many people had given up hope of ever rebuilding worldwide prosperity and a viable economic system, this book offered a theoretical analysis diagnosing the patient as seriously ill but not beyond hope and prescribing remedies that could restore its health. Keynes and his suggested policies immediately became the center of controversy among professional economists and politicians. Although damned by left-wing radicals and right-wing conservatives alike, Keynesian economics nevertheless swept aside almost all opposition among economists to establish a new orthodoxy within the profession. Together with *The Wealth of Nations* and *Capital, The General Theory of Employment* stands as one of the key books in the development of economics.

JOHN MAYNARD KEYNES

The man responsible for this revolution in social thought occupied a unique position in English public life. A member of the social and intellectual elite that had come to dominate public affairs in England, his unorthodox criticism of accepted economic policies seemed to fly in the face of all that the reigning leaders believed. Keynes was a critic of the Establishment from within the Establishment itself.

Keynes was born in 1883 in Cambridge, England, the son of a prominent economist and logician, John Neville Keynes. He was educated at Eton and Cambridge, where he studied philosophy and economics. A favorite and brilliant pupil of Alfred Marshall, he absorbed the essentials of neoclassical economics and always accepted its analysis of production and distribution. His special field was monetary economics, and he worked with the government on problems of Indian finance, and at the Treasury, in addition to lecturing at Cambridge. During the years before World War I, he became a member of the Bloomsbury set of artists and writers, which included such intellectuals as Lytton Strachey, E. M. Forster, Virginia Woolf, and Roger Fry. Typical of this group's attitude were Strachey's biographies debunking *Eminent Victorians*—brilliant, critical, but generally accepting the sense and order of the existing social system. The attitude was also typical of Keynes: himself a product of a comfortable social class that considered itself born to rule because of its intelligence, training, and dedication, he nevertheless sought always to achieve better ways of doing things within the framework of the old verities. By all accounts, Keynes was a brilliant snob with a most engaging personality, but he also had an analytical mind that could immediately probe to the essentials of a problem, perceiving its broader ramifications as well as its connections with other issues. If there had to be an intellectual elite, it was fortunate that a man like Keynes was part of it.

Keynes worked at the Treasury during World War I, making quite a name for himself as a financial expert, and in 1919 he was the Treasury's chief representative at the Versailles peace conference. With an intuitive understanding of world politics and a detailed knowledge of international finance, he knew that a stable peace depended on a magnanimous settlement and a realistic reparations burden for Germany. While statesmen argued over boundaries, frontiers, and national prestige, Keynes realized that the economic problems of Europe were more important than the political. When the peace treaty went the other way, demanding huge reparations and ignoring economic realities, Keynes resigned and returned home to write a slashing attack on the peace settlement and the men who developed it. In one of the most prophetic works of the age, *The Economic Consequences of the Peace,* he forecast the breakdown of the agreements and much of the economic turmoil that followed. The book was a sensation, but it largely destroyed Keynes' official contacts with government for a decade.

He went back to lecturing at Cambridge, became an executive of two insurance companies and several investment firms, speculated heavily in foreign exchange, stocks, and commodities to amass a substantial fortune, became active in the Liberal party, wrote extensively in *The Nation* and other journals, patronized art, music, and ballet, and married one of the great dancers of the Diaghilev Ballet. He lost his wealth in the stock market crash of

1929, borrowed to start over again, and made another fortune in the 1930s.

Keynes was critical of British economic policy, particularly the unwise effort to return to the gold standard in the mid-1920s, and from this controversy came his most important contribution to economics. Keynes attacked the policy primarily on the ground that its goal of achieving international economic stability was incorrect, that internal economic welfare was far more important. Stable prices and high levels of employment were more desirable than stability in the value of the pound on the foreign exchanges, he argued, pointing out that a return to the gold standard at the prewar exchange rate would seriously diminish British exports and cause domestic wages, prices, employment, and output to fall, just as they had a hundred years before, at the close of the Napoleonic wars, because of similar policies. Keynes advocated a managed monetary system in place of the automatism of the gold standard. But fiscal fundamentalism proved too strong: England went back to the gold standard, and disaster struck— unemployment, falling prices, and a nationwide general strike. Economic stagnation prevailed in England through the rest of the twenties, once again fulfilling Keynes' prophecy.

One reason no one listened to Keynes in 1923–1924 was that he had not developed a successful theoretical defense of his position. In order to demonstrate the deflationary effects of the government's monetary policy, he would have had to analyze the interconnections between the gold standard and the domestic level of employment and to prove that the orthodox economic analysis of those relationships, which applied Say's Law of Markets, was wrong. He was unable to do so at the time, but his keen mind saw that a thorough revision of the theory of employment and its relationship to monetary theory had to be developed. Keynes devoted the next twelve years to that task.

The first effort, a two-volume *Treatise on Money,* published in 1930 just after the stock market crash, did not do the job. In many ways Keynes' most scholarly book, it presented the basic framework of his new theory but left enough theoretical points unresolved to arouse more professional criticism than acceptance. Nevertheless, his point of view was important. The main argument of the book rested on the distinction between investment and savings and the different goals that motivated them. Say's Law insisted that the two had to be equal, but Keynes argued that they need not be. When savings exceeded investment, economic activity would decline; if the opposite was true, economic activity would increase. The remedies were those that Keynes had previously recommended—a managed monetary system to help maintain equality between savings and investment and hence to promote economic stability, supplemented by public works expenditures to mitigate the effects of whatever depression and unemployment should occur.

At the time the *Treatise* was published, economists as well as government officials were unaware of the seriousness of the depression, public opinion had not yet recognized the need for drastic remedies, and most people expected the market contraction to be short. Keynes, of course, did not share these views, but returned to his writing to attempt a second frontal attack on the accepted economic ideas.

THE CLIMATE OF OPINION
IN THE MID-1930s

The product of this phase of Keynes' labor was *The General Theory of Employment, Interest, and Money*. This book made an immediate sensation, not because it proposed a theory radically different from that in the *Treatise* but because, by the time of its publication in 1936, a path had been prepared for it. First, Keynes' previous publications had familiarized economists and policy-makers with his general point of view. Second, several other important economists had also broken through the orthodoxy of Say's Law of Markets to arrive at related conclusions. And third, the climate of opinion had shifted, particularly during the early years of the Great Depression, toward greater acceptance of ideas that tied the level of prosperity to total spending.

One vitally important element of the later Keynesian analysis was developed by a Russian economist with strong Marxist leanings, Michel Tugan-Baranowsky (1865-1919), who argued that a regular flow of savings comes into capital markets from consumers with relatively fixed incomes; that the investment process is, by contrast, highly volatile; and that the resultant disparities between the flow of savings and the flow of investment are at the root of the business cycle. These disparities could not be overcome by changes in the rate of interest, he declared, because many people who saved were motivated by reasons other than the rate of return they earned.

A far more important breakthrough was made by an eccentric Swedish economist, Knut Wicksell (1851-1926), who once spent a term in jail for violating a law that prohibited public advocacy of birth control and planned parenthood. Nevertheless, Wicksell was a brilliant scholar whose work made it possible for the next generation of Swedish economists and for Keynes to develop the contemporary theory of national income.

According to the orthodox theory of full employment embodied in Say's Law of Markets, any money saved would find its way to investment through the money markets. If there were a tendency for savings to exceed investments, a decline in the rate of interest would quickly right matters; if investment were to outrun the supply of savings, the rate of interest would rise and reestablish equality. If this equality of savings and investment occurred at relatively high price and wages levels that left some labor unemployed, wages would fall—bringing the price level down with them—until all resources were productively employed.

Wicksell noticed, however, that the actual course of events did not substantiate the theory. On the contrary, in depressions, when loans and investment were at low levels and hoarding of cash was widespread, interest rates were high and it was almost impossible to borrow; on the other hand, at the peak of a boom, when investment was high and cash balances were low, interest rates were also relatively low. This was, in fact, diametrically opposed to the theory, so Wicksell attempted a reconstruction. He postulated that there was a natural rate of interest consistent with full employment and with equality between savings and investment. However, the market rate of interest could differ from this natural rate for a variety of reasons, and when it did the economy would either expand or contract. The essential point was that the natural equilibrium was brought about not by changes in the rate of interest but by changes in the *level of economic activity*—that is, by increases or decreases in output and employment.

This was the great reformulation that ultimately led to the Keynesian revolution. Wicksell's concept of natural and market rates of interest was soon dropped, even by his brilliant followers among the Swedish economists, who included Gunnar Myrdal, Bertil Ohlin, and Dag Hammarskjöld, who later became a great Secretary General of the United Nations. But his fundamental concept of changes in the level of total spending as the equilibrating mechanism of the economy was retained and built into the economics of national income as we know it today.

Closer to Keynes than Wicksell was D. H. Robertson, one of Keynes' younger colleagues at Cambridge. In 1926 Robertson published a short book on the business cycle that stressed the importance of the relationship between savings and the demand for capital goods. The banks had a dual function, he pointed out, to provide the proper amount of working capital for business at the same time that they provided an amount of cash to the public consistent with the existing price level. The equilibrium was a precarious one, he argued, and the economy's efforts to achieve it resulted in the fluctuations of the business cycle. Here again was an analysis that emphasized the kind of variables with which Keynes was working and that familiarized economists with related ideas.

These theoretical inquiries were supplemented during the 1920s by statistical studies of national income, spending, saving, and investment that contributed significantly to the later development of Keynesian economics by providing it with a solid empirical foundation. In the United States the studies were carried on largely by the National Bureau of Economic Research under the direction of Simon Kuznets, in England by Arthur Bowley, and in Sweden at the University of Stockholm. Much of the support for all these studies came from various foundations supported by the Rockefeller family.

The path for a new economics was prepared by a shifting climate of opinion, as well as by developments in theory and statistics. In the United States in the 1920s, for example, William T. Foster and Waddill Catchings wrote a series of three widely read books that emphasized the need for high levels of consumer spending if production were to continue at a high level. They developed the concept of the circular flow of spending and argued that purchasing power must continually flow from producer to consumer and back to producer in order to sustain prosperity. Profits and savings had to be immediately spent or the circular flow would be interrupted, output would fall, and large-scale unemployment would occur. The basic argument that consumption must be stimulated to keep pace with production stood in direct opposition to the orthodox precept that production created its own demand.

This view was supplemented by the work of the so-called "monetary cranks," a group of writers who developed all sorts of monetary schemes designed to promote spending as a means of achieving full prosperity. They advocated several types of "funny money," as their detractors called it, such as money backed by reserves of commodities instead of gold, so that its quantity would be based on the level of production; "stamped money"—stamped with a date—which would gradually lose its value as time went on, a scheme designed to get people to spend money rapidly; or a requirement that banks hold reserves equal to their deposits, instead of fractional reserves, to prevent banks from creating money by their lending power and thereby stimulating overexpansion of the economy. These and similar ideas were spread widely during the 1920s by such people as the Nobel scientist Frederick Soddy, a persuasive English ex-army officer named Clifford Douglas, the German businessman Silvio Gesell, and even the prestigious Yale University economist Irving Fisher. Most economists laughed at the ideas, although the orthodox emphasis on the supply of and demand for money was partly responsible for them, but the concepts had wide popular appeal. For example, in the United States a Stable Money Association was formed to publicize Irving Fisher's ideas. Its members included bankers, railroad presidents, and even a former member of the Board of Governors of the Federal Reserve System.

All of these ideas reflected a fundamental change taking place in the economy. After more than a hundred years of economic growth and industrialization, the economic center of gravity was shifting from the investor to the consumer. In the days when industrialization was just beginning, the most important source of economic growth was capital investment in industries that largely supplied other industries—steel, coal, machinery, railroads. The classical economics of Ricardo and his followers had reflected that reality of the economic scene and had built a theory of economic growth largely upon the investment process and the concept that the purpose of savings was investment. But as industrialization proceeded, incomes rose and the spending and saving patterns of consumers became more important. Higher incomes enabled consumers to spend greater sums on durable goods like houses and home furnishings, automobiles, and electrical equipment. Installment plan methods of financing these purchases were developed. Savings began to flow into insurance policies and mortgage payments. The entire economy was transformed as consumer-oriented industries became the bellwethers of prosperity and economic growth. It was a slow process, which started in the United States in the years before World War I and developed more recently in Western Europe, but it transformed industry, finance, and public policy. In economics, it made the former emphasis on the investment process increasingly obsolete and made the idea of automatic investment of savings less and less applicable to the real world.

The Great Depression of the 1930s forced many people to recognize the changes and the consequent irrelevance of the old ideas. The very magnitude of the disaster would itself have been enough to evoke a reconsideration: in the major industrial nations better than one out of four workers were out of jobs, the banks of the world closed their doors in a disastrous wave of failures, business firms were bankrupted, farmers lost their land, and the entire economic system appeared to be grinding to a halt as incomes fell and spending declined. The commonsense explanation for the debacle seemed to be a huge decline in spending and the commonsense remedy to be a large increase in spending.

In most industrial countries, including the United States, this common-sense view led to large government expenditures on public works, financed by borrowing, and some of the hardships of depression and unemployment were eased. But the policy's justification was humanitarian and pragmatic, not based on economic analysis. Orthodox economic theory continued to call for tightening of the belt until "business confidence" could be restored, protection of the monetary system by fiscal restraint, and restoration of profits by wage reductions. The time was ripe for change.

THE GENERAL THEORY OF EMPLOYMENT

Keynes announced the revolution in economic theory in his book's emphatic one-paragraph first chapter:

> *I have called this book the* General Theory of Employment, Interest, and Money, *placing the emphasis on the prefix general. The object of such a title is to contrast the character of my arguments and conclusions with those of the classical theory of the subject, upon which I was brought up and which dominates the economic thought, both practical and theoretical, of the governing and academic classes of this generation, as it has for a hundred years past. Moreover, the characteristics of the special case assumed by the classical theory happen not to be those of the economic society in which we actually live, with the result that its teaching is misleading and disastrous if we attempt to apply it to the facts of experience.*

The book is an analysis of the causes of unemployment, written for the economic theorist and couched in the most esoteric language of the science. Indeed, Keynes created a new vocabulary within which the factors causing unemployment could be analyzed: the propensity to consume, the inducement to invest, the marginal efficiency of capital, liquidity preference, the multiplier. Together with the money supply, these variables determined the level of output and employment and had a major influence on the level of prices. Behind the esoteric terminology, however, lay the same simple principles that had been imperfectly developed in the earlier *Treatise on Money.*

Keynes first reiterated that unless savings were channeled back into the stream of spending, total spending would fall, creating unemployment and stagnation. Then he added something new—the concept of equilibrium at less than full employment. A fall in total spending caused by reduced investment would reduce incomes, which in turn would cause savings to decline until the desire to save was brought into balance with the desire to invest. At that point savings withdrawn from the income stream would be equaled by offsetting investment expenditures, and the decline in total spending would be halted. This "equilibrium" might well be established at a depression level, however, and unless there was a change in the relevant variables, the economy could stagnate indefinitely. Furthermore, the extent of the decline could be estimated fairly accurately by using the "multiplier"— the relationship between any change in consumption or investment and the level of total spending.

These basic relationships were then analyzed further, particularly the factors that determined the inducement to invest. Keynes argued that the amount of investment expenditure depended on the expected rate of return on new investment and the rate of interest. The former was the expected gain and the latter was the cost. If at any time the rate of interest could be lowered, and if there were no changes in business expectations of profit, the amount of new investment would be increased and would in turn have a multiplied effect on total spending. For this reason Keynes advocated easy money and low interest rates as one means of reducing unemployment. The rate of interest, in turn, depended on the quantity of money and the desire to hold it in cash or bank accounts. For example, if the desire to hold liquid assets remained unchanged while the quantity of money were increased, the rate of interest would fall, investment spending would rise, there would be a multiplied increase in total spending, and output and employment would increase. Here again, an easy money policy would help reduce unemployment.

Keynes' theory is illustrated in a figure on the next page. Employment depends on total spending, the components of which are consumer spending and business investment. The level of investment spending depends on the rate of interest and the expected rate of return on new investment. For example, if business firms expect to earn 10 percent on new investment and they can get the funds for 8 percent, investment spending will increase until the expected return falls or the rate of interest rises, or both, to bring the two rates into equality. The rate of interest depends on the desire to hold cash and the quantity of money available. When the amount of money people or institutions want to hold differs from the amount available, the rate of interest will either rise or fall until the two quantities are the same.

As an example of these relationships, let the central bank expand the reserves of the banking system, which causes banks to increase their loans, thereby increasing the supply of money. With no increase in the desire to hold cash, the increased supply of money will bring interest rates down. A reduced rate of interest will stimulate additional investment (as long as the expected rate of return on new investment does not change). More investment will then increase the national income by a calculated amount, because of the continued respending of the original increase in the circular flow of spending through the economy.

Keynes did not put all of his trust in monetary policy. He felt that the extremely depressed situation of the mid-1930s necessitated a large program of public works financed by borrowing. Such a program would add directly to employment, and the multiplied effect of the increased government spending would expand incomes, spending, and employment still further. This emphasis on deficit financing had been developed in several pamphlets and letters prior to the publication of the *General Theory*— including an open letter to President Roosevelt printed in the *New York Times* in 1933—and it became a major element in the Keynesian prescriptions for ending the depression.

Schematic Diagram of Keynesian Theory

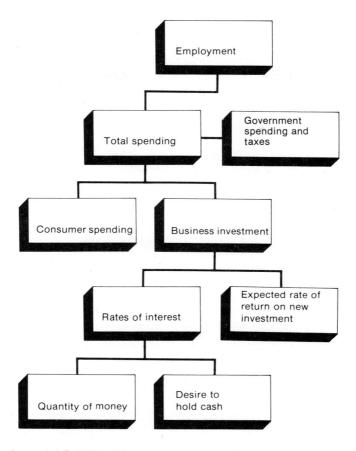

Fundamental Relationships:

1. *In a private enterprise economy, employment depends on the total amount spent for consumption and investment.*
2. *Consumer spending is essentially passive. It moves up or down as incomes rise and fall, and, in the short run, depends on the number of persons employed.*
3. *Business investment, however, may fluctuate widely in response to a) changes in rates of interest, which determine the cost of investment, and b) the expected rate of return on new investment.*
4. *Rates of interest in turn, depend on a) the quantity of money, which can be controlled by the monetary authorities, and b) the desire of people and business firms with financial assets to hold cash.*
5. *Government policy can influence the quantity of money directly, but not the desire to hold cash or the expected rate of return on new investment. This means that an economic stabilization policy may require direct government action to raise or lower total spending through changes in government expenditures or tax receipts.*

The analysis carried implications for long-range social policy as well as for the immediate problem of ending the depression. Keynes worried about the ability of a mature economy, which generated large amounts of savings annually, to sustain the high levels of investment necessary for maintenance of full employment. Thrift was not always a virtue, and high levels of spending might be more necessary than savings in an advanced, developed economy. So Keynes advocated a more equalitarian distribution of income, plus restrictions on unearned income, as a means of achieving better economic health in the long run, since the rich tended to save a larger proportion of their income than did the poor.

The basic ideas expounded in the *General Theory* stood in direct opposition to the old theory that the rate of interest determined equality between savings and investment and that wage reductions would lead to full employment. In terms of the events of the 1930s and the climate of political opinion, the new theory was far more realistic than the old. Right or wrong, it at least offered some hope that proper policies could cure the ills of the economy, and it laid down the general lines that those policies should follow.

THE MEANING OF KEYNESIAN ECONOMICS

The *General Theory* was given a mixed reception. To judge by the reviews in scholarly journals, the older generation of economists missed its significance or did not understand its obviously intricate theoretical complexities. But younger economists seized upon it avidly, seeking both to fathom its difficulties and to spread its gospel. In particular, a group of young economists in the United States government used its ideas to justify the already existing policy of public works, deficit spending, and easy money. They were aided by two somewhat older men, Gerhard Colm, a German refugee then in the Bureau of the Budget whose experience in Germany had given him an understanding of the need for expansionary economic policies, and Alvin Hansen, a Harvard professor who became the chief American exponent of the Keynesian point of view. Hansen produced a voluminous series of works publicizing the new ideas, while Colm and others worked quietly and anonymously within the government to build effective policies. But conservatives, young and old, reacted with horror against the ideas that seemed to be destroying the verities of hard money, savings, and fiscal restraint: "Keynesian economics" came to be a term of opprobrium in their circles.

Keynes, meanwhile, was *hors de combat.* Illness and a heart attack temporarily retired him within a year after the publication of the *General Theory,* and by the time he recovered, World War II had begun. During the war Keynes acted as an advisor to the British Treasury and helped negotiate major loans from the United States. After the war he helped formulate the Bretton Woods plan for an International Monetary Fund to help stabilize the world economy and avoid some of the pitfalls of the twenties. Knighted for his efforts, he died in 1946 at the age of sixty-two, recognized for what he was, the greatest economist of his time, overshadowed—perhaps—only by Adam Smith among economists of all time.

Keynes had almost single-handedly developed the rationale for the basic economic policies of the second half of the twentieth century in the nations of

Western Europe and North America. Keynesian economic policies using monetary management and an active *fiscal policy* (that is, government spending and taxing policies) were expected to maintain economic stability and promote economic growth. Yet most economists assumed that with the devil of unemployment exorcised from the body economic, the self-adjusting market mechanism could be relied upon to allocate resources. The welfare-maximizing consumer and the profit-maximizing producer, meeting in the competitive marketplace, would bring about a pattern of production that matched the wants of consumers. By and large, their argument ran, the free economy could be relied upon to allocate resources to the best advantage, assisted by laws to maintain competition and to resolve special conflicts. Although the overall level of economic activity had to be managed by government in the interest of the nation as a whole, the economy nevertheless could be left free to respond to the decisions of individual consumers and producers. The promise of Keynesian economics was that individual freedom and social order were consistent with each other within the framework of prosperity for all. As we shall see, however, the promise was far from reality.

CHAPTER **10**

Economic Planning

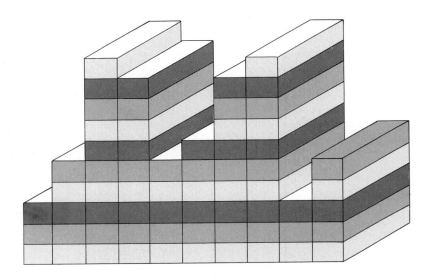

While Keynes was leading the way toward new policies designed to preserve and revitalize the market economy, a new challenge was arising. During the 1920s and 1930s socialist leaders in the Soviet Union devised methods of large-scale economic planning which brought rapid rates of economic growth and transformed a backward, rural economy into an industrial giant. The social costs of the program were high, but its basic goals were achieved.

Many Western economists argued at first that a planned economy must fail, but others examined the theory of planning in greater detail—explored its rationale and its operating techniques—and concluded that an efficient system was quite feasible. A number of underdeveloped, formerly colonial nations experimented with considerable success with a range of socialist and quasisocialist, planned and semiplanned economies. Both theory and practice have shown that economic planning can work effectively. The issue in recent years has been the compatibility of planning with economic and political freedom: is it possible to develop an effective system of economic planning that avoids centralization of power and authoritarian government?

PLANNING IN THE SOVIET UNION

The conclusion that economic planning can work was not always as obvious as it appears today. In Russia, in the years immediately after the Russian

Revolution, from 1917 to 1921, it seemed that the economy of the new Soviet state would gradually grind to a halt. Revolution, counterrevolution, and war destroyed most of the industry that had not been lost to foreign countries as the result of the peace settlement in Eastern Europe. The new government was not prepared to manage factories, and the former owners could hardly be expected to operate in a regime dedicated to their elimination. The peasants had seized the large agricultural estates and consumed most of the reduced output instead of marketing it to supply the cities. When the government sent soldiers to seize grain, a peasant revolt threatened. And with the old bureaucracy gone, tax collection failed, the government resorted to printing presses to obtain money, and inflation further complicated the economic chaos that developed.

Drastic measures were called for. The government shifted to a "New Economic Policy" that represented a retreat from full nationalization of trade and industry. Light industry and retail trade were returned to private enterprise, but the government retained the "commanding heights" of the economy—heavy industry, power, transportation, banking, and much whole-sale trade. The economy responded well. Output rose to its prewar levels in most industries by 1928. Reconstruction was rapid, and the government gained valuable experience in planning the nationalized industries. The first great crisis was over.

But new problems were at hand. Russia was still the most backward country in Europe. Its peasant agriculture was primitive by modern stan-dards, much of the population was illiterate, and a large part of its "industrial" production was carried on by handicraft methods. Yet here was a nation faithful to a Marxist ideology which postulated that socialism would naturally evolve in highly industrialized economies in which the industrial working class comprised a majority of the population. Compounding the problem was the fact that world revolution had failed and the fear that the U.S.S.R. might be attacked at any time by the antagonistic capitalist countries that surrounded it.

V. I. Lenin (1870–1924) had laid down the basic lines on which these problems could be resolved. He had led the Bolshevik revolution to a successful conclusion after convincing his followers that Russia could bypass the capitalist industrial era and move directly from an agricultural, semifeudal society into the socialist era. The instrument of transition was to be rapid and large-scale industrialization, building the working-class society in which socialism could flourish. The necessary social basis for the transition to an urban, industrial society would be an alliance between workers and peasants (but not the well-to-do peasants, the "kulaks") under a workers' dictatorship. Lenin died before his strategy could be translated into specific policies, and in the late 1920s a great public debate took place among Soviet economists and political leaders over methods of planning and rates of growth. Until it was ended by Stalinist authoritarianism in 1930, with the first of the purge trials, this debate produced some extremely revealing discussions of economic development policy.

One approach (called by Stalin the "right deviation") was advocated by the moderates, led by Nikolai Bukharin (1888–1938), the Communist party's leading Marxist theoretician. He had in 1920 coauthored a famous treatise on economics which announced that the economic laws of capitalism no longer applied to the new Soviet state, which therefore had tremendous freedom to experiment with planning and other policies. By the later twenties, he had shifted his position, however, arguing that the nation's rate of economic growth was limited by the amount of agricultural surplus that could be produced to feed the cities and to export in exchange for machinery. Industry had to grow, but two of its chief tasks were production of agricultural machinery and of consumer goods for sale to the peasants as an inducement for them to market their products. Bukharin was concerned about the loyalty of the peasantry to the regime—and well he might be—and was willing to restrict industrial development to the level made possible by expansion of agricultural production on a voluntary basis. This policy was based on the belief that fundamental economic relationships—such as those between industry and agriculture, heavy industry and consumer goods—determined the possible rate of economic development and that it was dangerous for planners to try to expand beyond the pace inherent in those relationships. Bekharin also tied his policies to foreign affairs. World revolution had to be temporarily postponed, he argued, because the first attempt had not succeeded. Moreover, the regime had to build firm support at home to resist the unfriendly capitalist powers; this meant gaining the allegiance of the peasants by not pushing them too hard.

A second approach, opposing that of the moderates, was put forward by the "left wing" of the Communist party, led by Leon Trotsky (1879–1940), Lenin's right-hand man during the revolution. The chief economist of this faction was Evgeni Preobrazhenski, who had been coauthor with Bukharin of the 1920 treatise but now opposed him. The development strategy proposed by this group was to press the economy to the utmost, to attain the maximum possible rate of industrialization at all costs, squeezing living standards in order to free resources for industrial development and using the power of the state to extract the maximum surplus from agriculture for food, raw materials, and export. Agriculture was to be transformed by mechanization and by the formation of large collective farms. The left wing scorned the balanced planning advocated by Bukharin in favor of rapid industrialization, even at the cost of economic dislocation. Like Bukharin, the left also related its policies to the international situation, arguing that the Soviet state could never be secure in a capitalist world; that the Soviet Union could best protect itself by fostering world revolution; and that the best way to foster revolution was to demonstrate the superior productivity of socialism through impressive economic growth, which would also bring the working classes of other nations to Russia's support to further hinder a capitalist attack.

The great industrialization debate clearly involved the gravest of issues for the U.S.S.R., and the wily Joseph Stalin (1879–1953) used it as a stepping-stone to full power. He took an intermediate position at first, supporting rapid industrialization and "taut" planning as advocated by the left but siding with the right against collectivization of agriculture, in order to conciliate the peasantry. On the issue of world revolution, he aligned himself with Bukharin and the right, and on the basis of this alliance was able to defeat Trotsky in a contest for power and drive him into exile. Then, in an amazing political turnabout, he suddenly advocated the left's agricultural policy, accelerated the rate of capital accumulation beyond even that faction's expectations, and used the support he thereby gained to purge Bukharin and his followers.

The debate was thus resolved by the establishment of ambitious development goals and a method of economic planning to achieve them, with Stalinist authoritarianism as a major driving force behind the whole system.

Stalin stated the U.S.S.R.'s basic goals in 1928. They included "the final victory of socialism in our country," "an adequate industrial base for defense," and economic growth "to overtake and outstrip the advanced capitalist countries." The goals were essentially political and ideological in nature, although economic means were to be used to achieve them. "Maximum capital investment in industry" to achieve a "fast rate of industrial development" was the path to be followed, said Stalin, and this required "a state of tension in our plans."

The planning technique in general was not complicated, although the development of administrative details required much experimentation. The desired expansion of the economy was determined by top government leaders, who selected targets that would press the economy to its limits. A few key industries such as coal, power, steel, and machinery were selected as "leading links" and given top priority. The rest of the economy was tied to the target industries by a system of "balanced estimates," which determined the inputs and outputs of all sectors of the economy needed to achieve the goals for the leading links and through them, for the economy as a whole. Production plans for individual enterprises were calculated on the basis of these industry-wide balances and supplemented by corresponding plans for finance and labor.

The ambitious goals and taut planning required that strong incentives be developed to draw forth the best efforts of the Russian people. Here the Soviet growth strategy ran into difficulty, because restrictions on output of consumer goods held back any significant increase in living standards. Any effort to increase production of consumer goods meant that less effort was available for expansion of industry; every ton of steel used for refrigerators meant one ton of steel less for electrical generators; every labor-hour spent for construction of housing meant one less labor-hour for building a power dam. For a time this problem was avoided by reducing unemployment, drawing women into the labor force, and shifting workers from agriculture to industry. Some incentive was provided by raising wages and salaries periodically, but with production of consumer goods held down, increased wages only drove prices up. Widening the differences between wage rates for jobs of differing skills also helped, but this practice was limited by its inconsistency with the equalitarian principles of socialism and by the fact that it brought lower standards of living to lower-income groups, who could afford to buy only a small share of the limited quantity of consumer goods. "Socialist" incentives were also tried—honors, medals, publicity, and various special benefits awarded to workers who exceeded existing production norms. But, in the end, the regime was forced to use compulsory methods, however reluctant it may have been to do so. Political goals required political incentives.

This was particularly true in agriculture. The shift from individual farms to collectives in the early 1930s aroused sharp resistance from the peasants and was the major cause of the terrible famine of 1933. The collective farms facilitated agricultural mechanization and substantially increased output, however, and enabled the regime to apply planning to agriculture and ensure that the entire increase in output went to the state rather than to farmers. Compulsory deliveries of farm products at low prices were instituted, and restrictions were placed on the uses of private farm plots. But these measures gave little incentive to individual peasants to improve farming methods, and production stagnated after the initial increase in output.

Other compulsory and restrictive measures became necessary for industrial workers as well. Regulations designed to reduce labor mobility were introduced in the late 1930s and, when World War II began, were extended to prohibit a worker from quitting his job without permission from the plant manager; legal penalties were imposed for tardiness, unexcused absence, consistent failure to fulfill work norms, and other economic "crimes." Perhaps justified under wartime conditions, these negative incentives for labor continued in force until the early 1950s.

The power of the state rather than economic incentives was used to ensure plan fulfillment. The Stalinist system of authority became as much a part of Soviet economic development strategy as the industrialization drive and taut planning. At the same time, of course, concentration camps—the Gulag Archipelago or "country within the country"—had appeared as part of the Soviet scene. Although their purposes were more political than economic, they further darkened the already gray picture.

The system couldn't continue indefinitely. After Stalin's death, his successors attempted to gain the support of the people by eliminating much of the repression and by producing more consumer goods to raise living standards. Inevitably, the rate of economic growth slowed down as the hard-driving Stalinist pattern of authority was eased. Agriculture remained stagnant and backward: after an initial increase in farm output in 1953–58, obtained by opening huge areas of new land in central Asia and by providing greater incentives to the peasants, production levels stabilized rather than continued to rise. Moreover, two major crop failures in 1972–73, and 1975 required large purchases of grain from abroad. Industrial expansion also began to level off, despite administrative reorganizations, greater flexibility for plant managers, improved systems of rewards and incentives, and other efforts to sustain high rates of growth. Major inefficiencies in resource allocation became apparent. Nevertheless, the essential elements of centralized planning in an authoritarian state remain.

THE THEORY OF PLANNING

While the Soviet Union was forging a system of planning based largely on political goals, economists in other countries debated whether or not planning as a purely economic system could be efficient. They had little experience with public ownership, they knew little about planned economies, and even the traditional socialist literature had little to say on the topic. Moreover, most orthodox economists were so imbued with the beauties of the theory of the self-adjusting private-enterprise economy that they tended to dismiss economic planning as impractical, and the early difficulties of the Soviet economy seemed to confirm these first impressions.

One of the leaders in the attack on planning was Ludwig von Mises (1881–1973), an Austrian neoclassical economist who argued that socialism and planning could not provide a rational basis for economic decision-making. Writing in 1920 at the height of the Soviet Union's early difficulties, he pointed out that public ownership of the means of production precluded the establishment of a market for capital. Without such a market there could be no price for capital, no rate of interest to express relative scarcities, and hence no rational basis for determining how much capital should be accumulated and how it should be used. These decisions could be made by planners, he said, but they would not be rational ones that used the resources of the nation efficiently.

Interestingly enough, Von Mises' argument had been refuted some years before by an Italian economist, Enrico Barone (1859-1924), who showed that accounting prices established by planners could substitute for prices set in competitive markets, at least in theory. However, followers of Von Mises continued the attack, dismissing Barone's theoretical solution as impractical because it would require literally millions of decisions based on a vast amount of information about consumer preferences which plainly was not available to any planning board. Even if the information were available, solutions would be obsolete by the time they were calculated—electronic computers were not known in the 1920s, of course.

This argument was answered by two economists who began from widely different viewpoints. One was a conservative American neoclassicist, Fred M. Taylor (1855-1932), whose presidential address to the American Economic Association in 1928 demonstrated that Barone's solution could be achieved by a trial-and-error process. Consumers could be left free to spend their incomes in any way they liked, according to Taylor, while planners simply established prices that cleared the markets—that is, precluded shortages and gluts—and that equaled costs of production. Production decisions would be determined by the quantities that could be sold at those prices. Once a balance had been achieved, the planners could be reasonably sure that resources were being allocated rationally.

The second answer was published in 1836-37 by the socialist Oscar Lange (1904-1965), a Polish economist trained at the University of Chicago who was to become an important participant in Poland's planned economy after World War II. In a much more elaborate analysis than Taylor's, he showed that a planning board could simulate the market process by a trial-and-error method of setting prices, together with a profit-maximizing rule for decisions by individual plant managers. The result would be maximization of consumer welfare along the lines of the competitive private-enterprise economy. Furthermore, the restrictions of monopoly could be eliminated and full employment ensured by planning the level of investment. Lange and Taylor showed that market socialism was feasible. To this the English economist Arthur Pigou added that the private-enterprise economy did not always work well, anyway, as attested by the disparity between its description in economic theory and its actual operation.

The arguments of Taylor and Lange carried the day. Few economists today will argue that planning per se must fail, or even that it must be inefficient, although many would say that excessively detailed central planning will not work effectively. There are obvious difficulties involved in planning, and its actual operation in a given country may be criticized, but the theoretical argument has been won by those who argued in favor of planning.

Critics, too, have shifted ground. Taking their cue from the Soviet Union and the European dictatorships of the 1930s, they now argue that planning may be workable in an economic sense, but only at the expense of personal and political freedom. The foremost statement of this position was made by Friedrich von Hayek (born 1899), another Austrian economist, in *The Road to Serfdom* (1944). This little book argues that once government intervention in the free market begins, it must inevitably lead to socialism, and that socialist planning leads inevitably to loss of freedom. There is no stopping place along the path to oppression.

The development of planning in recent years does not support Hayek's contention, no matter how realistic it may have seemed in the last days of World War II. The Soviet Union itself has significantly eased the authoritarianism imposed by Stalin. Yugoslav central planners have made a conscious effort to reduce their own power, develop management by workers themselves, and rely more on the operation of markets in making price and production decisions. Decentralization in planning and reliance on the market mechanism and its incentives, which are important elements in market socialism, are now a major feature of economic planning throughout the eastern European countries, including Hungary, Poland, Rumania, and Czechoslovakia. In France, a system of "indicative," or "target," planning has been developed in which goals for economic growth are fostered primarily by financial inducements to private enterprise, government management of some important nationalized industries, and control over the financial system—leaving individual decision making largely untouched. In the People's Republic of China the regime is admittedly authoritarian, but the system of planning involves an ingenious mix of central authority and local autonomy. In the less developed nations of the world, planning for growth takes place within many kinds of political frameworks. The great variety of social and political systems, with greater or lesser degrees of planning, indicates that no simple relationship exists between planning and authority, and that a planned economy need not be modeled on that of the Soviet Union or the dictatorships of the 1930s. Market socialism along lines analyzed by Lange and Taylor, in which planning is oriented toward consumer needs and decisions are made within a framework of democratic political institutions and individual freedom, may well be a feasible alternative to either authoritarian socialism or monopoly capitalism.

PLANNING IN LESS-DEVELOPED NATIONS

The less-developed nations are experimenting widely with a variety of planning methods. They emerged from World War II either independent or on the verge of independence, but backward in both living standards and economic development. Like the Soviet Union in the 1920s, they are seeking to break the fetters of traditionalism and accelerate their rates of economic growth.

These less-developed countries of Asia, Africa, and Latin America had been caught in a vicious circle. Low productivity and low incomes meant that savings were inadequate to achieve levels of investment that might accelerate economic growth. Low incomes also meant a consumer demand inadequate to attract capital investment from other countries. Low levels of investment, in turn, completed the circle of low productivity, low incomes, and backwardness. Low incomes also meant poor housing, poor sanitation, and poor health conditions, which reduced both vigor and length of life, resulting in a young population with a large proportion of unproductive dependents. Low incomes, furthermore, prevented innovation in economic affairs. Since innovation requires a surplus on which to rely in case of failure, a peasant family living at subsistence level cannot afford to experiment with new methods or machines; it must be conservative, for one crop failure means death from starvation. Also generating conservatism was the dominance in many less-developed areas of an economic elite with large land holdings and high incomes whose savings were usually not invested for national economic development but were used instead for acquiring more land, for money-lending at high rates of interest to the peasants, or for investing in more advanced countries. Meanwhile, population pressures were created by high birth rates among the peasant families. Birth rates in less-developed nations were always high, but they were counterbalanced by high death rates until the application of modern methods of sanitation and public health made populations soar.

Some economists pointed to economic dualism as another problem in some areas. The Dutch economist J. H. Boecke, for example, in describing the economy of Indonesia under the Dutch, pointed out that a market economy developed in some sectors of the economy under the aegis of European and American capital, that it was tied very closely to the import-export trade, and that it involved only a small part of the population. The bulk of the people remained isolated in a subsistence economy organized around village and family relationships. The two parts of the economy seldom came into contact, and the westernized sector imparted no growth impulse to the native sector.

The less-developed nations began, therefore, to plan for balanced economic growth, devising various methods to increase savings and to mobilize them for economic expansion under the auspices of government. A wide variety of combinations of public enterprise, public subsidies for private enterprise, and economic controls were developed, especially in the years following the Second World War. At one extreme countries like Mexico and Brazil rely very heavily on private enterprise and foreign capital. At the other extreme the Chinese economy is almost completely socialized, using both central planning of basic industries and local control of much small-scale production.

Many economists are hopeful that the problems can be solved, and that the poor nations can set in motion a self-sustaining process of economic growth. For example, the American economist Walt W. Rostow argues that any nation goes through stages of economic development as it moves from a traditional society to a modern mass-consumption economy. The process involves establishing certain preconditions—a stable government, improved education, a group of innovators and businessmen to utilize the savings, and expanded trade. Then comes the "take-off" into sustained growth, when the economy breaks its shackles and economic progress dominates. Crucial to this change, says Rostow, is an increase in savings and investment to 10 percent or more of the national income. Finally the development of industry and rising living standards lead to economic maturity and mass consumption.

Implicit in Rostow's analysis are policy recommendations that found great favor in the United States. First, social reform is needed to make the less-developed nations more like North America—"Do it the way we did," Rostow says in effect. Second, the concept of the take-off implies that economic aid to developing countries can be gradually phased out, even if it must be initially large to get the take-off started; this aspect of Rostow's ideas had an obvious appeal to the economy-minded. Third, Rostow's description of the growth process implies that once begun, it is not dependent on planning or state management: it is self-sustaining. Perhaps for this reason he titled his book *The Stages of Economic Growth: A Non-Communist Manifesto* (1960).

Other economists are less optimistic about the prospects for achieving a natural or self-sustaining process of growth. Gunnar Myrdal, a Swedish economist who helped develop the Swedish version of national income theory concurrently with Keynes and who wrote a sociological classic on the American racial problem, *An American Dilemma,* argued persuasively that the economic gap between advanced and less-developed nations is widening. The already industrialized nations have high incomes which generate large amounts of savings, he pointed out in *An International Economy* (1956), but the savings are not invested in less-developed nations because of higher profit rates at home. The industrial economy reached into some parts of the world with mines and plantations to produce for export, but these economic enclaves draw savings and the most talented people from the local economy, leaving it more starved for the means of achieving growth than it was in the first place. As a result, says Myrdal, less-developed nations cannot model themselves on advanced nations but must act radically within their own economies to reorganize imports and exports, diversify production, and plan for economic development. In a later study, *Asian Drama* (1968), he argued that economic advancement for the less-developed countries is possible, but only if population growth can be controlled.

Part of the growth problem for less-developed countries is their economic relationship with the more advanced industrial countries. Raúl Prebisch, an Argentine economist working with the United Nations, argued that the "terms of trade" have a long-run tendency to be unfavorable to less developed areas. These regions produce primary commodities for export—foodstuffs, minerals, and other land-based products—for which markets are highly competitive and which can easily be produced in excess. The result is low prices and low incomes for the producers, as well as highly unstable markets. Advanced countries, on the other hand, export manufactured goods, whose prices tend to rise, according to Prebisch, because of strong monopolistic controls by producers and demands by organized labor for higher wages. These nations, therefore, sell at high prices to less developed areas and buy at low prices from them. This would not be too bad if rising incomes in the advanced countries resulted in a larger demand for the products of the poor countries, but this is not the case: Prebisch showed that incomes in industrial areas rise almost twice as fast as do their imports.

Prebisch advocated regional economic integration—common markets, customs unions, free-trade areas, etc.—among groups of less-developed countries to widen local markets while retaining tariff protection against imports from advanced nations. Within regional free-trade areas nations could plan for industrial growth, having the twin effects of reducing their dependence on foreign manufactures and using more of their primary production domestically. In addition, Prebisch strongly supported international efforts to stabilize the prices of primary products on world markets, and this implies some kind of production restraint or planning in most cases.

Economic planning and foreign capital, however, helped many of the less-developed countries become developing countries during the 1950s and 1960s. Political independence freed some from colonial status and its hindrances to development. Modern health and sanitation facilities and improved nutrition brought greater efficiency in production, although those advances also brought explosive population growth that literally ate up the gains in some areas. Stress on education and literacy also helped. But the biggest economic gains were the result of planning to promote industrialization, with capital coming from government tax receipts, loans from foreign governments and international organizations, investment by foreign firms, and even from domestic savings and business profits. The most successful of the developing countries were those like Taiwan, Brazil, or Mexico that greatly favored private enterprise in their planning and that were therefore able to attract substantial amounts of private capital or assistance from foreign governments; or, like Yugoslavia and Hungary, socialist countries that used taxes to provide investment funds. Planning plus capital accumulation was the prescription for success.

The record does not show success in achieving satisfactory economic growth everywhere, and some of the aspects of planned economic development have not been favorable. Much of the less-developed world has continued to fall behind the advanced countries in overall economic growth and has not been able to raise per capita income significantly. In some countries growth is seriously unbalanced. In India, for example, perhaps some 50 million people are part of a modern, developing economy that compares favorably with any other in the world, but some 400 million others remain in a stagnant, backward, poverty-stricken economy that is making no progress whatever. In other countries, particularly some in Africa, a combination of corruption, waste, and bad planning has eaten up much of the potential gains from economic development programs. Even in some of the countries that can show the best successes using the private enterprise mode in conjunction with planning and strong investment programs, like Brazil and Mexico, the distribution of wealth and income has remained highly unequal; political authority and economic power are centralized; there are serious problems of mass unemployment; and foreign capital and foreign economic influence remain very important. As these problems became more significant in the 1970s, and as world economic growth slowed down, many of the countries whose growth record was good moved toward authoritarian political regimes to sustain the new patterns of wealth and power that had emerged during the process of economic growth.

THE CHINESE ECONOMY

Perhaps the most significant of all the "success stories" among the less-developed countries has been that of China. Although data on Chinese development is hard to come by and difficult to evaluate, the record since the victory of the Communist regime in 1949 shows an average annual rate of growth of output of about 6 percent. The growth rate of industrial production is estimated at above 10 percent each year. Population growth has been held to about 2 percent annually, while agricultural production has been growing at an annual rate of 3 percent. Consumption per person has also been rising at a rate of about 3 percent annually. This is not as good a rate of economic growth as some other Asian countries, such as Taiwan and South Korea, but it is considerably better than the Third World as a whole. For a country as large and as poor as China it is, in some respects, an exceptional record.

A bit of history is necessary before we can examine that record. Prior to the victory of the Communists in 1949, the Chinese economy was dominated by a precapitalist and capitalist elite: landlords, warlords, and moneylenders in rural areas and business, merchant, and financial interests in the cities. The government was both authoritarian and corrupt. The economy had been devastated by two decades of civil war and war with Japan; in the areas occupied by Japanese armies—over half the country with about three-fourths of the population—foreign dominance prevailed.

During this period the Communist party, headed by Mao Tse-Tung, developed its special character. Driven out of its earlier area of strength in south China, its army and leadership moved in the "long march" of 1934–35 to the province of Shensi, in northwest China. There the new model for Chinese development was first established: rural-oriented rather than urban-oriented; mass-oriented rather than elite-oriented; emphasizing collective economic organizations and participatory decision making rather than private property and central management; equalitarian distribution of income and economic self-sufficiency; and promotion of new behavior patterns and motivations based on an equalitarian and collectivist ideal. When the old regime fell in 1949 these principles were applied to the country as a whole.

The Maoist economic development strategy called for full use of the labor resources of the country. Public authorities took responsibility for providing jobs for everyone, either in small-scale and labor-intensive industries promoted by local governments or in large-scale, capital-intensive industries fostered by the central government. The new collectives organized at the local level to manage agriculture and small-scale industry introduced, in varying degrees, collective decision making, incentive systems for groups rather than individuals, and educational programs to raise the literacy, health, and skill levels of masses of people. A minimum level of material security and welfare was provided for each individual including a job, food, shelter, health care, and other essentials. The minimum was low, but survival and security were guaranteed. To complete the strategy, the planners of the central government sought to promote balanced economic development among regions of the country and between rural and urban areas.

This "mass-oriented" strategy used labor power instead of capital as the essential element in economic development. Where a private-enterprise economy like the United States relies on profits as the primary source of capital accumulation, supplemented by taxes and savings, and the Soviet Union uses taxes supplemented by profits and savings, the Maoist strategy was to use mass labor power itself as the primary source of economic development. The collective organization of production, participatory patterns of decision making, group incentives, equalitarian income distribution, and a balanced pattern of economic development were part of a unified strategy designed to make this type of capital accumulation feasible.

This strategy was never applied in its pure form. Nor was postrevolutionary Chinese economic development smooth and steady. Immediately after 1949 there were several years of reconstruction and land reform. Then followed the first five year plan, 1953-57, along the lines of the centralized, capital-intensive model of the Soviet Union, which was grafted onto the Maoist pattern. The Soviet model was abandoned during the "Great Leap Forward" of 1958-59, which turned out instead to be an economic disaster. Yet it was in these first ten years of the new regime that the basic strategy we have described was worked out. A second period of economic setback came with the "Great Proletarian Cultural Revolution" of 1966-69, which was a last-ditch effort to rid the ruling party and the country of "bourgeois" values and motivations. Relatively stable and balanced growth followed and continues.

After the death of Mao Tse-Tung in 1976 there were several years of political uncertainty, but no significant economic disturbances. The new leadership continues the program of economic development and modern-ization of agriculture, industry, national defense, and science and technol-ogy. Although the basic patterns established under Mao's leadership remain, there seems to be a shift in emphasis toward less authority for central planning, greater use of individual incentives in the form of wage differentials and bonuses, and increased authority for management in the various enterprises. How far these changes will go remains to be seen.

PLANNING IN THE PRIVATE-ENTERPRISE ECONOMIES

Most of the industrial nations of Western Europe and North America, including the United States, also moved toward a greater degree of economic planning after the debacle of the 1930s. Emphasis was on the level of economic activity, in an effort to maintain prosperity and encourage economic growth. However, planning for those goals led slowly into other areas: management of the conflict between business and labor, the direction of investment into sectors of the economy that governments deemed necessary, and stabilization of international financial relationships. The philosophy was that management of aggregate demand would allow the private sector to make its own decisions about consumption and production, but that ideal came to be modified in practice.

The instruments of economic planning were similar everywhere, including the United States. A national "economic budget" would be drawn up each year. It would show the expected amount of spending by consumers, business, and government. This amount would then be compared with the amount necessary to achieve full employment or a desired rate of economic growth. Any deficit in expected spending below the desired level could then be made up by government spending or by stimulating private spending through reduced taxes, monetary ease, or subsidies to private industry. Too much spending could be eliminated by manipulating the government budget, taxes, and monetary policy in the opposite direction. It was aggregative economic planning on the Keynesian model.

Most countries found it necessary to supplement national economic budgets by programs designed to channel business investment into relatively backward regions, such as southern Italy or southern France. The West German government fostered expansion of export industries, and so did most of the other countries of Western Europe, but with somewhat less success. In the United States, large government spending on armaments stimulated rapid economic growth in the southern and southwestern states. All of the advanced industrial countries also expanded the public provision of services like education and health, increased their welfare spending, and subsidized housing and transportation. In addition, the energy crisis (shortage) of the early 1970s and subsequent high costs led nearly all the Western industrial nations (including the U.S.) to set national goals and to coordinate and encourage output of coal, oil, natural gas, atomic energy, and other newer sources of energy. Democratic governments did not like to admit that they were trying to manage the production and distribution of goods, but they were doing it anyway.

In the United States, one key area in which the federal government moved toward planning was agriculture. The government's role changed from being the main provider of research and development and the main source of information to assuming the role of coordinator. Goals for output are not actually set, but rather projections or expectations of output in the various foodstuffs are indicated, and farmers are encouraged to base their plantings on the government's forecasts. This close monitoring of agricultural production is designed to promote stability of prices for both farmer and consumer, and to help in moving toward a more favorable balance of payments, since agricultural products are now this nation's most valuable export.

Another sensitive area was subject to increased intervention by all the Western governments: labor-management relations. Peaceful settlement of disputes between big business and big labor is essential to the smooth operation of the modern economy. For example, a national strike in trucking or the railroads can bring the economy to a standstill within a week. In addition, rapidly rising labor costs can seriously damage industries heavily dependent on export sales; this is especially true in Japan and the Western European countries, where prosperity is far more dependent on exports than in the United States. So these countries quickly moved to hold wage agreements within limits imposed by foreign competition. In the Scandinavian countries the unions and employers' associations, under the watchful eye of government, disciplined themselves. Even the United States government began to move into this area of economic planning in the 1960s and 1970s.

A new pattern began to emerge in virtually all of the industrial countries of the West. Both big labor and big business needed the national economic planning provided by big government to achieve full employment, prosperity, and economic growth. Big government, in turn, sought the economic stability provided by reasonable settlements in the rivalry between labor and management. Furthermore, economic and political stability—maintenance of the status quo—required government programs to provide for the poor and promote regional development. Big labor, big business, and big government found themselves in a situation that called for mutually cooperative relationships, mutually acceptable solutions to problems, and maintenance of existing relationships between economic interest groups. Economic planning moved all of the industrial countries down the path toward the *corporate state.*

This does not mean that conflict was eliminated. Far from it. A modern industrial economy generates conflict between labor and business enterprise, among labor unions, among firms within an industry, and between industries, between governments and business firms, between rich and poor, among groups at various levels of income. One role of government is to mediate and manage those conflicts in the interest of maintaining stability, and that was the fundamental drive behind much of the economic planning we are describing.

The symbiosis of big business, big labor, and big government is reminiscent of the post-World War I economies of Germany, Italy, and Japan, but without the accompanying authoritarianism and terror politics. The future may yet show us that a modern industrial society in crisis moves toward fascist-type solutions. But that was not the direction of politics in the twenty-five prosperous years after World War II. Nevertheless, the economic planning that developed in the advanced industrial countries showed striking similarities to the strictly economic aspects of the pre-World War II fascist states. We see here the same thread that ran through Veblen's turn of the century analysis of capitalism and the changes that took place in the New Deal era in the United States.

CHAPTER 11

The Mixed Economy

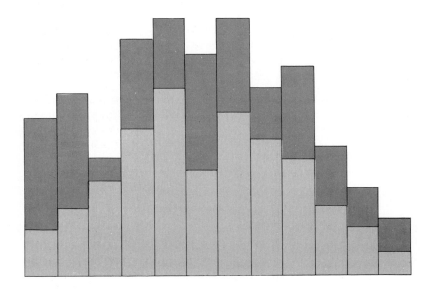

Nikita Khrushchev, the former Soviet premier, once toasted a group of Americans at a Moscow party with the now-famous remark, "We shall bury you." Although the statement was made half jokingly, it has come to symbolize the ideological conflict of our time. Two economic systems are contesting for the loyalties of people, and the rivalry exists at all levels— philosophical, economic, diplomatic, and military. It is expressed in the terms used by both sides: "iron curtain," "cold war," "peoples' democracies," "neoimperialism," "détente," and the like. Meanwhile, the economic system has itself changed, and economists are continually examining it with a view toward understanding the nature of those changes and their implications for public policy.

WILL CAPITALISM SURVIVE?

Joseph Schumpeter (1883-1950) did not think that capitalism would survive. Born in the same year as John Maynard Keynes, Schumpeter was usually bracketed with Keynes as one of the two greatest economists of his time. Since his death, economic theory has developed in directions other than those taken by Schumpeter, but economists will continue to value his three major works. All three books sing the praises of the capitalist entrepreneur, described as the innovating profit-seeker responsible for the constant change that makes a private-enterprise system dynamic.

In his first important book, *The Theory of Economic Development* (1912), Schumpeter analyzed the function of the entrepreneur in creating economic progress and change. The private-enterprise economy always offers large rewards for new products, new production methods, or new systems of organization. The first person to offer lower costs or new products with customer appeal earns high profits. The entrepreneur is that first person, and his continual innovation is the source of the growth and change that are characteristic of modern capitalist society.

Schumpeter carried the analysis a step further in *Business Cycles* (1939), where he argued that innovations tend to be bunched at certain times—one leading to another—creating large investment booms that promote long periods of prosperity. When investment declines from these high levels, the prosperous years are succeeded by stagnation and bad times. Super-imposed on these "long waves" of economic activity are business cycles as we know them: during a long wave of good times upswings are sustained and strong and the downturns short and shallow, while just the opposite effects occur during the long periods of bad times. In the process, the series of industrial revolutions characteristic of capitalism occur, each one ushering in a long period of good times rooted in a group of related innovations.

The book was one answer to the pessimists who felt that the Great Depression of the 1930s marked the ultimate failure of capitalism. Schumpeter's argument implied that the system was only in one of the troughs of its long waves and that a better future was in store as innovation and technological change turned the wave upward once more. The book also expressed Schumpeter's view of the inner dynamics of capitalism and his answer to Marx. The bad effects of capitalism were not the result of its faults but were caused by its strengths. The innovating, profit-seeking activity of the entrepreneur brought change, growth, and expansion, but the process was erratic rather than smooth and steady, and one result was the business cycle.

This theme—that the dynamic factors in capitalism lead to its inadequacies—Schumpeter developed in his finest book, *Capitalism, Socialism, and Democracy* (1942). He believed strongly in the effectiveness of capitalism in producing goods and services for all and estimated that the fifty years from 1928 to 1978 would see a more than doubled output in the United States, making it possible to eliminate poverty for all but the exceptional "pathological" case. In the process, however, several social characteristics of capitalism would become apparent.

One characteristic is the **gradual elimination of the entrepreneur.** The technology and organization of large-scale production are important innovations of capitalism, leading to big business and monopolistic markets. The bureaucracies created to run large enterprises are not places where individualistic, innovating entrepreneurs can function. These individuals are lone operators, dreamers of large schemes, and risk-takers, while bureaucracies tend to be run by committees, by people who conserve the status quo rather than change it. The very organizations created by entrepreneurs dispense with their services.

A second characteristic of developing capitalism predicted by Schumpeter is the **alienation of intellectuals** from adherence to the system. Thinkers, writers, and teachers are critics of the existing order, even though their position is made possible by the affluence of capitalist society. Their function is to point out faults in an effort to make the world better, and they succeed in creating a climate of opinion antagonistic to the capitalist way of life.

This environment of public opinion engenders a third characteristic, *government intervention in economic affairs.* The intervention is directed toward the faults of the economy—toward reducing inequality, smoothing out the business cycle, reducing speculation, controlling monopoly, subsidizing agriculture, and so forth. As a by-product, it also reduces the entrepreneur's freedom of action and serves to further reduce the dynamism of the economy.

These trends in economic organization, the climate of opinion, and public policy lead to the gradual elimination of the entrepreneur from economic life, and with him the economic advances that give capitalism its appeal. The growth of the economy is hindered, capitalism loses its ability to satisfy new wants, and the predictions of collapse made by the intellectuals are fulfilled. As the performance of the system becomes poorer, government intervention increases, which further reduces the vitality of the system and makes socialism inevitable. Schumpeter believed that socialism would replace capitalism in the long run and that it could be either democratic or authoritarian in political structure—the great choice of the future lay in the political sphere. To the question "Can capitalism survive?" Schumpeter answered, "No, I do not think it can."

THE CHANGING ECONOMY

Schumpeter was correct on one point: innovation, economic growth, and change occur together and reinforce each other. The quarter-century after World War II was a period of unmatched world economic growth and sustained prosperity. Contrary to the expectations and fears of many economists during the mid-1940s, the economy did not fall back into the doldrums from which it had been lifted by World War II. Instead of depression or stagnation, the postwar world economy surged ahead. With assistance from the United States, the countries of Western Europe recovered readily from the devastation and dislocation of war. Eastern Europe joined the parade of economic growth after a period of economic and social upheaval, and the Soviet economy continued its forward march. The U.S. economy experienced a steady pattern of growth, with the only major lull coming during the 1950s as the result of old-fashioned monetary and fiscal policies. Japan developed into the world's third major industrial power, and several underdeveloped countries transformed themselves into developing nations.

One of the most important reasons for this advance was the *investment boom* in electronics, plastics, atomic energy, and motor transportation. The result was a whole new world of automobiles, jet aircraft, computers, automated production, and extended ubranization that created vast areas of economic opportunity.

A second factor promoting growth was the *research revolution.* Innovation became an integral part of business enterprise and public activity. Basic and applied research expanded many times beyond the level of the 1920s and 1930s, and became an accepted function of both business and government. This research and development—the basic ingredient of innovation—provided a new dynamism to the whole economic system, even though much of it was associated with military needs and the race to the moon.

A third factor in the postwar expansion was the *emergence of the consumer* to a position of even greater importance. As incomes rose, more consumers had larger amounts of "discretionary income" over and above the amounts needed for satisfying basic wants, which enabled them to invest in homes and home furnishings, automobiles, other durable goods, and in securities and insurance policies. Recreational industries expanded as people gained more leisure time, and service industries grew. The "powerful consumer" was a greater determinant of the level and mix of economic activity than ever before.

A fourth element in postwar economic growth was large *government expenditures on armaments and warfare.* The cold war between the U.S. and the U.S.S.R. required large increases in military spending, and active war in Korea and Vietnam added to the thrust of government spending. Huge investments were necessary as the technology of warfare changed from guns, tanks, and aircraft to nuclear weapons, missiles, and electronic weaponry.

Business enterprise took advantage of these opportunities for expansion. The postwar years saw a huge increase in investment and plant capacity, which were not restricted to one or a few nations but became a worldwide phenomenon. World trade expanded, and an international program of reducing barriers to trade brought into being the General Agreement on Tariffs and Trade, as well as the European Common Market and other regional associations of nations.

Economic growth also stimulated rapid technological change. Computers and electronic controls made possible large-scale automation, particularly in manufacturing and business management. As capital was substituted for labor on a growing scale, the nature of work and the work force began to change. At the upper levels of the labor market new types of highly skilled occupations appeared, like computer programming and operation, and new skills were required of management. New types of scientific education and managerial techniques were necessary, and the technical-managerial elite both expanded and became more sophisticated.

At the lower levels of the work force automation both eliminated some jobs and transformed others. Tasks on the production line were subdivided into simpler component parts that could be done by machines rather than people. This process had been going on ever since the beginning of the industrial revolution, but it was greatly speeded and applied more widely with the new technology of the years after 1945. Automation greatly improved the productivity of the work force, of course. However, it also meant that enlarged output could be produced without increasing the number of workers. That is exactly what happened. In the United States after 1950, a greatly expanded manufacturing output was produced with little increase in the work force employed in manufacturing.

Perhaps the most striking example of this relationship between people and jobs occurred in agriculture, however. Great increases in farm production made possible by mechanization, hybrid plants, and the use of fertilizers were accompanied by a large shift of population from farm to city. Blacks, in particular, were heavily affected. Between 1949 and 1953 workable cotton and corn harvesting machines were introduced into southern agriculture; at the same time soybean cultivation, which uses relatively little labor, spread rapidly. The result was a huge decline in the use of unskilled agricultural labor in much of the South and a vast migration of blacks to northern cities. The impact of this migration, together with other social forces, was felt in the urban riots of the 1960s and contributed heavily to the continuing urban and racial crises of the U.S.

But that was only the most spectacular example of the impact of technical change. A persistent shift was taking place in the structure of the labor force. With few new jobs available in manufacturing (which paid high wages), more workers were employed in service industries (which paid relatively lower wages). The other outlet was in government employment, including education and health services, and in the white-collar administrative jobs of expanding corporate enterprise.

Subtle changes took place in the social classes of industrial capitalism. At the upper levels the high-income elite of expensively trained technicians and managers increased in numbers. At the bottom, there was a growing proportion of low-income workers in the expanding service industries. These workers required little training. Their wages remained low because of a surplus population of unemployed and partially employed recipients of welfare, food stamps, and other assistance. (In the United States, this part of the work force was heavily black, Hispanic, or immigrant labor, and many were women.) Within this framework, resentment, hostility, and lawlessness increased. Lenin had predicted something like this as far back as 1914, and one Swedish economist called it "the English sickness," because it seems to have appeared earliest in England. Similar patterns are seen in all the industrial nations of Europe.

Economists were laggard in appreciating the changes wrought by growth, capital accumulation, and technological change. Both neoclassical and Keynesian theory, which focused on market adjustments and aggregate demand, paid little attention to the changing institutional structure of the economy. There was, however, a flurry of interest in the effects of automation in the late 1950s and early 1960s and a controversy over "structural unemployment" in the mid-1960s. It was not until the late 1960s and early 1970s that a group of younger economists began to explain plausibly why unemployment rates continued to remain high in spite of Keynesian policies, a wartime economy, and rising prices. They found the cause in *dual labor markets,* in which one sector has high wages, relatively skilled workers, and union organization, while the other has low wages, unskilled labor, no unions, and high unemployment rates.

Other changes in the economy were more thoroughly documented: The growth of giant corporate enterprise, the rise of organized labor, and the expansion of government economic activity. Studies of these trends clearly showed that the traditional pattern of largely self-adjusting markets, which were the empirical basis of neoclassical economics, had changed significantly.

BIG BUSINESS, BIG LABOR, BIG GOVERNMENT

Capitalism survived the Great Depression and the economy prospered as never before. But the price of survival was a change of face. The capitalism we know is hardly that of our grandparents. Big business grew even bigger and in turn bred the growth of "big labor." Both fostered the growth of government.

One of the most important studies of the changing nature of business enterprise was *The Modern Corporation and Private Property* (1932) by Adolf A. Berle, Jr., and Gardner C. Means. It documented the dominant position of the large corporation in the modern economy, the growing dispersion of ownership of corporate stock, and the separation of ownership from control. Emphasis was placed on the new structure of power that had appeared, in which the officers of corporations dominated policies while owning only insignificant portions of the stock. The book also questioned the continued validity of the traditional "logic of profits": since profits went to stockholders rather than to management, production decisions were no longer necessarily in accord with consumer wishes. The close connections between consumer wants, profits, and business decisions were seriously loosened. Instead, business decisions might reflect the needs of management and the ability of their firms to control markets.

The two authors continued to develop these themes in later studies. Berle developed two ideas in a series of articles and books, the most important of which were *The 20th Century Capitalist Revolution* (1954), *Power Without Property* (1959), and *The American Economic Republic* (1963). The first idea is that the new place of the corporation in the economy has given big business both a public function and public responsibilities, which in turn has caused the firm and its management to exercise its economic power with restraint, to accept its public functions, and to modify its quest for profit. Needless to say, this is a highly controversial proposition. The second idea is that the nature of private property has changed significantly. Property in the hands of powerful corporations, because of its essentially public nature, is no longer private in the old sense, and the power it brings to those who control it can no longer be exercised freely, with regard only to private interests. As a result, we are moving toward a new relationship in which public interests prevail over private. As Berle put it:

> American society is not being used by, but, rather, uses the profit-seeking market-enterprise system, and certainly is not governed by it. Private enterprise in the United States is thus essentially an instrument of the state—not, as was formerly believed (perhaps accurately), an end for which the state exists.

In other words, property has remained private while its use has been partly socialized.

Gardner Means pursued other aspects of the place of big business in the economy, concentrating on prices and pricing policy. In 1934 he originated the term "administered prices" to describe the type of prices set by firms in monopolized sectors of the economy.* Means showed that such prices were relatively inflexible and did not respond readily to changes in demand. When demand fell during the depression years, certain firms maintained their prices and cut output and employment. This relative freedom of prices from the effects of market forces, together with the power of large corporations, has created a new type of economic system. According to Means in a later work, *The Corporate Revolution in America* (1964):

> *We now have single corporate enterprises employing hundreds of thousands of workers, having hundreds of thousands of stockholders, using billions of dollars' worth of the instruments of production, serving millions of customers, and controlled by a single management group. These are great collectives of enterprise, and a system composed of them might well be called "collective capitalism."*

Means came to differ from Berle. He argued that the corporate community dominated the economy and that the public interest was not paramount.

If there were any doubt about the importance of big enterprise and the monopolized nature of many sectors of the American economy, it was dispelled by the reports of the Temporary National Economic Committee (TNEC) published in the early 1940s. This joint congressional committee investigated the concentration of economic power in the United States in the late 1930s. Its hundreds of volumes of testimony and forty-three expert monographs documented the overwhelming influence of the large corporation, particularly in finance, transportation, heavy industry, and durable consumer goods manufacturing.

Other governmental studies showed the existence of a closely knit big-business community held together by interlocking directorates, financial ties, large family holdings like those of the Rockefellers and Mellons, and corporate stockholdings. While a continual struggle for economic advantage, power, and position goes on at even the top levels, the development of a corporate capitalism dominated by a few hundred major firms raises new issues of economic and social power and control. The ends of that power and the goals of the economic system become issues subject to conscious actions. Economics once more has become political economy. The very organization of productive enterprise has made laissez faire obsolete. Even if government did not seek to control economic activity, big business would.

If Berle and Means and the TNEC were worried about the power of big business and its management, Sumner H. Slichter was concerned with labor unions. This astute observer of the American economy argued that "a laboristic society is succeeding a capitalistic one." Power was shifting from business to labor as employees organized themselves into labor unions— "the most powerful economic organizations of the time"—to bargain collectively with management. Slichter pointed out in *Union Policies and Industrial Management* (1941) that bargaining between unions and management had developed a system of industrial jurisprudence that largely replaced free market relationships in determining the rights of the two parties and their economic gains. In *Trade Unions in a Free Society* (1947) he took

*The term was used in a confidential memorandum to the Secretary of Agriculture that was "leaked" to the press and to Congress, and later published as "Industrial Prices and Their Relative Flexibility," U.S. Senate Document 13, 74th Congress, First Session.

up the problem of the relationship of unions to the operation of free institutions. This well-reasoned book came at a time when the general public and Congress were also vitally interested in the problem—the Taft-Hartley Act was passed in the same year—but the political debate was polarized around extremes of opinion about unions and lacked the even-tempered appraisal that Slichter brought to the issue. He argued that responsible unions and cooperative union-management relations could be a great force for social good, while selfish and narrow viewpoints on either side could severely damage the economy and the social order as a whole. The problems were to keep conflict at a minimum, to ensure a fair distribution of freedom and opportunity, to limit abuses of power, and to achieve a satisfactory balance between individual and community interests. Slichter offered no solutions, but it was clear from his analysis that these problems would not solve themselves. An economist again was suggesting that wise social policies were required to correlate the emerging economic institutions of mid-century with the broad goals of society.

The growth of big business and big labor was paralleled by the growth of big government. This was one of the most heavily publicized changes in the American economy, with much of the publicity coming from the business community as part of its opposition to the trend. The opposition sometimes maintained that the growth of government economic activity was an alien development foisted on an unwilling society by political adventurers and demagogues, but economists produced different explanations.

Solomon Fabricant, for example, in his scholarly study *The Trend of Government Activity in the United States Since 1900* (1952), argued that economic growth itself was the chief reason for the expanded role of government. Population growth and its changing structure, the end of the frontier, advancing science and technology, urbanization and industrialization, the growing size of business enterprise, and growing economic interdependence—these developments created new problems that the free market could not easily solve and that demanded new government functions at all levels, federal, state, and local. Added stimuli were provided by recurring depressions, wars, and the increased possibility of war. Finally, Fabricant pointed out that the climate of opinion changed: there was growing confidence in the ability of government to meet new needs, confidence inspired in part by improved organization and efficiency within government itself. He noted that by mid-century the government was the nation's biggest banker, operated the largest insurance company, employed one-eighth of the labor force, exerted a major influence on wage and salary levels, and was the largest single buyer of commodities. He expected this share in economic activity to become larger as the economy expanded and incomes grew.

It has. Fifteen years later, Eli Ginzberg and his research associates, in *The Pluralistic Economy* (1965), showed that private profit-seeking enterprises— the traditional subjects of much economic theory and the central institution of capitalism—now share the scene with two other types of economic organization. One is limited-profit enterprise, such as public utilities and other regulated firms, and government-subsidized private enterprise, such as defense industries. The other is the "not-for-profit" sector, which includes government at all levels, hospitals, universities, and religious enterprises (such as some publishers of religious books). Focusing on the second group,

Ginzberg showed that the not-for-profit sector accounts for about one-fourth of the nation's income and up to two-fifths of its employment. It is a major contributor to innovation and technical manpower. In recent years it was the most rapidly growing sector of the economy: between 1950 and 1960, nine out of every ten new jobs were created, directly or indirectly, by the expansion of the not-for-profit sector.

The growth of big business, big government, and big labor makes it clear that the impersonal operation of market forces has now been at least partially supplanted by the ability of important groups in labor, management, and government to influence significantly the way the economy functions. The organization and locus of political and economic power influence economic decisions as never before.

THE NEOCLASSICAL SYNTHESIS

The changing economic system did not hold the center of the stage in economic thinking in the quarter century following World War II. Instead, attention centered on the more immediate problems of economic growth and economic stability.

All of the major industrial nations adopted policies designed to promote high levels of economic activity. Acceptance of the Keynesian point of view by policy makers in all of the advanced countries meant that government took responsibility for the maintenance of high levels of employment and acceptable rates of economic growth. The new attitude was typified by passage of the Employment Act of 1946 in the United States:

> *The Congress declares that it is the continuing policy and responsibility of the Federal Government to use all practicable means . . . for the purpose of creating and maintaining . . . conditions under which there will be afforded useful employment opportunities . . . for those able, willing and seeking to work, and to promote maximum employment, production, and purchasing power.*

A variety of techniques was developed to implement these policies. Monetary policies were used to stimulate the economy in poor times and to dampen economic activity when inflation threatened. Tax laws were changed to increase investment and consumer spending when an economic stimulus was needed. When recessions threatened, government expenditures were increased to fill the gap left by the decline in the private sector or taxes were reduced to give an added stimulus to private spending and investment. The goal was to balance the economy at full employment levels rather than to balance government budgets, and the budget was used as a means of achieving that economic balance. The ideal situation was seen as one in which the economy operated at full employment, with stable prices and a balanced government budget that neither stimulated the economy to inflationary levels nor held it back at less than full employment.

Keynesian economics taught that continuous prosperity was possible if the proper fiscal and monetary policies were followed by government. If the private sector showed signs of faltering, it could be stimulated by easy-money policies or given a direct boost by increased government spending. The important factor was the level of aggregate demand, and it could be kept at full-employment levels by consumer spending and business investment supplemented by whatever levels of government spending were necessary.

If the economy were prosperous decisions about what should be produced could be left to the private sector. As long as the public sector is adjusted to maintain full employment and to validate the growth pattern inherent in the private decisions to save and invest, the knotty decisions of whether to produce cars or houses, plowshares or butter, refrigerators or snowmobiles—and in what amounts—can be left to the freely made decisions of consumers in the marketplace. Consumers, spending their incomes as they see fit, will provide signals to producers about what should be produced, and the search for profits will channel resources into those uses. Keynesian macroeconomics seemed to have brought Smith's invisible hand back to life. A grand synthesis of Keynesian macroeconomics and neoclassical microeconomics was forged.

This neoclassical synthesis had to deal with the growth of big business, however. A number of leading economists denied that monopoly was a significant problem. Antitrust laws and public-utility regulation were needed, of course, and it was argued that they had helped make for workable competition even in oligopolistic markets. During the 1950s there was an upsurge of such ideas among economists, especially in the United States, the home of the giant corporation. John Maurice Clark argued in *Competition as a Dynamic Process* (1961) that the important criterion was the performance of an industry rather than its structure: whether it had a good record of innovation, growth, and labor relations rather than whether it met the theoretical criteria of competition. Morris Adelman argued that economic concentration was not increasing (later data showed that it was) and his empirical findings had a wide impact. Gardner Ackley, who was later to be chairman of the President's Council of Economic Advisors, wrote that administered prices were not a significant problem, and much of the profession agreed with his sentiments. Even John Kenneth Galbraith tried to show how an economy of big business and big labor could function effectively. In *American Capitalism* (1952) he argued that "countervailing power" is generated in the private sector. Big business begets big labor, and large manufacturers beget large retailers and large suppliers of raw materials. The power of one neutralizes the power of the other, and government stands as a balance wheel, ready to step in if any one power center becomes too important. Bargaining between small numbers of equally powerful organizations supplements the system of self-adjusting markets, and a reasonable pattern of production results. All these ideas added strength to the argument that the private sector would function effectively if high levels of total demand were sustained.

The neoclassical synthesis did not ignore the problems of income distribution and poverty, but there was little room in the synthesis for drastic changes. The medicine for poverty was economic growth and full employment. Jobs would be available for all, and economic growth would gradually make the poor better off. Inequalities would still exist, but that seemed to matter little. Economic growth would make everyone rich, and special assistance programs, particularly education and vocational training, could bring along even the disadvantaged. Although change and automation could not be ignored, the problems they raised could be resolved by education, growth, and full employment. Of these, economic growth was the key, since growth made more goods available to provide for the good life and ease the problems of an industrial society.

The less developed countries were a special problem, but they could be assisted by aid programs. Just as the Marshall Plan had helped put Europe back on its feet, a similar program of aid for less developed countries could help get them started. Walt W. Rostow's *Stages of Economic Growth: A Non-Communist Manifesto* (1960) was particularly influential. It pictured a growth process modeled after that of Western Europe and the United States, including a "take-off into sustained growth" requiring about twenty years. Economic aid would start the process and the developing nations would move forward in the image of the United States.

No one or two economists were primarily responsible for the neoclassical synthesis. It emerged almost as an unspoken consensus among economists and policy makers in the course of applying Keynesian macroeconomics to the policy problems of the period after World War II. Some of the theoretical groundwork focused on the determinants of the rate of interest and its effect on the level of economic activity, because these topics offered a connecting link between the "real" level of output and the "monetary" aspects of the economy. The most widely accepted analysis of these matters appeared in a 1937 article by the British economist John R. Hicks, "Mr. Keynes and the Classics: A Suggested Interpretation," whose very title indicates its attempt to unify the two approaches.

The economist most closely associated with the neoclassical synthesis, however, is the American Paul Samuelson (born 1915). His textbook, *Economics* (first edition, 1947), was the most widely used introduction to economics for college students for more than a quarter century. Its first edition concentrated on presenting the Keynesian analysis, but later editions broadened out to give equal emphasis to the neoclassical analysis of markets. Samuelson's doctoral dissertation, *Foundations of Economic Analysis* (completed 1941; published 1947), was essentially a translation of neoclassical and Keynesian economics into mathematical terms designed to lead economic theory into a new method of theoretical analysis based on mathematical models. A professor at the Massachusetts Institute of Technology at 32, Samuelson produced a series of professional papers that broke new ground at the highest levels of economic theory in a wide variety of fields.

Emphasis on abstract theory does not preclude concern with current issues of economic policy. Samuelson is a forceful advocate of the pragmatic use of monetary and fiscal policy to achieve full employment, stabilize the economy, and promote economic growth. He sees these objectives as the most important goals of public policy, to be achieved by government spending, tax changes, and monetary policy. The particular policy mix at any time depends upon the existing situation, and flexible use of those instruments is highly desirable. Even though the situation may be uncertain, Samuelson generally feels that hesitancy is worse than an active policy to push the economy in the proper direction.

The neoclassical synthesis was as much political economy as it was economic analysis. It supported the comprehensive macroeconomic planning of the Keynesian system and promoted such liberal ideas as antipoverty programs and aid to less developed countries. At the same time, it accepted the status quo as far as the structure of the economy was concerned: there was no need for significant change in either the distribution of income or the locus of economic power. As long as macroeconomic policies could produce full employment and economic growth, the annual growth dividend of increased output would make additional resources available to meet everyone's needs.

The neoclassical synthesis dominated economic policy during the Cold War conflict between the United States and the Soviet Union. In one sense it was a complement to the Truman Doctrine policy of containment of Communism. In the 1950s and 1960s that policy did not contemplate merely coexistence or détente. It postulated that political and economic tensions within the Communist bloc would ultimately bring a breakdown of that system. If Communism could be contained within its boundaries long enough for that to happen, the threat to western capitalism would disintegrate. Meanwhile, the western democracies, led by the United States, would be prospering. Full employment and rising living standards would bring contentment. Economic growth would solve the internal problems of poverty. Aid could be provided to the developing nations. And a growing economy could provide ample resources for a large defense establishment. The new system of political economy validated the position taken by the United States and its allies in the international struggle for world power after World War II, just as it validated the internal structure of power and the existing economic organization within those countries. The neoclassical synthesis defined the policy mix that would not only allow capitalism to survive, but to triumph.

THE CONSERVATIVE DISSENT

The interventionist monetary and fiscal policies of the neoclassical synthesis brought it under attack by a group of conservative neoclassical economists who reaffirmed the virtues of the competitive private enterprise economy. There were two parts of this reaffirmation, one old and one new.

The older part was the Austrian neoclassical economics of Menger and his followers as restated by a group of European scholars trained in that tradition. One was Friedrich von Hayek (born 1899) of the University of Chicago, whose attack on socialist planning we have already noted. Another was Ludwig von Mises (1881–1973) of New York University, who strongly advocated the free market as the only sure antidote to centralized political power and the only way to ensure the survival of individualism. His European counterpart is Wilhelm Röpke (born 1899) of the Institute of International Studies in Geneva, Switzerland. All of these men condemned equally the rise of modern socialism, the Keynesian interventionism of the modern reformers, and the welfare measures that contemporary governments have adopted. The best word to describe them is *libertarian*—individual liberty above all. They saw any type of government intervention as a threat to individual freedom.

The newer part of the conservative dissent became prominent in the 1960s. It has its home base at the University of Chicago, and its *chef d'ecole* in Milton Friedman (born 1912). Friedman is a strong advocate of the virtues of a competitive private-enterprise economy, but, in contrast to the libertarians, he stresses the need for government to establish a framework within which the free market can function more effectively. In taking that position, he follows in the tradition of Henry C. Simons (1899–1946), who taught Friedman as an undergraduate at the University of Chicago. Simons did not write much—his life's work is a group of essays and papers that comprise only one modest volume—but he was highly influential. A single essay, *A Positive Program for Laissez Faire* (1934), set out a program of reform to bring competitive private enterprise back to life and preserve its vitality:

> . . . *eliminate all forms of monopolistic market power, to include the breakup of large oligopolistic corporations and application of anti-trust laws to labor unions. A Federal incorporation law could be used to limit corporate size, and where technology required giant firms for reasons of low cost production the Federal government should own and operate them.*
>
> . . . *promote economic stability by reform of the monetary system and establishment of stable rules for monetary policy.*
>
> . . . *reform the tax system and promote equity through the income tax.*
>
> . . . *abolish all tariffs.*
>
> . . . *limit waste by restricting advertising and other wasteful merchandising practices.*

Simons' program was directed against artificially maintained privilege and market restrictions as much as it was in favor of competition and individualism. It did not ignore instability, inequity, and wasteful spending but sought measures that would reduce if not eliminate them.

A contemporary of Simons at the University of Chicago, Frank H. Knight (1885–1972)—the two men had joined the faculty there in the same year, 1927—was also important in helping formulate conservative neoclassical economics in the United States. He was the theorist who balanced Simons' policy emphasis. Neoclassical economics had come under attack in the 1920s from those who advocated a more equalitarian income distribution and greater government intervention in the economy. Knight's career was devoted primarily to answering those attacks by more careful definition of terms and greater precision in analysis. The result was an enriched statement of the theory of the free market based on the economic individual as the key actor. Knight recognized that the theory was not all-inclusive and that it was sometimes at variance with reality, but he argued that it was **useful.** This methodological position was a cornerstone of the Chicago "school" and the approach developed later by Friedman.

Milton Friedman is today's most important representative of the classical liberal philosophy that goes back to Adam Smith's economics. He argues that the benefits derived from a laissez faire policy are far more desirable than those obtained from interventionist policies that modify the operation of free markets in the interest of solving some immediate problem. Take minimum wage laws, for example. Designed to benefit low-wage workers by raising their incomes, Friedman argues that they have the opposite effect. By making it too expensive for employers to hire such workers, the laws increase unemployment and worsen the economic position of all those at the bottom of the economic pyramid. A whole series of similar examples are given in Friedman's widely read *Capitalism and Freedom* (1962), in which the root of the argument is that those measures which restrict the free market bring losses rather than gains, while economic freedom pays off in greater welfare in the long run.

The most significant example of government intervention in the economy today is Keynesian macroeconomic planning. Friedman's strongest criticisms are directed against the use of fiscal policy to stabilize the economy, and his strongest advocacy is in support of monetary policy—but of a special type that goes back to Simons' policy proposals for its base.

Friedman argues that it is extremely difficult to counterbalance the swings of the private sector with government spending or tax changes. Not only is it difficult to forecast the movement of the business cycle, but, in Friedman's words:

> There is likely to be a lag between the need for action and government recognition of the need; a further lag between recognition of the need for action and the taking of action; and a still further lag between the action and its effects.

The result is that "corrective action may itself turn into a further error," with a stimulus coming when spending should be dampened, or vice versa.

Friedman believes that the monetary system has a far more pervasive effect on economic activity than does fiscal policy. To support his position he revived and gave new life to the quantity theory of money—the idea that the quantity of money determines the general level of prices—by showing that the monetary system affects the level of aggregate demand and national output in a wide variety of subtle ways. The Keynesians had never denied the importance of monetary policies, and sought to use them as one of the twin arms of macroeconomic policy in coordination with fiscal policy. But even on that point Friedman parts company with the Keynesians. He does not like the active use of monetary policy. He wants neither easy money to promote full employment nor tight money to prevent inflation. The long-run effects of each, he argues, may be just the opposite of their intended short-run effects. He wants a neutral monetary policy oriented toward long-run growth needs. Friedman would prescribe a gradual and steady increase in the money supply at a fixed percent annually as an aid to economic expansion and growth.

But what about business cycles and depressions? Would not Friedman's policies leave the economy wide open to another severe depression? He argues that they would not, and to prove his point he and Anna Schwartz analyzed the monetary history of the United States to try to show that instability in the monetary system has always been the chief cause of instability in employment and output. These findings were published in *A Monetary History of the United States* (1963). A large section of that book was devoted to showing how the monetary policies of the Federal Reserve System first helped to bring on the Great Depression of the 1930s and then made it much worse when it came. The implication is clear: stabilize the monetary system and economic stability will follow.

Friedman and his supporters, who are called "monetarists" because of their emphasis on monetary factors, also contend that government spending designed to prevent recessions is a significant cause of inflation. Government securities sold to finance a deficit during a recession represent additions to the private and public debt that the economy normally generates. Thus, when the economy moves back to a full-employment level of activity, they argue, the money supply must be increased in order to support the extra debt. With a larger money supply the price level will be forced up as full employment is approached. Thus a recession-created deficit is "monetized" by action of the monetary authorities as the economy moves toward full employment, and prices rise. Recessions can be avoided, but only at the cost of inflation.

The attack on Keynesian policies by Friedman and the Chicago school broke the almost complete dominance of Keynesian macroeconomics in the formulation of government economic policy. It showed that money is important. Already much of the work of the monetarists is being integrated into the larger body of economic theory. But there remains a strong area of disagreement. It centers on the fundamental differences between the activist liberal who advocates strong government action to solve society's problems and the laissez faire liberal who sees that path as wrong. The latter wants government to follow only the path of establishing and maintaining a framework within which the free market can function effectively. The laissez faire liberal sticks with the neoclassical approach and does not accept Keynesian macroeconomics.

JOHN KENNETH GALBRAITH: LIBERAL CRITIC

John Kenneth Galbraith (born 1908) is probably the best-known critic of contemporary economics and economic policy and the values associated with them. A leading member of the liberal "establishment" in the United States and a strong advocate of activist public policies designed to promote prosperity, Galbraith nevertheless rejects both economic growth as a sufficient goal for economic policy and the market mechanism as an effective means of allocating resources.

Three major works present Galbraith's argument: *The Affluent Society* (1958), *The New Industrial State* (1967), and *Economics and the Public Purpose* (1973). Taken together, these three books provide the most incisive analysis of modern American capitalism since Veblen. The first attacks the "conventional wisdom" that economic growth and more output is necessarily a good thing, the second sketches the outlines of a society dominated by big enterprise and the "technostructure" that runs it, and the third argues for the dominance of the social good over private gain through democratic socialism and economic planning. Together they comprise a critique of modern society and its values and call for major changes in the ends economic activity ought to seek.

Galbraith argues that modern technology makes possible the abundant society that has always been one of humanity's dreams. But affluence has not brought happiness, because people still believe in the doctrine of scarcity, and continually seek greater and greater output of material things. The private-enterprise industrial economy creates additional wants, partly by suggestion and emulation, and partly by the deliberate action of producers through advertising and salesmanship. Higher levels of production merely bring higher levels of want creation: wants depend on the process by which they are satisfied. Galbraith calls this the **dependence effect,** and with it disposes of the rational consumer. If he is right, the whole economy becomes irrational: if producers can determine, or even significantly influence, the decisions of consumers, they can determine the forces to which their own decisions respond, and the self-adjusting market becomes merely a device for sustaining and enriching big enterprise.

In such an economy the giant corporation able to manipulate markets is the significant unit. Ostensibly managed by its highest officers, the decisions are really made by a **technostructure** of experts who are able to manipulate the complex technology of modern production and marketing. This hierarchy is interested in the firm's survival and growth, and in its own aggrandizement, but maximization of profits is not its chief concern. And without maximization of profits the neat adjustment of production to consumer wants postulated by neoclassical economics would not occur, even in the absence of the dependence effect.

Galbraith's analysis broadens out from there. The giant corporation abhors risk and requires growth and stable markets. This can be achieved only by the use of Keynesian macroeconomic policies. Government becomes a partner of the technostructure. The educational system becomes another partner, because the giant corporation needs the trained personnel and scientific advances it produces, with the costs borne largely by government. Labor unions are a junior partner, gaining security through collective bargaining in exchange for a regular supply of labor for the giant firm.

The values of the affluent society stress individual wants and starve the public sector. So we drive in our private cars on clogged expressways beside poisoned streams through polluted air to get to public parks that are too crowded for everyone to be admitted—in an affluent society.

The whole system moves toward irrational goals. The consumer continually seeks more and newer products under the influence of an unremitting sales effort; advancing technology creates a growing pool of unemployed and unemployable labor; government policies continually push the economy to higher levels of output; and the only forms of social consumption that get high priority are military needs and special research and development programs (the current one being new energy sources; the previous one was space exploration).

What can be done to bring the economy back toward more humane goals? In the third book of this trilogy Galbraith calls for a "new socialism" that would include, in addition to greater equality of income and wealth, steps to discipline the giant corporation by wage, price, profit, and salary controls, nationalization of the chief military supplying firms, and—surprisingly—nationalization of much of the less concentrated sectors of the economy, like health care, in order to achieve the advantages of planning that are already present in the giant corporate sector. Socialization of the "unduly weak industries and unduly strong ones," along with planning of the rest, would enable the public interest to triumph over private interests. All of this can be achieved, however, only if there is a new belief system that recognizes the realities of the modern economy and no longer merely repeats the shibboleths of the past. This would enable a new people's movement to gain political power, bringing the new socialism through democratic political change.

RADICAL ECONOMICS

The deficiencies in modern society that inspired Galbraith's critique also brought about a revival of Marxism and an increased interest in socialism. Gathering force through the 1960s, the resurgence of radicalism was less an attack on the dominant economic theory and policy as it was a critique of the economic system and its effects. A new interest in Marxism appeared, along with a wide range of non-Marxist radical analyses of the modern world.

One book led the way in the United States for the resurgence of Marxism as a tool for analyzing the contemporary economy. It was *Monopoly Capital* (1966), by Paul Baran and Paul Sweezy. Baran, who died two years before the book was published, was Professor of Economics at Stanford University. An earlier book of his, *The Political Economy of Growth* (1957), had already marked him as a major contributor to Marxist economic theory. In it, he focused attention on monopoly as the distinguishing feature of highly developed capitalism, on the production of an economic surplus that had to be disposed of, and on a drive toward economic imperialism leading to inevitable conflict between the advanced and the underdeveloped economies. All of these themes were to be developed in the later book. Baran's coauthor, Paul Sweezy, had begun an academic career, teaching at Harvard University from 1934 to 1942 and writing two important pieces on interest groups among American corporations and on the theory of oligopoly. After government service in World War II he helped found in 1949 the leading U.S. Marxist journal, *Monthly Review,* and has been one of its editors since then. He also wrote an important Marxist work, *The Theory of Capitalist Development* (1942), which is still the best restatement of basic Marxist economic theory for the contemporary reader.

Monopoly Capital made a major contribution to Marxist theory by shifting attention away from the assumption of a competitive economy, which was basic to the original analysis developed by Marx, and by focusing on the monopolistic aspects of giant enterprise in the contemporary economy. In doing so it also de-emphasized the role of the working class and the class struggle, as it worked out the logic of an economy dominated by privately owned big corporations. The argument runs as follows:

> *Monopolistic large corporations are able to maintain selling prices at relatively high levels while competing with each other to cut costs, advertise and sell, and develop new or modified products, all in a gigantic race for profits. An economic surplus is the result, which can't be absorbed by consumer spending, however wasteful, or business investment, which only increases the surplus. Part of the surplus is absorbed in mammoth sales and marketing efforts and part through government employment. But the major thrust of monopoly capital is to imperialism and militarism as the easiest and surest way of utilizing otherwise surplus productive capacity. In the process, exploitation centers on low-wage workers at home, especially blacks and other minority groups, and on underdeveloped areas overseas that provide opportunities for profit even larger than in the home economy. For the average person the profit nexus and exchange relationship destroy meaningful human relationships, leading to widespread alienation, hostility, and purposelessness. The entire system is essentially*

irrational, for although individual economic units may be operated with the utmost emphasis on rational decisions, the system as a whole is directed toward irrational goals. Nevertheless, the system continues to function effectively because of military spending and Keynesian full employment policies. It will continue to do so until the less developed countries throw off the yoke of neocolonialism and the worldwide system of industrial capitalism collapses.

This brief summary can only suggest the richness and breadth of the analysis and the angry condemnation of modern life the book contains. If it had been written by anyone other than the two leading U.S. Marxists, it might have been a major best seller, just as some non-Marxist critiques were. Baran and Sweezy were clearly describing the same economy as Galbraith, and much of their analyses were parallel. As it is, *Monopoly Capital* has had a steadily widening influence both in the United States and abroad.

Perhaps equally influential in stimulating radical analyses of modern society was an earlier book, *The Power Elite* (1956), written by Columbia University sociologist C. Wright Mills (1916-1962). Mills argued that the United States is ruled by an elite group of business, political, and military leaders who manage the large bureaucratic organizations that dominate modern life. Recruited from a relatively narrow stratum of society, this group of several thousand elite managers selects itself by an informal process in which the older leadership passes on a value system that stresses acquisition of wealth and private enterprise. Oligarchy rather than democracy dominates modern America, along with the corrupt values of individualistic materialism, according to Mills.

A third radical analysis, James O'Connor's *The Fiscal Crisis of the State* (1973), centered attention on conflicts within the advanced industrial nations. In contrast to Baran and Sweezy, O'Connor argued that industrial capitalism was approaching a crisis because of internal difficulties. The fundamental problem was Marx's: rapid expansion of output capacity and inadequate growth of purchasing power. Business firms seek to resolve their individual problems of inadequate sales by spending large amounts for advertising. This helps a little, but isn't enough. Government must step in with enlarged spending programs to sustain prosperity, including government employment, welfare programs, and military spending. These programs must be financed, however. Taxes are raised, but that brings political opposition, so government turns to borrowing, which causes inflation. Spending programs are reduced, therefore, which allows unemployment and unrest to increase. The economy is then caught in a three-pronged tradeoff between rising unemployment, increasing taxes, and growing inflation. As the crisis approaches, all three plague the economy. O'Connor's analysis seemed to fit the actual events of the mid-1970s.

Other dissidents focused on the effects of industrial capitalism on the daily lives of people. Istvan Mészáros, in *Marx's Theory of Alienation* (1970), and Walter A. Weisskoff, in *Alienation and Economics* (1971), dealt with the psychological effects of modern capitalism, arguing that personal satisfactions diminished in spite of growing material wealth. Harry Braverman, in *Labor Under Monopoly Capitalism* (1975), maintained that work was degraded as industrial capitalism moved toward higher levels of technology and greater managerial control of the workplace. These books pictured a crisis in everyday life to supplement O'Connor's general crisis in the economy as a whole.

These themes—dominance of the economy by giant corporations led by a self-selecting elite and the ultimate breakdown of the capitalist economy—are the distinguishing features of radical analyses of the modern economy. The implications, both for overall economic performance and for the life of the individual, are a major concern of a significant portion of the young economists who are just beginning their careers. Such topics as the nature and effects of government spending and the distribution of income are receiving new attention from radical perspectives. In the United States, the Union for Radical Political Economics publishes a journal, sponsors national and regional conferences, and is a feature of the annual meetings of the staid American Economic Association. In England, a group of young economists at the major universities has taken up radical interests and Marxist ways of analysis. On the continent, the student movement of the 1960s in Germany, France, and Italy was heavily Marxist in its orientation. The leading theoretician there is Ernest Mandel, whose *Marxist Economic Theory* (1968) combines a review and restatement of basic Marxist economics with an analysis of how the modern western economies can move from capitalism to socialism.

The Marxist revival and related radical economic thought are not particularly associated with support for the Soviet Union and its brand of socialism. Many radicals, including strong Marxists, look with dismay upon the centralized bureaucratic methods of planning of the Soviet Union. They are more favorably inclined toward decentralized administration and market socialism, and look toward the system of workers' management developing in Yugoslavia as more of an ideal. The market orientation of planning applied in Hungary and other east European countries in the late 1960s, which gives substantial stress to consumer wants and the signals they give to planners through buying decisions, is also creating strong interest. A worldwide search is underway among radicals for alternatives to both private enterprise capitalism as practiced in the United States and Western Europe, and the centralized state planning of the Soviet Union.

CHAPTER **12**

The Contemporary Crisis

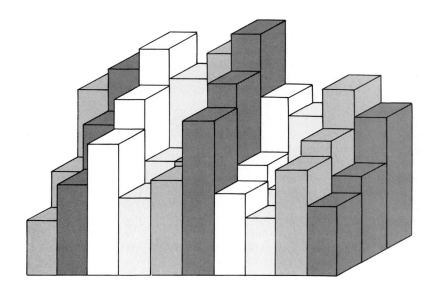

As the last quarter of the twentieth century opened, the United States prepared to celebrate its 200th birthday in the midst of a time of troubles. A disastrous war in southeast Asia had just ended and a President had been forced to resign under a cloud of scandal. The accelerating inflation of the early 1970s brought on the most serious recession/depression since the 1930s. Financial difficulties in New York City were matched by a massive bankruptcy of the northeastern railroads. A cartel of oil-producing nations imposed a fivefold increase in the price of oil. The tenuous détente between the U.S. and the U.S.S.R. in international affairs began to disintegrate, raising the possibility of a renewed arms race and the spectre of nuclear war. Economic difficulties in England and political instability in Spain, Italy, Portugal, and France threatened the stability of European politics. The old international financial system established at Bretton Woods in 1945 was already gone, a victim of U.S. inflation and balance of payments deficits, and was replaced by an improvised and untested pattern of freely floating exchange rates.

Although the neoclassical synthesis seemed to be not only dominant, but triumphant, in the era of prosperity after World War II, its position was by no means secure. It was attacked, as we have seen, by Friedman and the conservative monetarists, Galbraithian liberal critics, and radicals of various sorts. In the political spectrum it occupied the broad middle ground, accepting the chief contours of the existing economic society while attempting to make marginal reforms that would improve things a bit. In the 1970s this mainstream approach to economics came increasingly into disrepute. Keynesian macroeconomics and the policies derived from it could not handle the simultaneous appearance of both unemployment and inflation, called "stagflation" by some to indicate inflation in a period of economic stagnation. At the same time, new ideas at the highest levels of pure theory seriously weakened some of the chief doctrines and basic preconceptions of neoclassical microeconomics. As this is written, economics as a theoretical and policy science is in disarray, with the Keynesian, activist approach under strong attack for failing to explain and remedy the many economic ills of the 1970s. A reformulation of Keynesian theory is in its embryonic stages. When it will come to fruition and the form it will take cannot yet be perceived, but this is a great time to be studying economics, for the subject is in ferment at all levels.

UNEMPLOYMENT AND INFLATION

Keynesian macroeconomics explained the existence of both unemployment and inflation in terms of aggregate demand, or total purchasing power. If there was too little purchasing power, output would fall and unemployment increase. The remedy was found in economic stimulation: more government spending, or an increase in the money supply, or a combination of the two. Inflation, on the other hand, was seen as caused by too much spending, and the remedies were less government spending and monetary restraint. In the middle was the "impossible dream"—an economic balance of full employment, stable prices, a balanced government budget, and an "appropriate" monetary policy.

With respect to causes of inflation, however, economists recognized three exceptions to the general explanation or "rule." Prices could rise if production bottlenecks appeared in key industries, like steel, prior to full employment in the economy as a whole. And prices could rise if labor shortages or union power caused wage rates to rise, driving costs up; rising total spending would enable this "cost push" to be translated into higher prices. Finally, the entire cost structure of the economy could be raised by increased costs for a basic input, such as occurred when the cost of oil jumped in the early 1970s (although most economists didn't think of this exception until it actually happened). Nevertheless, the fundamental idea remained: unemployment was caused by too little spending and inflation by too much spending.

These Keynesian explanations for inflation could not fully account for the behavior of price levels from the 1950s on, however. For example, prices rose steadily in the late 1950s in spite of rising unemployment rates and an increasing gap between output capacity and actual output. When a recession occurred in 1958-59 and prices rose even faster during the recession it was clear that the theory was inadequate. One response was to argue that changes in demand during a recession were uneven, with demand down in some industries and up in others. Where demand fell, prices didn't drop because prices were *inflexible downward;* that is, the large corporations would quite willingly raise prices to meet increasing demand, but were powerful enough to refuse to lower prices when demand fell. But that addition to the theory could hardly account for the worsening inflation of the 1960s at a time when unemployment and unused plant capacity were general throughout the economy. At that point the so-called "Phillips Curve" doctrine appeared. Named after the English economist A. W. Phillips, who published a study of wages and prices in England, the Phillips Curve presumably showed a tradeoff between unemployment and prices: when unemployment was high and a good deal of slack existed in the economy, prices tended to remain stable or rise slowly; but as unemployment fell and economic slack was reduced, prices started rising more rapidly. This idea was very popular among economists in the late 1960s, because it seemed to accord with the facts, to show that prices would rise as unemployment fell.

The Phillips Curve doctrine was an attempt to explain the phenomenon of "structural unemployment," that is, the persistence of significant numbers of unemployed workers even while prices were rising. This phenomenon had begun to appear in the 1950s, for a variety of reasons: automation and other forms of substitution of capital for labor in high-wage, capital-intensive industries like automobiles and steel; large-scale migration of relatively poorly educated and ill-trained workers from Puerto Rico and the southern states; a growing shift of women into the labor market; and the slowed economic growth of the Eisenhower years. The problem was worsened during the 1960s with large-scale shifts in industrial production by international corporations to relatively low-wage countries like Taiwan, South Korea, and other less-developed countries. For a time these changes in the labor market were masked by the strong economic expansion of the 1950s and 1960s and by relatively rapid increases in government employment. But strong growth ended in the early 1970s, as government employment stabilized, and large numbers of young workers—the "echo" of the World War II baby boom—began flooding into the labor market. The result was a large surplus of young, relatively unskilled, and inexperienced workers in labor markets that were not expanding fast enough to absorb them. Even when "full employment" prevailed among "prime" workers—married white males between the ages of twenty-five and forty-five—and further increases in aggregate demand or costs of production pushed prices upward, many young, black, latino, and women workers were unemployed, or partially employed, or working in low-wage, dead-end jobs they were eager to leave. Thus, in the 1970s the Phillips Curve relationship was discredited: prices continued to rise no matter what the unemployment rate or the extent of slack in the economy.

Meanwhile, the critics of mainstream economics developed alternative theories of inflation. Friedman argued that Keynesian economic policies brought about increases in the money supply that caused inflation. Galbraith argued that the wage bargains between big business and big labor caused inflation: firms granted wage increases greater than increases in productivity and raised prices to make up the difference and protect their profits. Radicals claimed that inflation was due to the enlarged military spending and wars inherent in the capitalist system, or, like O'Connor, that the inherently unstable capitalist economy could be stabilized only by measures that themselves were inflationary. None of these arguments could be satisfactorily answered because the orthodox Keynesian theory did not itself have an adequate explanation for the unfortunate disparity between theory and events.

One English economist, Nicholas Kaldor, worked out a Keynesian analysis of simultaneous inflation and unemployment, however. According to Kaldor, negotiations between big business and big labor brought higher wages and increases in total spending no matter what the level of aggregate demand happened to be. If the economy was prosperous and output expanded at the same rate as the increase in wages, all would be well. But if a recession came, output would fall while purchasing power continued to rise, pushing prices up while unemployment rose because of the decline in output. Kaldor's remedy was highly unorthodox, however: if economic expansion were stimulated, output would rise and ease the upward pressure on prices, curing both the inflation and the unemployment. Few economists listened to Kaldor, primarily because the accepted remedy for inflation was to cool off the economy rather than heat it up. Nevertheless, U.S. experience in 1974–76 seemed to support Kaldor's analysis: inflation accelerated during the worst part of the recession and slowed down when recovery began. But aside from Kaldor, the mainstream of Keynesian thinking seemed out of tune with events.

PROBLEMS OF ECONOMIC GROWTH

Part of the difficulty lay in continuing changes in the structure of industrial capitalism. Economic growth and accumulation of capital, the economic forces analyzed by the classical economists from Adam Smith to David Ricardo to Karl Marx, caused slow but persistent changes in the economy that Keynesian macroeconomics was unable to deal with, since it was oriented toward short-term changes in total spending and assumed the existence of a given structure of economic institutions.

The classical economists had emphasized the continuing transformation of labor into capital as a basic characteristic of capitalism. Adam Smith and David Ricardo stressed the growth aspects of capital accumulation, while Marx emphasized the creation of private accumulations of wealth and high incomes for a few. In the modern economy the polarization of society predicted by Marx was ameliorated by the action of governments, through taxation, welfare spending, and other programs. But while growing disparities of personal income and wealth were partially checked, most nations encouraged accumulation of capital by business firms. Retained earnings plowed back into enterprises enabled the capital of enterprises to grow. Concentration of capital in the hands of giant corporations was promoted, and enabled the largest to become multinational in scope. Simultaneously, technological change continued to promote substitution of capital for labor, particularly in the high-wage, capital-intensive industries where labor unions were strong and could lay claim to a large share of the gains from growth and increased productivity. High wages in those industries also promoted investment by multinational corporations in the labor-surplus areas (with their low wages) of less-developed parts of the world. As we shall see, modernization there tended to promote more population growth and increase the labor surplus, thereby encouraging further investment by multinational firms. Meanwhile, in the advanced industrial countries a growing work force found relatively little opportunity in the high-wage unionized sector dominated by big corporations and big unions. The result was "structural" unemployment, rising numbers of workers in the low wage service industries and increased government spending that in the long run could be financed only by rising taxes or inflation, or both. With variations due to different circumstances, this process was at work throughout the industrial areas of North America and Western Europe.

These trends were masked for a time by economic growth and technological change itself. New technologies brought the development of whole new industries—electronics, television, and computers, for example—and rapid expansion of some others, such as air transportation and plastics. The new jobs created there kept the economy dynamic and unemployment relatively low through the 1950s. But as growth in those industries began to slow down, the other forces described above became more evident. Other sectors of the economy that had contributed to the great surge of economic expansion in the 1950s and 1960s also stopped expanding, particularly armaments and government spending on items like education and highways. As the great boom of 1945 to 1970 gave way to the relative stagnation of the 1970s, it became clear that the process of economic growth itself created problems of unemployment and low incomes deep within the structure of industrial capitalism, and that the relatively simple remedies of Keynesian economics were inadequate.

Economic growth also raised issues of resource use and pollution, particularly in the 1960s and 1970s when the impact of continued growth could be clearly seen. A growing economy must have increasing inputs of raw materials as it uses increasing amounts of energy to produce enlarged output and more wastes. Present technology is based very heavily on exhaustible resources and energy supplies, and uses the reservoirs of air, land, and water for waste disposal. Both resources and reservoirs are limited. If one resource starts to run out, another can be substituted for it—but it, too, is exhaustible. And a continuing build-up of wastes can so burden the environment that health and life can be threatened.

Economists began to examine these issues. Donella H. Meadows and others, in *The Limits to Growth* (1972), reported on a computerized simulation of world economic growth in an environment of limited resources, and showed that the economic growth rates of the recent past could not be sustained. While no one limiting factor, such as too little iron ore, for example, could bring growth to an end, the combined effects of a number of interrelated factors would. For example, irrigation of deserts may make available large increases in the food supply, but even if the water can be found, such projects require huge amounts of energy and capital whose production is subject to limits elsewhere. Improvements in technology and inventions still to come may provide further space for growth, but limits are inherent in the limited resources available on this planet. That point was made in a much-quoted article by Kenneth Boulding, "The Economics of the Coming Spaceship Earth" (1966). Boulding finds the solution in the ultimate development of a "closed" economic system, which, like a stable biological system, uses all of its outputs as inputs, including wastes. Herman E. Daly defined the viable economy of the future in somewhat more specific terms. His article on "The Steady-State Economy: Toward a Political Economy of

Biophysical Equilibrium and Moral Growth" (1971) called for a constant population, constant physical wealth, and socially controlled distribution of goods, while growth can take place in the moral sphere. One further requirement may be smaller economic units using technologies that enhance human work skills rather than replacing them with machines, as pointed out by E. L. Schumacher in his book, *Small Is Beautiful: Economics As If People Mattered* (1973). There may not be enough time to make the necessary changes, however. Robert L. Heilbroner, in *An Inquiry Into the Human Prospect* (1975), contrasts the present trajectory of world economic growth with the converging problems of population, food, resources, and pollution, and sees a series of potential or actual catastrophes in the future that can bring "convulsive change." The human race can survive this doomsday prospect, he concludes, but only if human society is reorganized on a basis very different from the present.

We face the prospect of a slowdown in economic growth. Yet growth has always been necessary to satisfy the acquisitiveness that motivates capitalism. A steady-state economy will require different attitudes toward material things, and that suggests drastic changes in economic institutions. Furthermore, modern capitalism has a highly unequal distribution of income, wealth, and power that is accepted by most people because of the material benefits they obtain. When material gains slow down or stop, the average person, heretofore relatively content, will no longer so easily accept inequality. Without growth, redistribution of income and wealth is far more likely. Capitalism, as we know it, is not likely to survive in an era that moves toward a no-growth economy, and is likely to face conflicts over the distribution of income and wealth.

THE INTERNATIONAL ECONOMY

Equally unsettling issues emerge from the international economy. Economic growth after World War II featured a large increase in world trade. Reductions in tariffs and trade barriers helped, and the international financial system established by the Bretton Woods Agreements of 1945 provided a stable financial base for international trade and investment. A new era of world prosperity founded on the benefits of specialization and trade seemed to have arrived—until fissures began to appear in the 1960s.

One new problem was presented by the development of a worldwide banking system largely independent of the banking systems and controls of any one country. This so-called "Eurobank" system deals in loans, deposits, and investments in a wide variety of national currencies, but mostly in dollars. Even though the banks that participate have their home offices in individual countries, like the United States, Japan, or Germany, their dealings in other currencies are largely unregulated by monetary authorities. For example, if a Swiss bank lends Italian lira to a Greek shipowner to finance purchases of German machinery, the loan does not come under the authority or regulation of the monetary authorities of any of those countries and is not subject to their monetary policies. The world monetary system now has a significant component that is substantially free of all controls except those provided by the private managers of the international banks themselves. There is a large potential for monetary overexpansion and instability in the world economy that did not exist as late as 1968.

For example, expansion of credit in the Eurobank system was one of the chief features of worldwide inflation in the 1970s. From perhaps $50 billion in 1968, total Eurobank credit grew to an estimated $1000 billion by the end of 1979. Some idea of the magnitude of that figure can be obtained by comparing it with the entire money supply of the United States in 1979, about $350 billion. On a worldwide basis, Eurobank credit now represents about 40–50 percent of the entire money supply of the countries outside the Soviet bloc and China, up from only a tiny percentage just ten years earlier. To put it another way: Eurobank credit expansion almost doubled the world's money supply in approximately ten years.

One reason for the rapid increase in Eurobank credit is the need to finance imports of oil by countries with little or no domestic oil production. The oil is necessary for continued functioning of their domestic economies. When OPEC raises the price of oil, the funds to pay for it must be borrowed: the value of exports doesn't increase just because the price of a major import has risen. In the late 1970s, loans for this purpose may have reached as much as $100 billion annually. The loans are made in dollars, partly because oil is priced in dollars by OPEC and partly because control of credit expansion by the European central banks limits the amounts of loans their banks can make in domestic currencies. For example, the Swiss central bank limits the amount of loans Swiss banks can make in Swiss francs, but not the amount they can lend in dollars. The result is that the world's money markets have been flooded with U.S. dollars. Inflation is the result: the new dollars created by the loans merely refinance an existing flow of oil purchases at a higher level of total spending, without increasing output. Yet without the loan, economic activity in the oil-importing country would fall.

By the mid-1970s, then, the international financial and monetary system had introduced a new and as yet uncontrolled source of instability into the world economy. Erratic expansion and contraction of the world money supply was now possible, uncontrolled by monetary policy. Economic difficulties in one country could spread quickly to others, through rapid shifting of capital via the Eurobank system and a system of floating exchange rates between national currencies. The central banks of the leading industrial countries, like the Federal Reserve System in the United States, found themselves with considerably reduced influence over economic events.

Other, more fundamental problems developed in the international economy as industrialization spread into less developed areas. Capital was mobilized from the advanced countries, and from inside the less-developed countries as well, to promote industry, mining, and commercial agriculture, with international corporations and government aid programs leading the way. There is a great debate now going on among economists and among the people of the less-developed countries over whether the effects of this development are thoroughly desirable, and all the evidence is not yet available. One result has certainly been rising incomes and living standards for many people. But the benefits have been uneven. A relatively small number of very rich people have emerged in most of the less-developed countries, along with masses of very poor. This uneven development brings political instability that in turn is often answered by repression when unrest occurs. Economic development of this sort in many parts of the world is incompatible with democracy.

In addition, many of the less-developed countries began to feel a strong economic squeeze during the 1970s because of their financial relationships with the advanced industrial nations. During the 1950s and 1960s many of the less-developed countries borrowed heavily to finance ambitious plans for industrialization. Some, like Brazil, were able to start successful and continuing development. Others, like Egypt, were not. All became heavily indebted to foreign banks, governments, and international lending organizations. This indebtedness was complicated by often inefficient use of the borrowed funds—"one third wasted, one third for graft, and one third for development," is the standard cynical quip—which has led to serious problems of repayment. The loans were supposed to have been used to stimulate production of goods to sell abroad (or to substitute for imports), thereby creating earnings in foreign currencies to pay back the loans. But inefficient use of the borrowed funds plus large expenditures on imports by the newly affluent brought balance of payments deficits. The problem was seriously worsened by greatly increased costs of imported oil after the OPEC cartel raised prices and reduced production in the 1970s. By the mid-1970s it became apparent that most of the less-developed countries were unable to repay their foreign loans and were resorting to inflation to resolve their financial problems. Financial collapse has been avoided, up to now, by renegotiating repayment of the loans: foreign banks have agreed to stretch out the repayment period and some of the foreign governments and international organizations have agreed to forgive part of their loans. To achieve those agreements and avoid bankruptcy, the debtor countries had to agree to reduce inflation and cut their imports. But cutting imports can be achieved only by reducing incomes—that is, by reducing government spending and raising taxes. Reduced economic activity, more unemployment, and lower living standards are the costs today's less-developed countries are being asked to pay for yesterday's development planning. Those less-developed countries that have successfully established a continuing process of growth (Brazil, Taiwan, South Korea, for example), or those with large oil production (Nigeria, Mexico) do not have these financial problems, but many others are in trouble.

Slowed economic growth in Third World countries also affects the developed countries. If less-developed countries reduce their imports, developed countries must reduce their exports. Moreover, the financial problems of the Third World governments threaten the banking system of the developed countries. The international economy is a close-woven web of fragile relationships, so that difficulties in one sector are quickly transmitted elsewhere.

Modernization also brings high rates of population increase. Modern public health measures and sanitation programs brought death rates down while birth rates remained high. The resultant surplus population pushes wage rates down, which attracts capital investment on the part of multinational firms. Economic expansion attracts more of the surplus population from rural areas into urban slums, where poverty keeps birth rates up and adds more downward pressure to wage rates while owners and managers become wealthy. Meanwhile, back on the farm, the peasant families react to the population lost by migration to the cities as they always have, by generating more children. A vicious circle of modernization is set up, which can perpetuate itself indefinitely. This pattern is seen in much of Latin America and Asia, but to a lesser extent in Africa, with its tribal rather than peasant social structure. In all of the less developed world, however, the problems of uneven development are worsened by production of agricultural exports like sugar or cocoa instead of basic foods for home consumption. Economic development and modernization may be increasing population pressures and poverty rather than reducing them.

World population continues to increase rapidly. Under one billion only two hundred years ago, it was four billion in 1975, and if unchecked will reach more than ten billion in perhaps fifty years. Population will not go unchecked, however. Famine, disease, and perhaps war will bring a leveling off. United Nations population experts now foresee a world population of six to seven billion by the middle of the next century. At that level, and with foreseeable supplies of food available, more than half of the world's population will be at or near the starvation level. Any break in food supplies from droughts could then set mass starvation in motion and perhaps trigger huge political upheavals. We have already entered an era in which the relationship between food and population is a major concern.

Another major concern is the unequal international distribution of control over resources. The relatively affluent countries, with their relatively stable populations and rising living standards, use the bulk of the world's resources. They also hold the largest portion of the world's wealth and control most of the world's capital. The less-developed countries have much lower living standards and consume less per person, but their populations grow rapidly. Even if they were to bring their population growth under control over the next fifty years, they probably could never catch up to the affluent countries in consumption per person. There just are not enough resources in the world to make that possible, at least with the present patterns of consumption and resource use.

One group of less-developed countries, the oil producers, have gained control over their own resources. Led by the Arab countries, the largest and cheapest producers of petroleum, they form the Organization of Petroleum Exporting Countries (OPEC). OPEC was ineffective at first in dealing with the large international oil companies. But in the 1960s the Arab nations took steps to gain control over oil production within their own borders; then they moved to gain control over the pricing of oil by imposing higher royalties and taxes on the oil companies. Finally, during the 1973 war between Egypt and Israel, the Arab countries embargoed deliveries of oil to the United States, and OPEC raised the price of oil fivefold. OPEC was now a cartel that controlled the price of petroleum. In 1978 and 1979, it took advantage of reduced production in Iran, caused by the political revolution there, to engineer another large increase in prices. Oil that was selling for under three dollars per barrel in 1973 was bringing thirty dollars a barrel by the end of the decade.

The immediate result of these price increases was to shift huge amounts of income from consumers in the oil-importing countries to the oil-producing countries. The bulk of the gains went to the personal fortunes of the chief Arab families and political leaders, to economic development in the Arab countries, and to an armaments race in that area of the world. A portion of the gains moved into the other less-developed countries through loans from the now rich Arab nations. But oil-importing less-developed countries, such as India, Pakistan, and a number of African nations, were hard hit. The advanced industrial countries were also deeply affected, partly by temporary shortages, but primarily by increases in production costs as energy prices soared, and by subsequent increases in prices. In addition, the new "oil deficit" stimulated worldwide inflation through its impact on expansion of credit in the Eurobank monetary system. The OPEC price hikes contributed heavily to worldwide inflation, first by increasing the cost of energy, and second by triggering massive expansion of the world's money supply. Yet, ironically, the OPEC leadership argued that continuing increases in the price of oil were needed because inflation was raising the cost of the things they bought!

The world economy in the 1970s was in trouble: the emergence of an uncontrolled Eurobank monetary system, economic development problems in the less-developed countries compounded by debt repayment issues, continuing population growth that seems to be generating a Malthusian population trap in many areas, and the disruptive effect of OPEC oil pricing and production control signalled the end of an integrated world system. Where the international economy in the 1950s and 1960s was a source of economic expansion, as a result of growing world trade and stable financial relationships, in the 1970s it became a source of economic instability.

IDEOLOGICAL CONFLICT AND MILITARY SPENDING

Large-scale military spending also contributed to the problems of the world economy. Division of the world into capitalist and communist blocs, one led by the United States and the other by the Soviet Union, brought on military as well as political and economic rivalry. The American policy of containment sought to preserve as much as possible of the world from communist influence, and had the effect of keeping the noncommunist areas open for expansion of trade and investment. In this way the policy of containment helped promote the great era of world prosperity that followed World War II.

Containment and political-economic rivalry brought large military expenditures on the part of both the U.S. and the U.S.S.R., along with development of nuclear weapons, missiles, and electronic supporting equipment. The new weaponry contributed heavily to the technological changes that helped promote investment and rising productivity in all of the industrial nations, and large military expenditures helped support the high levels of aggregate demand that brought prosperity and economic growth through the 1950s and 1960s. In these respects military spending provided a positive support to the industrial economies. In the U.S.S.R., however, large military expenditures held back increases in production of consumer goods, and the inability of the Soviet government to provide adequate improvements in living standards undoubtedly contributed to continuation of political authoritarianism—which adds fuel to the international rivalry and antagonism with the U.S.

But military spending has two faces, even in a private enterprise economy: weapons are used for destruction, not for human benefit; and modern weapons become obsolete quickly. Instead of using labor and resources to produce either goods for consumption or capital that increases output in the future, weapons production is always wasteful. It may be deemed politically necessary, but it does not directly increase economic welfare. This is why economists of all political persuasions prefer peace to war: resources used to produce guns mean that less is available to produce either butter or plowshares.

Furthermore, the money spent on weapons becomes purchasing power for consumers, but weapons do not enter the marketplace to absorb purchasing power. If weapons production is increased when the economy is at or near full use of its production capacity the result is inflation: purchasing power rises, but the amount of goods available for sale is reduced by diversion of production capacity from civilian to military goods.*

The Vietnam war had particularly strong inflationary effects. The U.S. government tried to finance the war without raising taxes significantly, so as not to make an unpopular war even more unpopular. Prices rose because of diversion of output to military uses, large budget deficits, and increases in the money supply. The inflation, together with the large military spending abroad, brought huge deficits in the U.S. balance of payments in the early 1970s. The payments deficits, in turn, thrust large amounts of U.S. dollars into the world's money markets, with three results: it helped promote the great expansion of Eurobank loans already mentioned, which added to world inflation; it forced devaluation of the dollar, which promoted more inflation within the U.S.; and it contributed to the breakup of the Bretton Woods system of stable exchange rates. An era of worldwide economic growth was ended in the early 1970s with military defeat and a discredited U.S. foreign policy, and economic wreckage strewn across the landscape.

THREE UNSETTLING THEORIES

Up to this point we have discussed aspects of the contemporary crisis in economics that relate to macroeconomic problems: unemployment and inflation, changes in the structure of the economy wrought by growth and technological change, a changing international economy and financial system, and the distortions of militarism. A changing world brought new problems whose scope and nature went beyond the framework of traditional Keynesian theory and policy.

Neoclassical microeconomics was also in trouble, but its difficulties lay far more in theoretical and conceptual problems. At the borderlands of pure theory some of the most advanced work done by neoclassical economists themselves—often highly abstract and mathematical—was undermining the conceptual foundations of mainstream economics.

The basic idea of the post-Keynesian synthesis was that maintenance of full employment growth would enable the private sector to operate with reasonable effectiveness. Consumers seeking to maximize their welfare, interacting with producers trying to maximize profits, would bring about a pattern of output that satisfied both consumers and producers. In the process, a distribution of income fair to everyone would emerge, based on the individual's contribution to output. Effectively competitive markets were

*Even an increase in taxes is not sufficient to eliminate these inflationary pressures. Tax receipts are immediately spent, returning the purchasing power to consumers, while the diversion of output to military purposes continues.

necessary, and provision would have to be made for public needs through government spending, but, in general, the economy could be expected to move toward a satisfactory "best position," or equilibrium, through the rational action of producers and consumers interacting with each other in the marketplace. This was the vision, and it was maintained in the face of institutional changes that seemed inconsistent with the theory: the market power of big business, wage determination through collective bargaining, large expenditures for advertising, and the effects of high levels of government spending. These elements of the modern economy were treated largely as modifications of the basic analysis of economic forces at work in self-adjusting markets.

Nevertheless, the neoclassical vision began to disintegrate in the face of three new ideas that came to prominence in the 1960s: analysis of uncertainty, the theory of the second best solution, and the theory of social choice. In each case theoretical analysis that sought merely to extend the theory of market adjustment resulted instead in conclusions that undermined the theory itself. Instead of determinate, equilibrium solutions that pointed toward maximization of welfare, these new inquiries led to indeterminate results and serious questions about the validity of the assumptions that lay at the heart of the discipline.

Exhibit I: The Analysis of Uncertainty. As early as the 1920s some neoclassical economists began to wrestle with the problem of uncertainty. Since consumers and producers do not have full knowledge of all the alternatives open to them, and knowledge of the future is impossible, how can rational decisions be made? One of the first efforts to deal with this issue was made by Frank H. Knight (1885-1972). In *Risk, Uncertainty and Profit* (1921) he argued that risk, which involves the probability that an event will occur, can be estimated on the basis of experience. Like insurance, the economic costs of risk can then be included in the cost relationships used in decision making. Knight went on to argue that profit was the economic reward received for taking the risks inherent in business enterprise. Uncertainty, unlike risk, was created by the presence of unique events for which probabilities (and costs) could not be readily calculated, or by lack of information, or by the presence of random events generated outside the economic system. True uncertainty introduced indeterminateness into economic affairs.

Knight's conceptual breakthrough was only partially accepted into mainstream economic theory. His concept of risk was consistent with the idea of the determinate equilibrium of the market, and so it was built into the main body of economic theory. His concept of uncertainty was largely ignored, however, and it was not until the 1950s and 1960s that economists began to reexamine the problem of decision making under conditions of uncertainty, dealing successively with increasingly complex problems. First, uncertainty about the future implies that different individuals will assess differently the probability that a future event will occur. And some events occur only once, like choosing a career or selecting a line of business; with no experience to go by, how does one determine the probable outcome? Finally, suppose that pure chance—completely random occurrences—are a significant element in human experience; what will be the outcome? By the late 1960s economic theorists had progressed from the first to the last of these problems, with fascinating, if tentative, results. Subjective probability — different assessments by different people—was not a great problem theoretically. It merely meant that decisions had to be kept flexible and subject to revision or change. In this case Knight's solution was only modified. But when taken in conjunction with the once-and-for-all irreversible decision, it meant that costly mistakes could readily be made. In economic terms, the welfare-maximizing results of the competitive market economy could be aborted. And where pure chance is involved, like rolling dice or a "random walk," theorists concluded that even a perfectly competitive system of self-adjusting markets may or may not be able to determine prices, quantities, and other results. Here is a theoretical time-bomb ticking away in the center of the neoclassical model: if the world is truly subject to random events, we must expect not only a failure to maximize welfare, but also (possibly) a failure to produce any results other than random variations. One might argue that in the real world events are determinate, that we do see prices, outputs, and incomes being determined by market forces. However, if these economic analyses of the influence of uncertainty and chance are even close to being correct, we can no longer argue that the results will be optimal. Indeed, results may not even be desirable or beneficial, depending on the outcome of pure chance.

If all this seems highly theoretical and not particularly relevant to the world we live in, reflect for a moment on the earlier discussions in this chapter of the unsettling events of the past quarter century, the attempts of policy makers to cope with them, and the outcomes of those events. The world of the twentieth century, with its two world wars, inflations, depressions, genocide and concentration camps, political terrorism and authoritarian repression, is hardly consistent with a world view that emphasizes rational, purposive behavior as the path to maximization of welfare. In this environment of events and ideas, the new developments in economic theory that stress the role of chance and uncertainty in human affairs mean that economic theory itself is turning away from the mechanistic determinism of general equilibrium theory to an entirely different way of looking at the economic world.

Exhibit II: Second Best Solutions. The neoclassical model has another problem. Conditions in the real world are quite different from the conditions assumed in the theory. Results in the real world, therefore, will differ from the conclusions derived from the theory. But economists were inclined to take for granted the proposition that the theoretical conclusions could be approximated in the real world to the extent that reality approximated the theoretical model. For example, antitrust laws were expected to improve the functioning of the economy by making it more competitive, and public utility regulation was expected to replicate the results of competition.

Now we know that this simple assumption is not correct. Theorists examining the nature of less than optimal situations arrived at a "general theory of second best," that might be summarized in the following terms:

In a complex and interrelated economy, any variation from the conditions assumed by the theory of perfectly competitive markets produces a less than optimal solution. There is no way to determine how far from the optimum the result will be (that is, a slight deviation from the assumptions could bring a large shift in the results). Furthermore, efforts to improve the results by changing other conditions will bring a different result, but we can't tell whether that will be just as far from the optimum as before, closer, or further away.

Put it another way: we are at position A, which differs from the ideal position B. We try to move toward B and, in this imperfect world, get to C. But once there, we don't know whether C is closer to B or not.

Here is an example from public utility regulation. It might seem obvious at first glance that reduction of the monopoly power and profits of a public utility through government regulation would bring economic benefits, particularly to consumers in the form of lower charges. But hold on—not so fast. With other industries earning high monopolistic profits, a reduction of profits in the public utilities sector could discourage investment in that sector and service would deteriorate, leaving consumers and society worse off in the long run. Since the "best" solution (making all industries competitive) is not available, a "second best" solution (replicating competitive results in one sector) is tried, but the result may be worse than the original position. In this example, prices are lower but service is poorer.

If this is not enough, link together the findings from analysis of uncertainty and the theory of second best: the results of pure chance may be better than the results of purposive and rational choice! Furthermore, it may be impossible to determine which result is preferable. In an imperfect world, in which all solutions are second best, we can no longer claim that the results obtained from the free operation of self-adjusting markets are necessarily desirable. We just don't know.

Exhibit III: The Theory of Social Choice. Mainstream economics always had a place for public expenditures. They were fitted into the general model without difficulty by showing that rational social choices could be made by comparing benefits with costs. As long as benefits exceeded costs, expenditures could be increased until the increased benefits were just matched by rising costs. Voters or their representatives would make those choices for government much as consumers make choices about their individual spending. There were complications, of course, but the basic principle was simple enough.

Then in 1951 came a blockbuster of a book, *Social Choice and Individual Values* by Kenneth J. Arrow, which laid out what has since been called "Arrow's impossibility theorem." Stripped of its theoretical apparatus, it can be stated simply:

If there are more than two fundamentally different ideological positions, none of which constitutes a majority, and there are more than two policy alternatives, it may not be possible to achieve a decision satisfactory to a majority.

A simplified example uses three separate groups of equal size, A, B, and C, each one of which has a different order of preference among three different policy alternatives, X, Y, and Z. The table below shows the three groups and their preferences:

	Group A	Group B	Group C
1st choice	X	Y	Z
2nd choice	Y	Z	X
3rd choice	Z	X	Y

That is, group A chooses X in preference to Y or Z and Y over Z, and so on. Inspection of these preferences shows that if X is proposed as a policy both B and C would form a majority to select Z, which they prefer to X. If Z is then proposed, A and B would form a coalition to choose Y. But if Y is the proposal, A and C will combine to choose X—and that brings us back to the unstable starting point. Either no firm decision is reached, or one that a majority would oppose is taken by an outside authority.

Arrow's puzzle engendered a long debate and further analysis. It became clear that with only two parties and two choices a firm decision would emerge—which shows the practicality of the American two-party system and the legislative practice of dealing with single pieces of legislation on a yea-nay vote. And the problem disappears if there are no ideological groupings of voters. But in a complex industrial society multiple groups can develop in situations with intricate patterns of alternative choices. Arrow's original proposition still holds, and the traditional neoclassical conclusions about social choice no longer stand firm: rational social choices in a democratic framework may not be possible in a complex industrial world.

A NEW PARADIGM?

As the twentieth century reached the end of its eighth decade, modern economics was in trouble. Many problems—simultaneous unemployment and escalating inflation, relative economic stagnation, pollution, population growth and dwindling food supplies, and an unstable international economy —seemed beyond the reach of accepted modes of analysis and traditional policies. The concept of a self-adjusting economy supported by government programs to promote economic stability seemed not to be particularly relevant to the analysis and solution of the large-scale interrelated difficulties that plagued the economy.

At such a conjuncture of new problems and old theories, new ideas emerge as people seek better answers. The present is no exception. We can already observe a new point of view, a new way of understanding the modern economy, that began to emerge in the 1960s and gathered momentum in the 1970s.

The new approach is called "neo-Keynesian" in England and "post-Keynesian" in the United States. It takes from Keynes a heavy emphasis on the instability of a modern private enterprise economy and on the uncertainty that surrounds much economic behavior. In particular, it stresses the volatility of the level of investment that results from changes in anticipations and expectations about the future.

The investment decision must be made in the present, but, because capital equipment is long-lasting, the payoff can never be accurately known. As expectations about the future change—and they can change widely in a short time—investment decisions can also fluctuate widely and cause wide swings in the level of economic activity.

To these Keynesian foundations are added some key ideas of the Polish Marxist economist, Michael Kalecki (1899-1970, pronounced "Ka-let-ski"). During the 1930s and 1940s Kalecki developed an analysis that unified the macroeconomics of the level of economic activity, the microeconomics of price formation, and the theory of income distribution. He argued—to vastly simplify and strip the ideas to their essentials—that business investment determines the rate of expansion of economic activity, which determines the rate of profit, which determines investment expenditures. Prices consistent with the three macroeconomics variables emerge as part of a mutually determined system, since the prices firms charge must enable them to earn the profits required to finance the investment implied by the rate of economic growth.

Post-Keynesian economics also draws on the work of Piero Sraffa (born 1898), an Italian economist who worked in England after fleeing from Mussolini's fascism in the 1920s. In 1960 he published a 90-page book with the unlikely title of *Production of Commodities by Means of Commodities*. This book was a highly abstract mathematical description of an economy in which technological relationships determine the production of commodities. That is, commodity X is produced with inputs of given quantities of corn and iron (which symbolize food for workers and intermediate manufactured goods), commodity Y by different quantities of inputs, and so on. Note the conceptual breakthrough here. Outputs are determined by technical relations in the process of production, not by the interaction of demand and supply in the market.

Other economists had developed similar ideas in the 1920s and 1930s, particularly the Russian economist S. V. Kantorovich (born 1912) and the Russian-American Wassily Leontief (born 1906), who independently worked out a system of input-output analysis, also heavily mathematical, that related quantities of outputs to quantities of inputs through the technological relationships of the production system. These input-output theories assumed, however, that price relationships consistent with production relationships would be established, by central planners in the Kantorovich system and by the market in the Leontief system. Sraffa went one step further and completed the theory by demonstrating that prices consistent with patterns of output based on technological relationships could be established if the tradeoff between wages and profit was given.

That conclusion feeds back into Kalecki's macroeconomics, in which rate of economic growth, investment, profits, and price markups are mutually determined. The profits of Kalecki's macroeconomic theory close the gap in Sraffa's microeconomics by defining the distribution of income between wages and profits. It enables post-Keynesians to analyze the economy as a system in which all the major variables are functionally related to each other.

These ideas were developed initially at Cambridge, England, where Joan Robinson became their chief advocate. We have already noted her earlier contribution to the theory of imperfect competition and monopoly. In the 1960s she issued a direct challenge to the orthodox line of thinking, first by reviving the emphasis Keynes had given to the instability inherent in an economy in which uncertainty about the future creates a potential for wide fluctuations in investment spending. Secondly, Robinson mounted an attack on the most vulnerable part of neoclassical microeconomics, its treatment of capital and the time-consuming process of production.

The issue here concerned the role of capital goods in the production process. In the neoclassical theory of production, producers are presumed to minimize their costs of production. But costs of production are only the prices of inputs, like capital. Capital goods, however, get their value from the value of the final products they produce. This makes the argument circular: the cost of inputs depends on the value of the goods they produce, but the goods they produce cannot be priced until the costs of inputs are determined. The circularity would make no difference if all this were happening simultaneously, but that is not the case. Production takes place over time, and the business firm must value its inputs before it has information about what it can get for its output. Furthermore, since capital cannot be adequately valued in independently measurable units, how can we show that it earns a return equal to its contribution to production? The only ways out of this difficulty are to define capital as Marx did—as an intermediate product only, standing midway between labor and final output; or to find some way to define and measure capital independently of the value of final output—and this has not been done. These were some of the issues raised by Joan Robinson in a 1953 article on "The Production Function and the Theory of Capital." This article started a long and acrimonious debate on the nature of capital and its relationship to economic growth, prices, and the distribution of income.

The "capital controversy" that followed may well be one of the most important turning points in the history of economics. Robinson and her post-Keynesian supporters won the day. Prevailing ideas about the determination of prices and the distribution of income were shown to be logically inconsistent and of little or no relevance, particularly in a modern world of long-lasting capital goods and a complex technology. As long as the theoretical questions asked by economists are limited to exchange of goods within a market, the older ideas retain their robust conclusions: the interaction of demand and supply determines market price. But when production involving the use of capital goods in a time-consuming process determined by the technologies available must be analyzed, the neoclassical synthesis no longer provides adequate answers. Victory in the capital controversy went to the post-Keynesian critics of orthodoxy.

Post-Keynesian economics is being extended. A new view of the financial system is emerging: where monetarists see the supply of money as a major determinant of prices and traditional Keynesians suggest that management of the money supply can help stabilize the economy, post-Keynesians argue that the level of economic activity determines the money supply and that little can be accomplished by attempting to manage or control the monetary system. Inflation is seen as the result of big unions, big business, and big government attempting to enlarge or maintain their incomes in the face of changing levels of output and changing rates of economic growth. The economy is analyzed as a dual system, the more important sector being dominated by big business and monopoloid pricing, while the competitive, small-business sector is both less important and diminishing in significance, even though the traditional theory of competitive markets is still relevant there. The labor market is also analytically divided into two chief parts, a primary sector in the industries with advanced technology, labor unions, and big business, and a secondary sector, with more labor-intensive technology, few unions, and relatively small, competitive business enterprise. From the post-Keynesian standpoint, there is no presumption of a general equilibrium, prices are not determined primarily by supply and demand, the level of economic activity is volatile, the process of growth is unbalanced, and income distribution is the result of conflicts between the chief claimants, labor and capital, and the strength of their organized power.

This view of the economy implies that any tendency toward a harmonious and orderly outcome of the economic process is swamped by counter-tendencies toward fluctuations, conflict, and disorder. If orderly and desirable outcomes are to be achieved, government must intervene. Advocacy of economic planning is the logical outcome of the post-Keynesian position.

NEW BOTTLES FOR OLD WINE

Simultaneously with the emergence of post-Keynesian economics, with its emphasis on imbalance, disequilibrium, and the need for government direction of the economy, there has come a new conservatism that stresses greater reliance on self-adjusting market forces, a reduced economic role for government, and efforts to promote increased output rather than increased demand. In the case of post-Keynesian economics we find a revival of the mercantilist view of the economic world: the market is not self-adjusting, does not, by itself, generate socially desirable outcomes, and therefore needs substantial intervention by government to achieve social goals. In the case of the new conservatism, on the other hand, we observe a return to the conceptual framework of Adam Smith and the economic liberals of the eighteenth century: the market is self-adjusting, leads to socially desirable results, and could benefit from a substantial return to laissez-faire. If all this has an air of *déjà vu,* note Fusfeld's first law of intellectual history: if it's a good idea somebody else thought of it first.

The new conservatism has a theory to support its reformulation of laissez-faire doctrine. It is derived in large part from the monetarist critique of Keynesian economic policies, but it moves away from the monetarist preoccupation with the money supply to concentrate on the relationship between unemployment, inflation, expectations, and the "supply side" of the economy. The analysis, reduced to its key elements, runs as follows:

There is a "natural rate of unemployment," say 5 percent, at which the rate of inflation is zero. Efforts to reduce the actual rate of unemployment to a level below the natural rate, say 4 percent, by using fiscal and monetary policy to increase aggregate demand, can be successful in the short run, but will set inflationary pressures in motion. Prices will start rising because wages start to rise as unemployment falls (the "Phillips Curve" presumably showed that relationship), causing labor markets to tighten and the bargaining position of unions to strengthen. As prices rise, consumers, business firms, and labor unions begin to expect further price increases. Consumers start buying now instead of later, to avoid rising prices. Business firms also increase their advance buying of inputs, and raise their prices as well. Unions, expecting higher prices, demand wage increases now. The entire economy moves toward a higher price level. In this situation, according to the theory, something odd starts happening to the unemployment rate: it rises toward its "natural" level. The reason given is that under the impact of inflation the tradeoff between wages and prices changes. In the economists' language, "the Phillips Curve shifts upward," as a result of higher wage rates and increased costs of production. The result is that policies designed to reduce unemployment raise prices and have only a short-run impact on the unemployment rate.

Complicated? Yes. Controversial? You bet! The two most controversial aspects of the theory are, first, that expectations of inflation cause inflation, which is a classic unprovable proposition; and, second, that there is a changing tradeoff between unemployment and inflation as prices change, which is extremely difficult to demonstrate either theoretically or empirically.

The underpinning of the theory is the idea of "rational expectations." As people learn that stimulation of aggregate demand leads to inflation they adapt more quickly. Instead of a reduction in unemployment followed by inflation and then followed by an increase in unemployment back to the "natural" level, the time sequence is compressed until, after several experiences, the intermediate steps are eliminated. The economy responds immediately to increased aggregate demand with inflation, while unemployment is unaffected.

The policies derived from this analysis are strongly probusiness. The most obvious policy prescription is to abandon the classic Keynesian demand management program. Increased aggregate demand only causes inflation. On the other hand, programs to affect the "supply side" of the economy could be very helpful. Costs of production should be reduced through lower taxes on business enterprise and less regulation. Investment should be stimulated by enlarged tax credits. Transfers of income from productive workers to the poor through welfare and other payments should be reduced, providing greater incentives to work for both productive workers and the unproductive poor. The dominant theme here is a reduced role for government and an enlarged role for private enterprise.

Particular attention would also be given to reducing the "natural" rate of unemployment. The new conservatives recommend a number of programs developed earlier by the Keynesian liberals, but with the caveat that costs and benefits should be carefully assessed. Among the recommended programs are those that would train low-skilled workers, improve mobility of workers out of chronically depressed areas, reduce job discrimination against minorities and women, and improve public employment services. But many new conservatives also advocate elimination of minimum wage legislation, lower unemployment insurance benefits, and revision of national labor laws to reduce the bargaining power of labor unions. These aspects of "supply side economics" imply using the political process as part of the class conflict that always lies just beneath the surface of the modern private-enterprise economy.

THE ECONOMICS OF THE FUTURE

Economics is entering a new era: a dramatic change in direction and orientation impends. The older system of thought based on Keynesian macroeconomics and neoclassical microeconomics—what we have called the neoclassical synthesis—no longer commands the respect and authority it held a decade ago, and no longer provides adequate guides to public policy. A reformulation to fill the vacuum in theory and policy will have to come.

The breakup of the neoclassical synthesis was not caused primarily by faults in its internal logic. It came because the world of which the theory was a part reached a crisis. As the institutions and modes of thought of that world change, economics will change also. The macroeconomic problems of the 1980s are quite different from those of the 1930s, so the Keynesian economics developed to meet the difficulties of fifty years ago are increasingly seen to be inappropriate to current problems.

At the microeconomic level the growth of big business, big labor, and big government changed the environment within which market adjustments take place. Collective bargaining, new rigidities in labor markets, and national tax and spending programs may well be more important than market forces in determining the distribution of income. Control of markets by big corporations is now a significant influence on the pattern of production; the effect of advertising on consumer demand is no less significant. Failure to take these forces adequately into account has left the orthodox model of market exchange and adjustment to equilibrium in an increasingly unrealistic position.

Some general trends in the reformulation of economics can be discerned. Much of the fundamental wisdom and concepts accumulated over two hundred years will be retained. But these ideas must be treated as building blocks only, because they are parts of a general structure that no longer holds together. A reformulation will undoubtedly put the building blocks together in a different pattern, and at least partially reconstruct the damaged ones. We should expect, first, much greater attention to the changing institutional structure within which economic activity takes place. One of the lessons of the past quarter century is that the institutional structure changes and evolves; this in turn affects the way the economy functions. Analysis of this pattern of change, which characterized the work of Marx, Veblen, and Galbraith, for example, seems to be due for greater emphasis.

Second, the economic theory of the future will probably move away from certainty and determinateness toward acceptance of a world characterized by doubt and chance. The first stage in the application of mathematical logic to economic analysis is drawing to a close. In that stage the view of the world was one of stable relationships within known boundaries, much like the world view of the old Newtonian physics in which a determinate equilibrium emerged from natural forces. But modern physics as well as much twentieth-century philosophy has moved toward a world view that does not have neat boundaries and in which chance and uncertainty are basic elements. Economics, in some respects, is also coming to that view. Furthermore, belief in social progress through reason may have been one of the casualties of the twentieth century. That belief is hard to maintain in the face of a series of destructive wars, depression and inflation, extermination camps, famines, and similar horrors. An economic theory based on the idea that rational individual action and public policy can lead to optimal outcomes must surely be as difficult for a modern Candide to accept as an earlier Candide found the idea that "all is for the best in this best of all possible worlds." The old certainties and self-assurance are gone. Economics as it develops will reflect these changes in viewpoint, which are themselves rooted in the events of the modern world.

Third, the older emphasis in theory and policy on national economic conditions and national policies is now outmoded. New international money markets and multinational business firms, the growth of world trade, expansion of international transport and communications, emergence of the Third World as an independent force, and the rivalries of competing ideologies suggest that theoretical analysis of both macro- and micro-economic problems will have to be more general and international in scope. Internationalization of the economy means internationalization of the theory and policy that seeks to explain and manage that world.

Fourth, the economics of the future will surely put greater emphasis on *political economy*—the analysis of economic power, its sources, limits, and uses. Relationships between big business, big labor, and big government involve the acquisition and use of economic power in the struggle for advantage and gain. Much of the outcome of this struggle depends on which groups are able to use their economic strength to gain and hold political power: "money to get power, power to protect the money" is once again a central issue, made so by the changing nature of the economy itself. These aspects of political economy also include the age-old conflict between haves and have-nots, within both the domestic and the international economies. Economists will once again have to wrestle with the relationships between conflict (Marx) and harmony (Adam Smith) within a framework of changing ideas and institutions (Veblen and Galbraith).

These are not simply theoretical issues in a world of ideological conflict, struggles for power, and nuclear weapons. Modern industrial society has created the means of its own destruction. Even if the present generation succeeds in avoiding nuclear war or poisoning the environment, these deadly possibilities will be passed on to the next generation. Perhaps the greatest challenge to the economics of our time is the need to develop the economic foundation for an environmentally sound system of production, an ethically acceptable pattern of income distribution, and a world system that eliminates the threat of nuclear war.

Suggested Reading

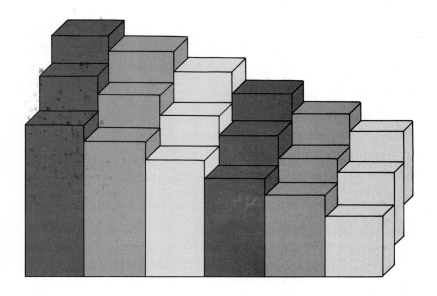

The literature of economics is vast and complex. It is no longer possible for even professional economists to be familiar with all of it, although a century ago Karl Marx could devote a lifetime to the subject and read just about everything that had been written in the field.

There are some good textbook surveys of the history of economics. The more readable of these comprehensive works are Erich Roll, *A History of Economic Thought* (third edition, 1956); John F. Bell, *A History of Economic Thought* (second edition, 1967); and Charles Gide and Charles Rist, *A History of Economic Doctrines* (second edition, 1948). Two surveys interesting for their points of view are Leo Rogin, *The Meaning and Validity of Economic Theory* (1956), which emphasizes the uses to which economic theories are put, and Joseph Schumpeter, *A History of Economic Analysis* (1954), an encyclopedic volume that stresses the development of economics as a science. More recent textbooks include Irene H. Rima, *Development of Economic Analysis* (revised, 1972); Mark Blaug, *Economic Theory in Retrospect* (revised, 1968); and Robert B. Ekelund, Jr. and Robert F. Herbert, *A History of Economic Theory and Method* (1975). Note the emphasis on theory, analysis, and method in the titles. Several recent books resurvey the history of economics from the viewpoint of recent critics of orthodoxy, indicating how changing ideas bring about reexamination of the past: Maurice Dobb, *Theories of Value and Distribution since Adam Smith*

(1973); Phyllis Deane, *The Evolution of Economic Ideas* (1978); and Guy Routh, *The Origin of Economic Ideas* (1975).

The early history of capitalism is covered in the standard treatises on the economic history of Europe, but few analyze the rise of the market economy. Two books that do are Karl Polanyi, *The Great Transformation* (1944; published in paperback 1957), and Richard H. Tawney's great work, *Religion and the Rise of Capitalism* (1947).

A good compendium that gives the flavor of mercantilism, physiocracy, and early economic liberalism is Arthur E. Monroe, *Early Economic Thought* (1945). A recent paperback edition of Bernard Mandeville's *The Fable of the Bees* (1962) has made this work available to modern readers. Two books that deal with economics before Adam Smith are Edgar A. Johnson, *Predecessors of Adam Smith* (1937), and William Letwin, *The Origins of Scientific Economics* (1963).

There is a large literature on classical economics. The very best discussion is Wesley Mitchell, *Lecture Notes on Types of Economic Theory* (1966), which originally appeared in mimeographed form during the 1930s; it consists of notes taken by students from Mitchell's lectures at Columbia University, and has the unique characteristic of being equally absorbing for both specialists and the general reader. A more demanding book, but one well worth studying, is Werner Stark, *The Ideal Foundations of Economic Thought* (1944). The best readily available editions of the major works of classical economics are the Modern Library Giant edition of Adam Smith's *Wealth of Nations;* the Ann Arbor Paperbacks edition of Thomas Malthus' *Population: The First Essay;* and the Dutton paperback edition of David Ricardo's *Principles of Political Economy and Taxation.* Smith is not easy to read, Malthus is a delight, and Ricardo is quite difficult. Perhaps the best overall survey of classical economics for the general reader is John Stuart Mill, *Principles of Political Economy,* which is available in most good libraries. Mill's *Autobiography* is a fascinating account of his education and early life, and *The Life of John Stuart Mill* by Michael St. John Packe (1954) is well worth reading. John Rae, *The Life of Adam Smith* (1965; first published in 1895) is rich in information but not written in a very interesting style. There are no good biographies of either Malthus or Ricardo, but useful brief accounts of their lives are Keynes' essay on Malthus in his *Essays and Sketches in Biography* (1956), which also contains interesting accounts of Alfred Marshall and William Stanley Jevons, and "A Memoir of Ricardo," written by one of his brothers and published with addenda in Piero Sraffa, ed., *The Works and Correspondence of David Ricardo,* Vol. X (1955). A fine account of Jeremy Bentham and his influence is Elie Halevy, *The Growth of Philosophic Radicalism* (1952), and classic accounts of Bentham, James Mill, and John Stuart Mill are in Leslie Stephen, *The English Utilitarians* (1900; reprinted in 1950). Two books that deal effectively with the differences between classical and modern liberalism are Harry K. Girvetz, *From Wealth to Welfare* (1950), reprinted as *The Evolution of Liberalism* (1963), and William D. Grampp, *Economic Liberalism* (2 vols., 1965). Economic policy in classical economics is the subject of three books: Lionel Robbins, *The Theory of Economic Policy in English Classical Political Economy* (1961); Warren J. Samuels, *The Classical Theory of Economic Policy* (1966); and A. W. Coats, *The Classical Economists and Economic Policy* (1971). Recent reinterpretations of classical economics include Samuel Hollander, *The Economics of Adam Smith* (1973); Thomas Sowell, *Classical Economics Reconsidered* (1974); Robert V. Eagly, *The Structure of Classical Economic Theory* (1974); and D. P. O'Brien, *The Classical Economists* (1975).

There are several good introductions to socialist thought. Probably the most interesting and stimulating is Edmund Wilson, *To the Finland Station* (1953), available now in paperback. Two more comprehensive surveys are Harry W. Laidler, *Social-Economic Movements* (1948), and Philip Taft, *Movements for Economic Reform* (1950). A fine selection of readings from the socialist literature is in Albert Fried and Ronald Sanders, eds., *Socialist Thought: A Documentary History* (1964). Peter Kropotkin's *Memoirs of a Revolutionist* (1906) is a very human document, written by one of the leading anarchists, that gives fascinating insights into the socialist movement in its heyday.

The most readily available edition of Marx is the Modern Library Giant edition of the first volume of *Capital,* and a fine translation of all three volumes has recently been published by the Foreign Languages Publishing House in Moscow. The novice should not tackle *Capital* directly, however. A good place to start is Ernst Mandel, *An Introduction to Marxist Economic Theory* (1969), chapters 1–2. Two pamphlets by Marx provide an excellent introduction to his economic analysis of capitalism: *Wage-Labour and Capital* (1849) and *Value, Price and Profit* (1865), chapters 6–14. Two early writings by Marx, which were not published until recently, give the flavor of his humanist concern for people and his dialectical-historical way of thinking: "Estranged Labor," in *Economic and Philosophical Manuscripts of 1844;* and *Pre-Capitalist Economic Formations,* which consists of extracts from early unpublished notebooks. *Capital,* if you tackle it, should be read in conjunction with Paul M. Sweezy, *The Theory of Capitalist Development* (1942), which is the best summary of Marxist economics available in English. The best biography of Marx is Franz Mehring, *Karl Marx: The Story of His Life* (1936). Friedrich Engels' classic work, *The Condition of the Working Class in England in 1844* (1952; first published in 1845), presents the picture of early industrial capitalism that Marx had in mind when he wrote *Capital;* it is essential reading for anyone who wishes to understand Marxism.

Most of the writings of Marx's dialectical and historical method are biased toward the author's preconceptions or political prejudices. Marx published almost nothing on these matters in his lifetime other than a few brief paragraphs in the "Author's Preface" to *A Contribution to the Critique of Political Economy* (1859). His early training was in philosophy, and the philosophical background to his economic thought is analyzed in Sidney Hook, *From Hegel to Marx* (1950). Friedrich Engels explained Marx's "historical materialism" (a term invented by Engels after Marx's death) in Part IV of *Ludwig Feuerbach and the Outcome of Classical German Philosophy* (1888), but this little essay was the first step in the simplification and rigidification of Marx's approach, culminating in the Stalin era interpretations of Maurice Cornforth, *Dialectical Materialism: An Introduction* (3 vols., 1952–54; 4th ed., 1971). Reading Marx's early unpublished writings on his conceptual framework, followed by Engels, Lenin and the Stalinists, provides an education in how rich philosophical ideas can be reduced to political dogma. There are, however, two useful survey-critiques of Marx and the economic interpretation of social change: M. M. Bober, *Karl Marx's Interpretation of History* (1927), which is a bit outdated, and Melvin Rader, *Marx's Interpretation of History* (1979).

I did not discuss later Marxist writings, some of which are fascinating and important. Basic Marxist theory was further developed by V. I. Lenin in *Imperialism: The Highest Stage of Capitalism* (1933), and Lenin's *State and Revolution* (1932) is the bible of orthodox communist political action. "Revisionist" Marxism received its classic statement in Eduard Bernstein, *Evolutionary Socialism* (1961), and was refined in Karl Kautsky, *Social Democracy versus Communism* (1946). Leon Trotsky's reply and amplification in *The Defense of Terrorism* (1921) and *The Permanent Revolution* (1965) are especially valuable for the light they throw on the policies followed by the Chinese communists in the 1950s and 1960s.

There are a variety of interesting books on the philosophy of individualism and the environment out of which it emerged. My favorite is Sidney Fine, *Laissez Faire and the General-Welfare State* (1964), closely followed by Richard Hofstadter, *Social Darwinism in American Thought* (1955). A more specialized but equally interesting study is Edward C. Kirkland, *Dream and Thought in the Business Community* (1956). Brief collections of the writing of the individualists and their antagonists include E. David Cronon, *Government and the Economy: Some Nineteenth-Century Views* (1960) and *Democracy and the Gospel of Wealth* (1949). There are some fascinating histories of the era of great wealth: Charles Francis Adams, Jr., and Henry Adams, *Chapters of Erie* (1956); Gustavus Myers, *History of the Great American Fortunes* (1936); and Matthew Josephson, *The Robber Barons* (1934). The flavor of individualism can best be obtained from the protagonists themselves, however: Herbert Spencer, *Social Statics* (1851); William G. Sumner, *Essays* (1934); and Andrew Carnegie, *Triumphant Democracy* (1886), *The Gospel of Wealth* (1900), *The Empire of Business* (1902), and *Autobiography* (1920).

There is no good general survey of neoclassical economics and very little interpretive literature below the scholarly level. Alfred Marshall's *Principles of Economics* (eighth edition, 1920) is ponderous but not difficult; it remains the authoritative statement of the neoclassical system. Three small volumes in the Cambridge Economic Handbook series are a better introduction: Hubert Henderson, *Supply and Demand* (1958); E. A. G. Robinson, *The Structure of Competitive Industry* (1959); and Dennis H. Robertson, *Money* (1959). All three were written by eminent economists, students, and followers of Marshall, and all were intended for the person who has no prior knowledge of economics.

Although surveys of modern economics tend, of necessity, to be highly selective, two general works are T. W. Hutchison, *A Review of Economic Doctrines: 1870-1929* (1953), which is essentially a historical summary of major trends, and Ben B. Seligman, *Main Currents in Modern Economics* (1962), a broad and inclusive volume full of useful insights into the social theories and political assumptions underlying the doctrines of academic economics. Paul T. Homan, *Contemporary Economic Thought* (1928) is an older but useful book that emphasizes the split between neoclassical theorists and institutionalists led by Veblen. Abram L. Harris, *Economics and Social Reform* (1958) covers somewhat the same ground with a broader perspective and the advantage of a longer view. G. L. S. Shackle, *The Years* of *High Theory: Intervention and Tradition in Economic Thought* (1967) deals with economic theory between 1920 and 1940. Wiliam Breit and Roger L. Ransom, *The Academic Scribblers* (1971) is an excellent survey of recent economics.

Allan G. Gruchy, *Modern Economic Thought* (1947) is a laudatory survey of Veblen and other institutionalists. Gruchy's *Contemporary Economic Thought: The Contribution of Neo-Institutional Economists* (1972) brings the treatment up to date. Rexford G. Tugwell, ed., *The Trend of Economics* (1924) presents essays by the leading American institutionalist economists that emphasize both their criticisms of orthodox economics and their advocacy of economic reforms. Two books by J. M. Clark, *Preface to Social Economics* (1936) and *The Social Control of Business* (1939), develop those themes further, as do the essays of Wesley Mitchell in *The Backward Art of Spending Money* (1937). John R. Commons was a prolific, obtuse, and turgid writer; his books are almost impossible to read—with one exception, his fascinating autobiography, *Myself* (1934; published in paperback 1963). The best of Thorstein Veblen's thought is in *The Theory of the Leisure Class* (1899; published in paperback 1954) and *The Theory of Business Enterprise* (1904); his essays in *The Place of Science in Modern Civilization* (1919) are also interesting.

The best introduction to the Fabian socialists is still George Bernard Shaw, ed., *Fabian Essays* (1948). Nearly all of John A. Hobson's books have been reprinted in hardbound editions; the only one available in paperback is *Imperialism* (1965). Three major works by R. H. Tawney are available in inexpensive editions: *Religion and the Rise of Capitalism* (1947), *The Acquisitive Society* (1960), and *Equality* (1961). The papal encyclicals on social problems, *Rerum Novarum, Quadragesimo Anno,* and *Mater et Magistra,* are readily available in pamphlets published by The American Press or the Paulist Press.

Keynes' *General Theory of Employment, Interest and Money* (1936) is far too difficult for the ordinary reader. One might start with *The Economic Consequences of the Peace* (1920), *The Means to Prosperity* (1933) or *Essays and Sketches in Biography* (1956). Two good summary-introductions to the *General Theory* are Dudley Dillard, *The Economics of John Maynard Keynes* (1948), and Alvin Hansen, *A Guide to Keynes* (1953). R. F. Harrod, *The Life of John Maynard Keynes* (1951) is a full-scale biography, while Seymour Harris, *John Maynard Keynes* (1955) is shorter and contains a more extensive evaluation of Keynes' ideas. Robert Lekachman, *The Age of Keynes* (1966) is an excellent book for the general reader.

There is a huge literature on the Soviet economy. Maurice Dobb, *Soviet Economic Development Since 1917* (1948) is old, but unexcelled in its treatment of the policy debates of the 1920s that preceded adoption of the present strategy of planning. Much of the debate itself has been translated and published in Nicolas Spulber, *Foundations of Soviet Strategy for Economic Growth* (1964). Three other recent surveys of the Soviet economy are Robert W. Campbell, *Soviet-Type Economies* (third edition, 1974); Alec Nove, *The Soviet Economy* (revised edition, 1969); and Nicolas Spulber, *The Soviet Economy* (revised edition, 1969). The debate over the theory of planning is best represented by Oskar Lange and Fred M. Taylor, *On the Economic Theory of Socialism* (1938); Friedrich A. Hayek, *The Road to*

Serfdom (1944); and John M. Clark, *Alternative to Serfdom* (1948). There are several interesting books on the practical applications of the theory of market socialism, including Branko Horvat, *Towards a Theory of Planned Economy* (1964); and Ota Sik, *Plan and Market Under Socialism* (1967) and *The Third Way* (1976). The "new revisionism" of western European Marxism, which rejects the Soviet Union as a model to be emulated, is explained in Santiago Carrillo, *Eurocommunism and the State* (1978). Horvat is a prominent Yugoslav economist, Sik is a former head of economic planning in Czechoslovakia who now lives in Switzerland, and Carrillo is a Spanish Marxist leader. The Chinese economy changes so rapidly that almost anything written about it is out of date before it can be published. Nevertheless, John G. Gurley, *China's Economy and the Maoist Strategy* (1977) is an excellent analysis of developments under Mao Tse-tung.

The underdeveloped countries have been analyzed exhaustively in the current economic literature. Three widely different approaches are presented by Barbara Ward, *The Rich Nations and the Poor Nations* (1962); Pierre Moussa, *The Underprivileged Nations* (1963); and L. J. Zimmerman, *Poor Lands, Rich Lands: The Widening Gap* (1965). Gunnar Myrdal's *An International Economy* (1956) deals with problems of underdevelopment, and is one of the most important economics books of the post-World War II years; an abridged version was published in 1957 under the title *Rich Lands and Poor*. Walt W. Rostow's *The Stages of Economic Growth* (1960) should be supplemented with the later chapters of Bert F. Hoselitz, ed., *Theories of Economic Growth* (1965). A recent short book on the subject is Edward Marcus and Mildred Rendl Marcus, *Economic Progress and the Developing World* (1971).

So much has been written on the changing economies of Western Europe and North America that it is hard to know where to begin. Start with two fundamental works: Joseph A. Schumpeter, *Capitalism, Socialism and Democracy* (1942), and Karl Polanyi, *The Great Transformation* (1957). Books dealing with the changing organization of the American economy include Sumner H. Slichter, *The American Economy* (1948); Adolf A. Berle, *The American Economic Republic* (1965); Gardner C. Means, *The Corporate Revolution in America* (1964); Solomon Fabricant, *The Trend of Government Activity in the United States Since 1900* (1952); and Eli Ginzberg et al., *The Pluralistic Economy* (1965). A trio of books provide a larger view of the changing economies of the free world: Gunnar Myrdal, *Beyond the Welfare State* (1960); Angus Maddison, *Economic Growth in the West* (1964); and Andrew Shonfield, *Modern Capitalism* (1965). These three books show how far the West has progressed toward economic planning and the welfare state, in a highly varied pattern.

The neoclassical synthesis is so widely dispersed throughout the writings of a wide variety of economists that it is impossible to give just a few references. The interested reader might look at Paul Samuelson's textbook, *Economics* (eleventh edition, 1980). If he has a good command of mathematics, he can try Samuelson's *Foundations of Economic Analysis* (1947), or dip into Samuelson's *Collected Scientific Papers* (1966). The classic statement of Keynesian fiscal policy, together with a restatement of neoclassical welfare economics, is Abba P. Lerner, *The Economics of Control* (1944). Beyond that, the *Annual Reports* of the President's Council of

Economic Advisers for the years 1962 through 1968 provide a running account of post-Keynesian macroeconomic policy in the context of the problems to which it is applied. Michael Stewart, *Keynes and After* (1967) and Herbert Stein, *The Fiscal Revolution in America* (1969) document the importance of Keynesian theory for economic policy. The best critique of Keynesian economics is Axel Leijonhufvud, *On Keynesian Economics and the Economics of Keynes* (1968).

A fascinating contrast between the interventionist liberal and the laissez-faire conservative in contemporary economics is found in the works of John Kenneth Galbraith and Milton Friedman. Galbraith's key books are *American Capitalism* (1952), *The Affluent Society* (1958), *The New Industrial State* (1968), and *Economics and the Public Purpose* (1973). Friedman is less readily accessible to the general reader, except for *Capitalism and Freedom* (1962). His monetary theories are presented in *The Optimum Quantity of Money and Other Essays* (1969), in the long and difficult *Monetary History of the United States, 1867-1960* (1963), which he coauthored with Anna Schwartz, and in essays published in *Dollars and Deficits* (1968). His methodological position is stated in the first chapter of *Essays in Positive Economics* (1953).

Key works in the revival of Marxist economics are Paul A. Baran, *The Political Economy of Growth* (1957); Paul A. Baran and Paul M. Sweezy, *Monopoly Capital* (1966); and Ernest Mandel, *Marxist Economic Theory* (1967). An influential book that applies a Marxist analysis to problems of economic development is Andre Gunder Frank, *Capitalism and Underdevelopment in Latin America* (1967). Another on the same topic is Samir Amin, *Accumulation on a World Scale: A Critique of the Theory of Underdevelopment* (2 vols., 1974); in *The Modern World System* (2 vols., 1976 and 1980), Immanuel Wallerstein argues that capitalism is a world system that has always featured exploitation of peripheral regions by the capitalist center.

Leftist criticism of the Soviet Union began early. Leon Trotsky, *The Revolution Betrayed* (1937) was a virulent attack on bureaucratic authoritarianism there. Trotsky's position was developed in detail in Isaac Deutscher, *Russia After Stalin* (1953) and *Russia in Transition* (1957). More recently, Charles Bettleheim, *Class Struggles in the U.S.S.R.* (2 vols., 1977-78) argues that Soviet authoritarianism is an outcome of a new type of class struggle in a socialist society. The entire Marxist theory of the state has come in for searching reanalysis in recent years, partly because of developments in the U.S.S.R. and partly because of the continued stability of the mixed capitalist-welfare state of the post-World War II years. Two of the leading volumes in this revival of Marxist political economy are Ralph Miliband, *The State in Capitalist Society* (1969) and Nicos Ponlantzas, *Political Power and Social Classes* (1973).

Meanwhile, a group of German Marxists of the so-called "Frankfurt School" have revived the humanist aspects of the early Marx: Herbert Marcuse, *Soviet Marxism: A Critical Analysis* (1958); Erich Fromm, *Marx's Concept of Man* (1961); and Jurgen Habermas, *Theory and Practice* (1973) and *Legitimation Crisis* (1975). A recent and stimulating critique of the American economy written from the point of view of U.S. democratic socialism, is Michael Harrington, *The Twilight of Capitalism* (1976).

The era of crisis in the contemporary economy has yet to be carefully documented. The persistence of poverty has been forcefully presented in Michael Harrington, *The Other America* (revised edition, 1970). Other good treatments include Oscar Ornati, *Poverty Amid Affluence* (1966); and David Hamilton, *A Primer on the Economics of Poverty* (1968). The other extreme of the distribution of income and wealth is shown in G. William Domhof, *Who Rules America?* (1967), and Ferdinand Lundberg, *The Rich and the Super Rich* (1968). The problem of achieving equitable income distribution is discussed in Arthur M. Okun, *Equality and Efficiency: The Big Tradeoff* (1975).

Criticisms of contemporary economics can be investigated in Benjamin Ward, *What's Wrong with Economics?* (1972); Jesse G. Schwartz and E. K. Hunt, eds., *A Critique of Economic Theory: Selected Readings* (1972); and Robert Lekachman, *Economists at Bay* (1976). Landmarks in the theory of social choice, in addition to the Arrow volume discussed in the text, include Anthony Downs, *An Economic Theory of Democracy* (1957); Mancur Olson, *The Logic of Collective Action* (revised edition, 1971); and James M. Buchanan and Gordon Tullock, *The Calculus of Consent: Logical Foundations of Constitutional Democracy* (1962).

Discussions of recent economic policy in the U.S., from the Keynesian viewpoint, are James Tobin, *National Economic Policy* (1966); Walter W. Heller, *New Dimensions of Political Economy* (1967); and Arthur M. Okun, *The Political Economy of Prosperity* (1970). The monetarist-Keynesian argument is illustrated by Milton Friedman and Walter W. Heller, *Monetary vs. Fiscal Policy: A Dialogue* (1969), which reproduces a debate between the two authors. Probably the best presentation of the social philosophy of the post-Keynesian synthesis and its relation to U.S. Cold War strategy is Eugene V. Rostow, *Planning for Freedom* (1959), in which "planning" is Keynesian economic policy and "freedom" the private enterprise economy. A useful and radical counterpoise is Harry Magdoff, *The Age of Imperialism: The Economics of U.S. Foreign Policy* (1969) or Seymour Melman, *The Permanent War Economy* (1976). *Gobal Reach: The Power of the Multinational Corporation* (1975) by Richard J. Barnet and Ronald E. Mueller is a highly critical treatment of multinational corporations, but is one of the few that deals in depth with their impact on the domestic economy as well as on the less-developed countries.

A number of important writings on the relationship between growth, population, food, resources, and pollution are reprinted in *Growth and Its Implications for the Future,* Part I, Hearings, Subcommittee on Fisheries and Wildlife, U.S. House of Representatives (1973). An older book with new relevance is K. William Kapp, *The Social Costs of Private Enterprise* (1950). Lester R. Brown, *In the Human Interest: A Strategy to Stabilize World Population* (1974) has an excellent treatment of population problems. Readings on the steady-state economy are included in Herman E. Daly, ed., *Toward a Steady-State Economy* (1973) and Mancur Olson and Hans H. Landsberg, eds., *The No-Growth Society* (1973). Two very provocative little books noted in the text, Robert L. Heilbroner, *An Inquiry Into the Human Prospect* (1975) and E. L. Schumacher, *Small Is Beautiful* (1973) deal with those larger issues at the level of the general reader, while Nicholas Georgescu-Roegen, *The Entrophy Law and the Economic Process* (1971) is slowly coming to be recognized as a key treatise on the physical limitations to economic growth.

There is a growing literature on post-Keynesian economics, but the only material readily accessible to the noneconomist is Alfred S. Eichner (ed.), *A Guide to Post-Keynesian Economics* (1978). The books by Michael Kalecki, *Essays in the Theory of Economic Fluctuations* (1939) and Piero Sraffa, *Production of Commodities by Means of Commodities* (1960), and Joan Robinson's paper, "The Production Function and the Theory of Capital" (1953), are for professionals, as are the two best books on the capital controversy, Geoffrey C. Harcourt, *Some Cambridge Controversies in the Theory of Capital* (1972) and Mark Blaug, *The Cambridge Revolution: Success or Failure?* (1974). American developments of post-Keynesian ideas are Sidney Weintraub, *Capitalism's Inflation and Unemployment Crisis* (1978), Paul Davidson, *Money and the Real World* (2nd ed., 1978), and Alfred S. Eichner, *The Megacorp and Oligopoly* (1976).

There is no single source for further reading on the new conservatism. One highly popularized version is presented in Milton and Rose Friedman, *Free to Choose: A Personal Statement* (1980), which emphasizes ideology and policy rather than economic analysis. A good statement of the natural rate of unemployment hypothesis is Milton Friedman, "Nobel Lecture: Inflation and Unemployment," *Journal of Political Economy,* Vol. 85 (June 1977), pp. 451–472, especially pp. 456–459. The seminal paper on the tradeoff between unemployment and wage rates, which the new conservatives have modified to a trade between unemployment and prices, is A. W. Phillips, "The Relationship Between Unemployment and the Rate of Change of Money Wage Rates in the U.K., 1861–1967," *Economica,* Vol. 25 (Nov. 1958), pp. 283–299. The theory of rational expectations is presented in Thomas J. Sargent and Neil Wallace, "Rational Expectations and the Theory of Economic Policy," *Journal of Monetary Economics,* Vol. 2 (April 1976), pp. 169–183. These articles in professional journals are rather esoteric, however; they are not for the ordinary reader.

Finally, let me note my own paper that develops more fully the idea that a growing alliance between big business and big government, in spite of the obvious conflicts between those centers of economic and political power, is leading us to the authoritarianism of a "corporate state": Daniel R. Fusfeld, "The Rise of the Corporate State in America," *Journal of Economic Issues,* March 1972.

Name Index

Hargreaves, James, 23
Harvey, William, 24
Hastings, Warren, 22
Hayek, Friedrich von, 42, 131
Hayes, Rutherford B., 64
Heilbroner, Robert L., 144
Hicks, John R., 130
Hobbes, Thomas, 25
Hobson, John A., 84-85, 86
Holmes, Oliver Wendell, Jr., 65
Hood, Thomas, 49
Hoover, Herbert, 76
Hornick, Philip von, 12
Hume, David, 17-18, 21, 22

Jefferson, Thomas, 16
Jevons, William Stanley, 72, 75
John XXIII, Pope, 83

Kaldor, Nicholas, 142
Kalecki, M., 154
Kantorovich, S. V., 154
Kay, John, 22
Keynes, John Maynard, 1, 3, 95-97, 100-105, 114, 120
Keynes, John Neville, 96
Khrushchev, Nikita, 120
Knight, Frank H., 132, 150-151
Kuznets, Simon, 99

Lange, Oscar, 111-112
Lavoisier, Antoine, 24
Lawrence, William, 67
Lenin, Nikolai (Vladimir Ilich Ulyanov), 84, 107-108, 125
Leo XIII, Pope, 82-83
Leontief, Wassily W., 154
Lincoln, Abraham, 16, 64
Locke, John, 18-19, 25
Louis XIV, 14
Louis XV, 16
Lynd, Helen, 89
Lynd, Robert, 89

Malthus, Thomas Robert, 33, 35-37, 43, 47
Mandel, Ernest, 138
Mandeville, Bernard de, 17-18, 31
Mao Tse-Tung, 116
Marshall, Alfred, 73, 74n, 77, 96

Marx, Karl 1, 2, 3, 29, 51-60, 71, 72, 73, 74, 80, 81, 121, 142, 155, 158
Meadows, Donella H., 143
Means, Gardner C., 89, 125-126
Menger, Karl, 72, 77, 80, 131
Meszaros, Istvan, 137
Mill, James, 42, 46
Mill, John Stuart, 42, 46
Mills, C. Wright, 89, 137
Mises, Ludwig von, 110, 131
Mitchell, Wesley, 89
Morgan, John Pierpont, 68-69
Myrdal, Gunnar, 99, 114

Newton, Isaac, 24
North, Dudley, 17-18

O'Connor, James, 137-138, 141
Ohlin, Bertil, 99
Owen, Robert, 50-51

Paine, Thomas, 34
Pareto, Vilfredo, 77
Parrington, Vernon, 89
Phillips, A. W., 141
Pigou, Arthur, 111
Pitt, William, 21, 34
Pius XI, Pope, 83
Prebisch, Raul, 114
Preobrazhenski, Evgeni, 108
Price, Richard, 21n
Proudhon, Pierre Joseph, 52
Pullman, George, 69

Quesnay, Francois, 16, 21

Reynolds, Sir Joshua, 22
Ricardo, David, 33, 37-39, 43, 46, 47, 73, 100, 142
Richardson, Samuel, 22
Robertson, Dennis H., 98
Robinson, Joan, 77, 155
Romney, George, 22
Roosevelt, Franklin D., 63n, 76, 90, 102
Ropke, Wilhelm, 131
Rostow, Walt W., 113, 130-131
Russell, Bertrand, 78

Samuelson, Paul, 130
Say, Jean Baptiste, 33, 42-44
Schumacher, E. L., 144
Schumpeter, Joseph, 77, 120-122
Schwartz, Anna, 133
Shaw, George Bernard, 84
Sidgwick, Henry, 79
Simons, Henry C., 132-133
Sismondi, Jean Simonde de, 42
Slichter, Sumner H., 126-127
Smith, Adam, 1, 3, 17, 20-21, 23,
    25-32, 33, 34, 40, 45-46, 73,
    77, 79, 132, 142, 156
Smith, Hubert Llewellyn, 76
Soddy, Frederick, 99
Sombart, Werner, 85
Spence, William, 42
Spencer, Herbert, 62-63, 65,
    73, 79
Spinoza, Baruch, 25
Sprague, Oliver M. W., 76
Sraffa, Piero, 154-155
Stackelberg, Heinrich von, 77
Stalin, Joseph, 108, 110, 112
Steele, Richard, 22
Strachey, Lytton, 96
Sumner, William Graham, 62-63,
    73, 79
Sweezy, Paul, 136-137

Tawney, Richard H., 84-86
Taylor, Fred M., 111-112

Thornton, Henry, 43
Tilden, Samuel J., 64
Townshend, Charles
    (Grandfather), 21
Trotsky, Leon, 108-109
Tugan-Baranowsky, Michel, 98
Tull, Jethro, 23
Turgot, Jacques, 19, 21

Vancouver, George, 22
Vanderbilt, William, 67
Veblen, Thorstein, 86, 89, 134,
    158, 159

Wallas, Graham, 84
Walras, Leon, 72, 77
Webb, Beatrice, 84
Webb, Sidney, 84
Weber, Max, 85
Weiser, Friedrich von, 80
Weisskopf, Walter A., 137
Wells, Herbert G., 84
Whitehead, Alfred N., 78
Whitney, Eli, 23
Wicksell, Knut, 99
Wicksteed, Philip, 80
Wilson, Thomas, 6
Woolf, Virginia, 96
Wright, Carroll, 75

Young, Arthur, 23

Subject Index

Division of labor, 30
international (comparative
advantage), 39-41
Dual labor markets, 124
Du Pont chemical enterprise, 16n

Easy money policies, 13, 128
criticism of, 132-133
Economic activity, level of
and interest rates, 98, 102
managed by government,
104-105
*Economic Consequences of the
Peace, The,* 96
Economic dualism, 113, 145
Economic equilibrium, 73, 77-78,
99, 100-102, 128, 156
international, 39-41
Economic fluctuations, 75-76
Economic freedom, 25-27
Economic growth, 12, 30-31, 37-
39, 49, 79, 122-125, 128-131,
142-144, 156, 158-159
limits to, 143-144
shift from investor to
consumer, 100
slowdown of, 47, 142-144
in underdeveloped nations,
114, 129-130, 145-146
Economic justice, 74-75, 82-83
Economic liberalism, 16-19
Economic life and religion, 8-10,
82-83
Economic Table of Quesnay, 16
Economics
analytical framework of, 31
and the climate of opinion, 4,
34-35, 48-50, 98-101
as a science, 4, 33, 77-79
as a system, 3
defined, 2-3
development of, 3-6
reconstruction of, after Marx,
62, 71, 80
scientific method in, 77-79
Economics, 130
*Economics and the Public
Purpose,* 134
Economists, 1-2
theologians as, 8

Eighteenth century
classical liberalism, 46
development of science and
mathematics, 24
economic liberalism, 17-19
guilds, power of, 14
individualism in English life,
22-24
liberal democracy, theory of,
24-25
social philosophy and
structure, 22
Electoral Commission of 1876, 64
Elite ruling class in the U.S., 88,
137-138
Eminent Victorians, 96
Empire of Business, The, 66
Employment, Keynes' general
theory of, 101-104
Employment Act of 1946, 91,
128-129
England
economic difficulties of, in
1815, 42
economic growth in seven-
teenth century, 14
economic issues of American
colonies in, 15
economic policy in 1920s, 96
guilds, seventeenth-century,
disintegration of, 14
"hungry forties" (1840s) in, 49
individualism, in, 22-24
mercantilism in, 13-15
nineteenth and twentieth century reforms in, 84
prosperity of, in eighteenth
century, 18
radical economists in, 138
reaction to the French
Revolution, 34-35
technological changes of the
Industrial Revolution in, 23
welfare-state philosophy in,
84-86
Entrepreneur, 77, 121-122
elimination of, 121
Environment, 143
Equality, 86
Equilibrium. *See* Economic

equilibrium
Erie Railroad stock, illegal
  watering of, 67
"Establishment, the," in the
  eighteenth century, 35
Ethical systems, Smith's theory
  of, 20-21
Eurobank system, 144-146, 148
European economy
  after World War II, 122
  prior to Middle Ages, 6
  reconstruction after World
    War II, 3-4
  transformation to market
    economy, 6-7
Evolution, Spencer's theory of, 62
*Evolution of Modern Capitalism,
  The,* 84
Exploitation of labor, 54-55, 59,
  74

Fabian Essays, 84
Fabian socialists, 84
Fabian Society, 84-85, 86
Fable of the Bees, The, 17
Fascism, 83, 88
Faust legend, 86
Federal budget, New Deal use of,
  92
Federal Reserve System, 76, 134,
  146
Feudal lords, opposition to
  nationalism, 11-12
Fifteenth century social and
  economic changes, 6-8
Finance, international, problems
  of, 144-145
Fiscal Crisis of the State, 137-138
Fiscal policy, 129, 133-134
Flying shuttle, 23
Folklore of individualism, 65-67
Folkways, 63
"Forgotten Man, The", 63n, 63
*Foundations of Economic
  Analysis,* 130
Fourteenth Amendment to
  Constitution, 64-65
Fragment on Government, 21, 44
France
  economic planning in, 112

government regulation of
  production, eighteenth
  century, 15-16
mercantilism in, 14
Freebooters, great age of, 67-70
Free markets, 41, 73, 80, 131-134
  analysis of, 27-29
  limitations of, 29-30
Free society, 36
Free trade, 22-23, 39-40
French Revolution, 34-35, 49
Full employment, 98, 128-129,
  131, 134, 140-142
"Funny money", 99

General Agreement on Tariffs
  and Trade, 123
*General Theory of Employment,
  Interest and Money, The,* 95,
  98, 101, 102, 104-105
Glut of commodities, 41-43, 55-56
Gold standard, return to, 97
Gospel of Wealth, The, 66
Government
  growth of big, in U.S., 127-128
  liberal role of, 19, 26-27, 28
  intervention, 121, 133
  spending, 122, 128-129, 133, 148
    (on public works), 100-101,
    102-103
  welfare role of, 84
Great Depression of 1930s, 42,
  44, 69, 91, 98, 100, 121,
  133, 134
Guilds, establishment of, 14

Habeas Corpus Act, 34
Halley's Comet, and natural
  law, 24
Happiness, as an economic
  value, 44-45
Hard Times, 49
Haymarket Square riot (Chicago,
  Illinois), 69
Hedonistic calculus, 45
History of England, 22
Homestead Act, 64
Homestead, Pennsylvania,
  labor battles at, 69

Imperfect competition, 77
Imperialism, 84
Incentives in the New Industrial Order, 84
Income distribution, 29, 74, 79, 130
Individual welfare and neoclassical economics, 72-74, 79
Individual's place in society, New Deal view, 92
Individualism, 81
   development of, 21
   in eighteenth-century England, 22-24
   folklore of, 65-67
   law and, 63-65
   limitations of, 70
   philosophy of, 62-63, 79
   results of, 67-69
   survival of, 131-132
Indonesia, dual economy of, 113
Industrial Revolution, 14, 23-24, 29, 35, 41, 48-49, 80
Industrialism, 59
   foundations of, 23-24
Industrialization, 35, 36, 37, 42, 49, 68, 75, 100, 127
Inflation, 41, 129, 134, 137, 140-142, 145, 148
Innovation, 77, 120-121, 122
Inquiry into the Human Prospect, An, 144
Institutional economists, in U.S., 86-91, 124-128, 133-134
Intellectual genealogy, 5
Interest rates, role of, 43-44, 76, 99, 102
International Economy, An, 114
International economy, classical theory of, 39-41
International Monetary Fund, 104
Interventionist liberalism, 44-46, 84-90, 131-132
   policies of the New Deal, 90-94
Introduction to the Principles of Morals and Legislation, An, 44-46
Investment boom, post-World War II, 122, 141
Investment, dual effects of, 122
"Invisible hand" doctrine, 26, 92, 129

Keynesian economics, 104-105, 116-117, 128-129
   Friedman's criticism of, 133-134
Keynesian revolution, 95-105

Labor theory of value, 18-19, 53-54, 79, 80
Labor Under Monopoly Capitalism, 137
Labor unions, 83, 92, 126-127, 128
   formation of, 36
   growth of, 60
   position in modern economics, 126-127
Laboristic society, 135
Labour party (England), formation of, and Fabian Society, 84-85
Laissez-faire, 46, 61, 65, 67, 71, 79, 82-83, 126-127
Laissez faire, laissez passer, 16
Large-scale production, and the entrepreneur, 121
Law and individualism, 63-65
Law of Markets. *See* Say's Law
Legal profession, rise of, 12
Leisure class, Veblen's theory of, 87
Less-developed nations, 47, 116, 132
   aid programs for, 130-131
   economic growth in, 114-115, 130-131, 145-146
   economic planning in, 112-115
   modernization and population, 145
   take-off into sustained growth, 113, 130
   transition to mass-consumption economy, 113
Liberal democracy and natural law, 24-25
Liberalism, economic, 17-19, 25-31, 44-47, 78-80, 83-85
Libertarian advocates, 131-134
"Liberty, equality and fraternity," 49
Life of Samuel Johnson, 22
Limited-profit enterprise, 127
Limits to Growth, The, 143
Lombard Street, 76

London, University of, and
Bentham's cadaver, 44n

*Main Currents in American
Thought,* 89
Majority rule, 25, 46, 152-153
Malthusian principle of popula-
tion, 35-37
Marginal analysis, 45, 72-74, 78
Marginal productivity, 74
Marginal utility, 72-74
Market equilibrium, 27-29, 31,
72-73
Market-oriented people, 7-8
Market socialism, 112
Markets, Say's Law of. *See* Say's
Law
Marxism, 2, 60, 81-82, 136-138
and the Russian Revolution,
106-107
influence on other economic
theories, 61, 71, 75, 79-80,
81, 154, 158-159
Marxist Economic Theory, 138
Marx's Theory of Alienation, 137
Mater et Magistra, 83
*Mathematical Investigations into
the Theory of Value and
Price,* 78
Mathematical logic, 77, 158
*Mathematical Principles of,
Natural Philosophy,* 24
Mathematical Psychics, 78
Mathematical techniques of
analysis and exposition, 77-78
Maximization of individual
welfare, 73
Maximization of satisfaction,
72-74
Mediation of labor disputes, 90
Mercantilism, 11-15
opposition to, 15-19
Middle Ages, economic activity
in, 7
economic philosophy of
(parable), 8
functional society of, 85
structure of society during, 22
universal law governing social
order, 22

Middletown, and *Middletown in
Transition,* 89
Migration of blacks to north, 123
Military spending, 93, 122, 148-149
Minimum wage laws, conservative
view of, 132
*Modern Corporation and Private
Property,* 125
Monetarism, 133-134
Monetary controversy, 41, 42-44
"Monetary cranks", 99
*Monetary History of the United
States, A,* 133
Monetary policy, 13, 41, 76, 128,
130, 133-134, 140
Monetary system, 64, 76, 97, 133,
144-145
Monetary theory of business
cycles, 75-76
Monopoly, 27, 29, 64, 68, 79,
129-130
Monopoly Capital, 136
Monopoly grants, 14
Morrill Tariff, 64
Multinational corporations
142-143, 158

Nation, The, 97
National Bank Act, 64
National Bureau for Economic
Research, 89, 99
National economic budget, 117
Nationalism, 11, 12
National Labor Relations
(Wagner) Act, 91
National Recovery Administra-
tion (NRA), 91
Natural environment, 47, 143-144
Natural law, 16, 22, 24-25
Natural liberty, system of, 25-27
Natural price, 27-29
Natural sciences, development
of, 24
Natural selection, 62
Neoclassical economics, con-
servative affirmation, 131-134
New Deal, 63n, 86, 90-94
New Harmony, Indiana, 51
New Industrial State, The, 134
New Lanark, Scotland, 50-51

Stalinist authoritarianism,
108-110, 112, 129
transition from agricultural to
socialist society, 107-108
Specialization in production,
30-33
international, 39-41
Spectator, The, 22
Speculators, great age of, 67-68
Spinning machine, 23
Spinning mule, 23
Stable Money Association, 99
*Stages of Economic Growth: A
Non-Communist Manifesto,
The,* 114, 130
Stagflation, 140
"Stamped money", 99
Steady state economy, 144
Steam engine applied to factory
machinery, 21n
Stock market crash of 1929, 76,
96, 97
Strikes, 68-69
Structural unemployment,
124-125, 143
Struggles in human society, 53,
55, 90
Supply and demand, 27-29, 73
Survival of the fittest, in
individualist philosophy, 62
Symbolic logic, 78
Synthetic Philosophy, 62

Taft-Hartley Act, 127
Tatler, The, 22
"Taxation without representa-
tion", 15
Technological change, 23, 47,
121, 123-124, 129, 143, 147
Technostructure, 134-135
Temporary National Economic
Committee, 91, 126
Tennessee Valley Authority, 92
Textile mills, 50-51
Textile revolution, 23
*Theory of Business Enterprise,
The,* 87
*Theory of Capitalist Develop-
ment, The,* 136
Theory of Economic Develop-

ment, The, 121
Theory of the Leisure Class, The,
87
Theory of Moral Sentiments, The,
20
Tight money, 41, 128, 140
Tom Jones, 22
Trade Unions in a Free Society,
126
Treatise on Money, 97, 101
*Treatise on Political Economy,
A,* 42
*Trend of Government Activity in
the United States Since 1900,
The,* 127
Triumphant Democracy, 66
Truman Doctrine, 131
Turks, poverty of, 31
*20th Century Capitalist Revolu-
tion, The,* 125

Uncertainty, 150-151, 158
Unemployment, 48-49, 69, 95,
140, 142-143
Union for Radical Political
Economics, 138
*Union Policies and Industrial
Management,* 126
Unions. *See* Labor unions
United States Steel Corporation,
66, 68
United States Supreme Court,
63-65, 93
Utilitarianism, 44-46, 71
Utopian ideals, 84

Versailles peace conference, 96
Vested interests, 88

Wealth
accumulation of, 30-31, 67
Carnegie's theory of, 67
growth of, 54
production of, 18-19
Wealth of Nations, 21, 24, 34, 95
Welfare legislation, 59, 85-86, 92
Welfare state, 84-94

What Is Property?, 52
Work and Wealth, 84
World trade expansion, post-
World War II, 144-146, 157

Yugoslavia
Planning in, 112
worker management in, as
radical ideal, 138